See Sicily

See Sicily

Paul Watkins

a complete guide
with maps and
gazetteer

FORMAT

For Persephone

Acknowledgments

The author would like to express his
appreciation and thanks to the officers
of the Italian State Tourist Office in
London and the Assessorato del Turismo
in Palermo for their constructive assistance
in the preparation of this book.
Also to the provincial and local tourist
boards in Sicily who were particularly
helpful in assisting with the revisions
for the second edition.
The author is also indebted to Prof.
Giuseppe Bellafiore of Palermo University
for his information on the historic
buildings of Palermo and elsewhere.

Front cover photo: Church of St John of
the Hermits, Palermo, by R. Everts
Back cover: Mt Etna
Front endpapers: View of coast at Solunto
Back endpapers: Cloister at Monreale
Frontispiece: Church of S. Domenico, Noto

Photographs are by the author with the
following exceptions:
ENIT: 9, 12, 13 (top), 26, 32, 56 (left),
61 (below), 64/65, 68–71, 90, 101, 107
(right, and left below), 108, 128, 134
(left), 135, 138–139, 150, 152/153, 154/155,
156, 168/169, 170–171, 174/175, 177, 190;
Bromofoto: 177; Fotocielo: 163, 173;
Sonia Halliday: 29; Quiresi-Cremona: 130;
N. Teresi: 81

First published 1974
Revised edition 1980
© Paul Watkins 1974, 1980
Published by Format Books
23 Jeffreys Street London NW1

ISBN 0 903372 05 3

Filmsetting by Oliver Burridge Filmsetting
Ltd, Crawley, Sussex

Printing by Artes Graficas Grijelmo s.a.,
Bilbao

Contents

The island 'To have seen Italy without having seen Sicily is not to have seen Italy at all, for Sicily is the clue to everything.'

Making this comment in his *Italian Journey*, Goethe must have been thinking of Italy as a land of novel and enchanting experiences, in which Sicily with its live volcanoes, Arabo-Norman churches, Greek temples, and strange dialect encapsulated the image. The modern traveller will see—with greater ease than Goethe—how generously the island adds her physical and historical virtues to the splendours of the country.

With an area of 25,460 sq km Sicily is the largest island in the Mediterranean. It takes its name from the ancient inhabitants of the island, the Sicels. The earlier Greek name *Trinacria*, meaning 'three cornered', refers to the shape of the island.

Sicily is separated from Italy by the narrow Strait of Messina, but the geology of the island shows a close relationship to that of southern Italy, the mountains of northern Sicily being, in fact, a continuation of the Apennines. The principal ranges are the Monti Peloritani in the north-east and, to the west of these, the Nebrodi and the Madonie.

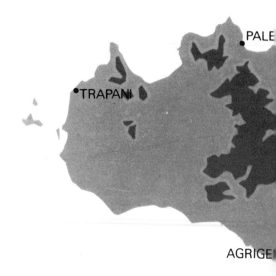

Further east are more isolated mountains (Monte Pellegrino, Monte Erice) which give the coastlines of Palermo and Trápani their characteristic bold contours. All these mountains are non-volcanic: by contrast, in the south-east of the island, the Monti Iblei are the result of ancient eruptions. The southern and eastern regions of Sicily are still subject to earthquakes and Sicily's famous volcano, Mt Etna, was in eruption as recently as 1979.

Without Etna, the drama of Sicily's landscape would lose its climax. A glimpse is enough: most perfect in spring when the countryside is green and the peak still has its white crust of snow. But a closer acquaintance with Mongibello will provide a climax of grand dimensions: the lava building its black and purple masses to the summit, broken here and there with the cauldron shapes of extinct craters. But one cannot think of Etna as merely the creator of desolation. At its foot is some of the most fertile land in Sicily, the volcanic soil working in combination with the temperate climate to produce the famous sweet wine of the region.

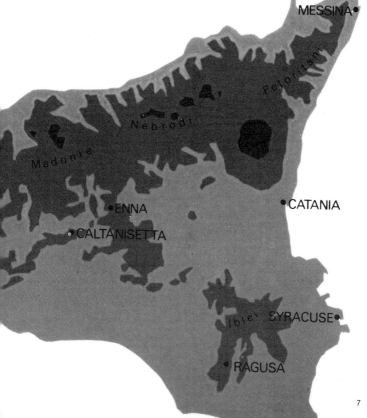

Sicily is at once barren and fertile. The coastal areas have their vineyards, citrus groves and olives; the Plain of Catania and the west and central regions their cornfields. The latter have been here since ancient times, the grain in great demand by the Romans during their period of occupation. Another natural product of the island, much exploited but not so easily replenished, was timber. Sicily was once largely covered by forest, but her rise to maritime power under Dionysius meant the cutting of large areas of timber for ship building. The export of timber and the increasing use of forested land for cultivation caused further depletion, and only 5% of Sicily is now wooded. The resulting erosion has created many of the island's barren regions, most noticeable in the hilly heartland of Sicily where the few rivers are dry for most of the year. But a drive through the stretches of empty, stone-covered landscape can never be boring. The contours of the interior—strongly defined in the north, more gradual in the south—offer endlessly changing perspectives.

This variety is reflected in Sicily's coastline, from which we can choose the dark dramatic rocks of the Riviera dei Ciclopi on the east coast, the superb resort beaches of Mondello and Cefalù, or the isolated, pine-screened beaches of white sand on the south-west coast—among the finest in the Mediterranean. This coastline is extended by Sicily's minor islands: lonely Ustica and the Aeolians to the north, the Égadi Islands to the west and Pantelleria and the Pelagic Islands to the south. Like their mother island many of these smaller islands are actively volcanic. Who can forget the smoking cone of Stromboli, or a warm bath in the thermal seas of Vulcano?

No description of Sicily's natural wonders can be complete without a mention of her flowers. The Sicilians show a touching awareness of this special gift of nature by their roadside planting. For most of the summer and autumn the pinks and reds of oleanders and geraniums make the little side roads seem like a winding driveway through the gardens of a country mansion. Only the less ordered sprinklings of anchusa, genista and other wild flowers reveal that nature is doing her own planting. In spring and early summer the fields of Sicily are a tapestry of reds, golds and purples from the poppies, daisies and wild gladioli: the observant eye will also spot the white and blue irises in the roadside verges. Whether it is an autumn crocus on the flanks of Mount Etna or a wild orchid on the banks of the Ciane, the element of surprise is always there to give an encounter with Sicily's flora its special appeal.

Man-made wonders are here too, stirring the mind and eye. History seems inexhaustible: echoed by the stone-age tombs of Pantálica, the Greek temples of Agrigento, Selinus and Segesta, the Norman palaces and churches of Palermo, the castles of 'Stupor Mundi', the Baroque fantasies of the Val de Noto. The traveller who follows Goethe on the roads to the past (see Exploring Sicily, p. 26 and Road Maps, p. 34) will certainly share his verdict on this fascinating island.

Sicilian fishermen

People and economy   Sicily has a population of over 5 million, the majority of them Roman Catholics. The modern Sicilian is a descendant of the many races that have inhabited the island since ancient times. His ancestry may be in part Phoenician, Greek or Roman, Arab or Norman, Swabian or Spanish: a compound that has produced an individual who cherishes his separate identity. With his sombre demeanour and slower, more primal way of life, his separateness from his compatriots in the busy industrial north of Italy is strongly marked.

The Unification of Italy in 1860 was a great military and political achievement. In its first ninety years however, it cannot be said that the new State—for all its good intentions—did much to improve the lot of the average Sicilian. Roads and railways were built and a programme of public works undertaken, but little done in the way of land reform or industrial development. The agriculture of the island was in the hands of a few landowners, with little incentive for the peasant farmer, and

industry remained in the North. This was very much at the expense of the Sicilians, who saw their young men emigrate in their thousands, year by year, to the factories of Milan and Turin.

Emigration was not only to northern Italy but to other European countries, America and Australia. After the war, politicians saw this continuing exodus of labour and the poor conditions in the South as an ultimate threat to the whole country's prosperity and stability. In 1950 the fund known as the *Cassa per il Mezzogiorno* was set up by the Central Government of Italy to revitalize the South. Money was allocated for the modernization of agriculture, including some land reform; to schools and hospitals; to roads, drainage and other public works; and to tourism. The emphasis was later switched to industry and the results of investment here may be seen in the petro-chemical plant at Gela, on the south coast of Sicily, the Fiat car assembly plant near Palermo, and the oil refinery and chemical industries between Augusta and Syracuse.

The impact of tourism and industrial development on Sicily is now clearly marked on her coastline, and for the greater offence to his eye the modern traveller can rarely choose between the shimmering, smoke-hazed refineries and the oblongs of concrete wedged into hillsides or poised on promontories, their only aesthetic virtue the view of the sea from their balconies.

More gradually, the people of Sicily are feeling the impact. Developments in the island have done something to stem the tide of emigration, but within Sicily itself have accelerated the movement of population from the country to the cities. The consequences of this movement are seen in the desolate countryside and in the skyscrapers of the new urban developments. These have put great pressure on cities which fifty years ago were for the most part small medieval towns, and whose services can now barely cope with the demands of a mushrooming population.

Sicily is a country where waste has become a tradition, whether it be the waste of human beings (through illiteracy, unemployment, emigration) or of resources (through ignorance, over-exploitation, neglect). This situation, explored in the works of Danilo Dolci (see Reference Books p. 25) is most desperate in western Sicily, where there is the added problem of the Mafia, the gangsters who control by graft and intimidation much of the resources of this part of the island.

With southern Italy, Sicily has been earmarked as a problem region of the European Economic Community. The future of the region is thus no longer the responsibility of Italy alone, and the *Cassa* has been helped in its great task by substantial loans from the European Investment Bank. Since 1950 great progress has been made in the region, but it remains one of the poorest parts of Europe. Sicily's development has been a test of the initiative, unselfishness and concern of her European neighbours. In the context of our new international community, the future of Sicily must be seen as the future of Europe.

Sicily in history

It is inevitable that the history of an island situated in the centre of the Mediterranean, midway between Europe and Africa, Asia and the Atlantic, should be dominated by a pattern of continuing occupation by rival powers. Whether it was for the expansion of an empire, the development of trade or just a need to break the ties of the mother country, the seafarers converged on Sicily. Some came from Africa—the Phoenicians, Carthaginians and Arabs—and some from Europe—the Greeks, Romans, Normans and Spanish. The African invasions were from the west, the European invasions from the east. The coincidence of the two brought the conflict which is written in the stones of Himera, Syracuse, Agrigento; the walls of fortresses taken by storm or given in deceit; the earth of battlefields long forgotten. The recurring overlay of conquests and cultures gives Sicily's history its special fascination.

Palaeolithic period Traces of human habitation have been found in Sicily dating back to the Late Palaeolithic period, c. 20,000 BC. The best-known discoveries of this early settlement (their precise date is as yet uncertain) are the incised drawings in the caves of Addaura near Palermo, and in the Grotta dei Genovesi on the island of Lévanzo, at that time part of the land mass of Sicily.

Neolithic period Between 4000–3000 BC there was a movement of population from the eastern to the central Mediterranean: a more advanced people who practiced agriculture and who combined pottery with the ability to make stone tools. Most of these people settled on the east coast of Sicily and in the Aeolian Islands, and the culture, known as the Stentinello, takes its name from the principal site to the north of Syracuse. The special characteristic of the pottery of this period—the earliest in Sicily—was the patterns incised and impressed on the clay, using sea-shells and animal bones.

Copper Age (c. 3000–2000 BC) A later immigration, also from the eastern Mediterranean, brought people with a knowledge of metal-working who are also identified with the first rock-cut tombs which remained the standard method of burial in Sicily up to the 5th c. BC.

Bronze Age (c. 2000–1000 BC) Apart from the use of bronze, this period was marked by increased contact with the civilizations of the Aegean. Imported Mycenaean pottery (c. 1400–1200 BC) has been found at many sites on the east coast and in the Aeolian Islands.

In approximately 1250 BC there was a further influx of new settlers, this time from the mainland of Italy. Of these tribes the *Ausonians* are identified with the Aeolian Islands and the *Sicels* with eastern Sicily. When they arrived in Sicily the Sicels displaced a race of people already established in the island, the *Sicans*, who are thought to have been a non-Aryan race from Africa or Spain. Also established in the island at the time of the arrival of the Sicels were the *Elymians* (descendants of Trojan refugees) who lived in the north-west.

Greek period (8th c. BC–241 BC) After establishing themselves on the west coast of Italy (Cumae) Greeks from the Aegean settled their first colony in Sicily at *Naxos* (757 BC). This site was chosen for its strategic position on the east coast of the island, on the sea route from Italy to Greece through the Strait of Messina. During the next two centuries the Greeks went on to colonize most of the eastern and southern Sicily, which with the colonies on the west coast of the Italian mainland constituted 'Magna Graecia'.

These colonies became independent city-states, taking their identity from the mother cities of their colonists. The most important, in order of their foundation, were *Megara Hyblaea* (750 BC) founded from Megara, *Syracuse* (733 BC) founded from Corinth and *Gela* (688 BC) founded from Rhodes and Crete. These cities in turn founded colonies further inland or further along the coast, many of which became rival cities later on. The most important of these were *Selinus*, founded from Megara Hyblaea in 650 BC, and *Akragas* (Agrigento) founded from Gela in 581 BC. The rivalry between these Greek cities, and their shifting alliances with foreign powers, is one of the features of Sicily's ancient history.

While the Greeks were founding their colonies in the east the Phoenicians were setting up trading enclaves in the west of the island. These included *Motya, Panormus* (Palermo) and *Solus,* all admirably located for communication with the Phoenicians' main base in Africa at Carthage. In an island the size of Sicily (large enough for two maritime powers to establish themselves but too small to contain both) it was inevitable that this rival colonization should lead to conflict.

The Greeks' power was centred at Syracuse, and a history of that city and its tyrants may be read as a history of the Greeks in Sicily (see the History of Syracuse, page 162). The two principal battles which helped to maintain this power were won against formidable rivals. In 480 BC the Carthaginians, who had succeeded the Phoenicians in the west, were soundly defeated by Greeks from Syracuse and Akragas at the Battle of Himera. In 413 BC the Athenians, who had sent their fleet to curb the power of Syracuse, were defeated by the Syracusans after a long siege. These victories left Greek Sicily one of the strongest powers in the Mediterranean: a position consolidated by the aggressive—and occasionally wise—rule of successive tyrants of Syracuse. Of these, the most noteworthy are Dionysius I (405-367 BC), Timoleon (343-336 BC), Agathocles (317-289 BC) and Hieron II (265-215 BC). The last two rulers, who styled themselves as kings, span the **Hellenistic period** of Sicily's history.

Roman period (241 BC–5th c. AD) The first Punic War (264-241 BC) between Rome and Carthage ended with the Roman conquest of Sicily. The Greeks, who had little control over events, could be little more than bystanders, although any Greek cities who did not align themselves with the Romans (such as Akragas, which at this time was in the Carthaginian camp) were destroyed. A timely

alliance made with the Romans by Hieron II of Syracuse ensured the preservation of the city, which was allowed to retain its independence. But during the second Punic War (218-201 BC) and after Hieron's death (215 BC) his successor made the mistake of transferring his allegiance to the Carthaginians. This resulted in the sack of Syracuse by the Romans in 211 BC.

After the Romans' triumph over the Greeks and Carthaginians, Sicily lost all her prestige and significance in the Mediterranean. As a province of Rome she was a subject territory. Her people, other than the Roman colonists themselves or the few natives accorded citizenship, were not Romans and had none of the rights of their masters. (This was not changed until the 3rd c. AD, when all inhabitants of the Empire were classified as Romans.) The island became an area of exploitation, both for the grain which she produced in great quantity for the Roman army and for any satisfaction she could give to the greed of her civilian rulers.

During the 2nd c. BC there were two serious revolts against the Romans by the slaves who worked on the land, the so-called Slave Wars (135-132 and 104-101 BC).

By far the worst individual oppressor of the province was the *praetor* (civilian governor) Verres who in the three years of his rule (73-71 BC) committed every conceivable excess, from wilful murder to the plundering of art treasures. The only blessing of this evil man was that he provoked the condemnation of Cicero, from whose speeches we learn much of the state of affairs in Sicily at the time.

Contributing further to the ruin of Sicily was the civil war between Sextus Pompey and Octavian, son of Julius Caesar. For seven years Sextus used Sicily as his stronghold, cutting off the supply of grain to Rome and consuming the forests for shipbuilding. Despite these efforts it was in a sea battle off Mylae (Milazzo) that Sextus was finally defeated by the Roman fleet under Agrippa (36 BC).

After Octavian became Emperor Augustus Caesar (27 BC) he turned a fresh eye on Sicily. The establishment of Roman colonies in some of the decaying towns did much to revive them, and Sicily entered a period of peace and relative prosperity. The island became a kind of feudal resort for the Roman nobility whose estates, the *latifundia,* were the basis for the subsequent ruinous exploitation of the countryside. The hunting lodge at Piazza Armerina (Casale), with its famous floor mosaics, dates from the tail-end of Roman colonization (late 3rd c. AD).

The later Roman period is associated with the advent of Christianity in Sicily. Legends surround the visits here of St Peter and St Paul, and there are extensive Christian catacombs in Syracuse (3rd-6th c. AD).

Syracusan Greek coin with head of Arethusa and dolphins (5th c. BC)

major town, Syracuse, was captured in 878. From their capital at Palermo the Saracens ruled Sicily with an efficiency impaired only by their domestic feuds. They introduced citrus fruits, sugar cane and other crops from their native lands and greatly improved the island's irrigation. The Fatimid dynasty established their emirate at Palermo, which became a city of great luxury.

Despite a brief occupation of Syracuse by the Byzantine general George Maniakes (1038-1042), the Byzantines were never able to recover the island. The next—and most celebrated—conquest of Sicily was by a small but intrepid band of Norman knights, under Roger and Robert de Hauteville.

Barbarian period (5th-6th c. AD) After Alaric, king of the Visigoths, had captured Rome in 410 AD Sicily was threatened by barbarian invasion. The island was finally overrun c. 440 AD by another German tribe, the Vandals, who invaded it from their base on the African coast at Carthage. From 493-526 Sicily came under the rule of the great Ostrogothic king Theodoric, who had won control over most of Italy.

As a result of these invasions the Romans had withdrawn to the new capital of their empire at Constantinople (formerly Byzantium). The recovery of the western part of the empire became the main objective of the Byzantine generals.

Byzantine period (535-827 AD) The island submitted willingly to the conquest of the Byzantine general Belisarius, who drove out the Goths in 535. Although the whole of Italy was subsequently won back from the barbarians, Sicily and the southern mainland were the only parts to remain attached to the empire when another Germanic tribe, the Lombards, overran the north. The 300-year connection with the Greek-speaking Byzantine Empire restored Sicily to the Greek world to which the island had belonged in ancient times, and it must have been a moment of fruition when the Emperor Constans II—harried by the Arabs at Constantinople—transferred his court to Syracuse in 662. (The imperial presence was however put to an end by an assassin in 668.) As the Arabs stepped up their attacks on the empire, its hold on Sicily weakened.

Arab period (827-1061) The treachery of a Byzantine admiral, Euphemius, who wanted to be the ruler of Sicily, prepared the way for an invasion by the Saracens, the mixed Berber and Arab people who by this time controlled most of the Levant and North Africa. Euphemius invited the military support of the Saracens, who landed at Mazara with a force of 10,000. Their conquest, however, was the hardest won in the history of Sicily. The Byzantines were defending their last outpost in the west and resisted desperately. Palermo was taken in 831; the last

Norman period (1061-1194) These adventurous knights, who had already captured the Lombard strongholds in southern Italy, had long had their eyes on Sicily. In 1061 Roger de Hauteville seized Messina, and in a series of campaigns lasting 30 years gradually won Sicily from the Saracens. He gave himself the title of Count of Sicily and became the first in the line of Norman rulers who did so much to restore the prestige of Sicily in the Mediterranean world.

Strong and cohesive administration was linked with an enlightened attitude towards the Saracens, whose Muslim faith was tolerated in the same way that the Saracens had tolerated the Byzantine Christians. These two cultures, with their legacy of co-existence, were harnessed by the Normans to create a cultural tradition that finds its best expression in the surviving buildings of the period (notably at Palermo, Monreale and Cefalù which combine with Norman architecture the decorative arts of Arab and Greek.

Count Roger (also known as Roger I) was succeeded, after a short regency, by his young son Roger (b. 1095) who became Roger II, the first Norman king of Sicily (1130-54). It was said of Roger that he

Left: Mosaic, Casale Right: Count Roger vs. Saracen, Cathedral, Mazara del Vallo   13

'accomplished more asleep than other men awake' and his rule was the high-water mark of Norman power in the Mediterranean. He was a patron of the arts, drew up the first written code of Sicilian law, and extended the kingdom of Sicily—which already included part of southern Italy—to Malta and part of the north Africa coast.

Roger's achievements were somewhat dissipated by his son, William I (1154–66). He was known as 'William the Bad', an apt title for a cruel and pleasure-seeking king who surrounded himself with favourites, quarrelled with his barons, and lost the territories won by his father in Africa. His son William II ('William the Good'), who ruled from 1166–1189, was by contrast a just and wise ruler, but unfortunately died without issue.

The main conflict abroad at this time was that between the Pope and the Holy Roman Emperor—the great spiritual and temporal powers of Europe. The contest was as much for territory as for the hearts of men and when the Norman succession in Sicily was disputed, the Holy Roman Emperor Henry VI seized the opportunity presented by his marriage to Constance, daughter of Roger II, to claim the throne of Sicily.

Swabian period (1194–1268) Henry VI, who was head of the Swabian house of Hohenstaufen, crowned himself king of Sicily in 1194. His primary interest was, however, his empire, which stretched from Germany to southern Italy. To Henry, Sicily was merely a source of revenue, its treasures to be plundered at will to line the imperial coffers. Fortunately he died of dysentery three years after his coronation and was succeeded by his infant son the Emperor Frederick II, who was crowned King Frederick I of Sicily in 1197.

Like his father, Frederick's activities were deployed throughout the Holy Roman Empire, and in quarrels with the Pope. Unlike his father—whose cruelty had stirred the Sicilians to revolt—he was a wise and just ruler and a man of prodigious learning, whose title 'Stupor Mundi' was rightly earned. He restored order to the island, built many fine castles, and created the first school of Italian vernacular poetry at his court in Palermo. There is no doubt that if his rule had been confined to Sicily the island would have reached its Golden Age, but his preoccupation was with his imperial authority, particularly in Italy where it was threatened by the temporal power of the Pope. After Frederick's death in 1250, this power was exerted in favour of the French prince Charles of Anjou, who was offered the crown of Sicily in return for his support of the Pope.

Angevin period (1268–1282) Once Frederick's natural successors had been dispatched (Manfred, the Emperor's son, was killed in battle in 1266; his grandson Conradin beheaded by the Angevins in 1268) Charles of Anjou seized the throne. The Sicilians, who had supported Frederick and his heirs, were resentful of their new French rulers, who did nothing to appease this resentment by an incredibly ruthless suppression of the people. Towns and villages which resisted the Angevins were shown no mercy, their inhabitants massacred: those which submitted were ground down by the taxation necessary to support Charles' military adventures. The whole affair was brought to an end in 1282 by the most spontaneous revolution in the history of Sicily. Known as the Sicilian Vespers, after an incident in Palermo which sparked it off (see History of Palermo, p. 117) this bloody rebellion speedily disposed of the French presence in Sicily.

In the subsequent war of the Vespers with France, the Sicilians were assisted by a Spanish prince, Peter of Aragon. His link with the Swabians (he was married to Manfred's daughter) made Peter a popular choice as the next king of Sicily.

Aragonese period (1282–1410) The war with France ended in 1302 at the Treaty of Caltabellotta, which confirmed Sicily as an independent kingdom under Aragonese rule. The ancient name of Sicily, 'Trinacria', was revived, and the Sicilians had the benefit of the wise and stable rule of Frederick II of Aragon (1296–1337). While fending off the continuing

attempts of the Angevins—now based in Naples—to reconquer the island, Frederick had the difficult task of keeping the peace between the Latin barons, established in the island since the Norman conquest, and the new Catalan nobles who had come to Sicily with the Aragonese succession (Catalonia had united with Aragon in 1137). These nobles were the forbears of the great Sicilian aristocracy which was to dominate the affairs of the island up to the 19th c.

In 1410 the Sicilian throne became vacant with the death of the last Aragonese king. A parliament was called at Taormina to choose a new king, but there were so many claimants that it was impossible to reach an agreement. The Spanish settled the issue by proclaiming Ferdinand of Castile the rightful successor. The kingdoms of Aragon and Sicily were united, and Sicily was ruled directly from Spain.

Spanish period (1410–1713) Initially the Spanish rulers of Sicily were resident in Spain, but in 1442, when Alfonso V (the Magnanimous) had occupied Naples, the 'two Sicilies' (southern Italy and Sicily) were ruled from here. After Alfonso's death in 1458, however, Naples and southern Italy were ruled by his successors and Sicily by Viceroys.

As Spanish power accelerated and Spain became a single nation, the status of Sicily declined. The Sicilian parliament had little power other than as a rubber-stamp to demands for the inevitable taxation that went with empire-building, and the land was divided among a few noble families who kept the favour of the Spanish court. The moral and spiritual freedom of the people was kept in tight check by the Spanish Inquisition and the island was scarcely touched by the Renaissance.

Such was the neglect of Sicily by the Spanish monarchy that during the period of the Viceroys the only Spanish king to visit the island was Charles V, who as Holy Roman Emperor passed through the island on his return from the conquest of Tunis (1535).

The 17th c. was a period of continuing decline for Sicily. Political oppression and financial exploitation reduced her to a peasant province, and the second half of the century was marked by the devastating eruption of Etna (1669) and the even more disastrous earthquake of 1693 which destroyed most of the towns in south-eastern Sicily.

When Charles II of Spain died, leaving all his lands to Philip of Anjou, the countries of the Grand Alliance (England, Holland and the German and Austrian states) went to war with France to prevent her taking over the Spanish territories (War of the Spanish Succession). In 1713 the Treaty of Utrecht awarded Sicily to Savoy; later on (1720) it was awarded, by the Treaty of the Hague, to

Austria. The Austrian presence in Sicily was extremely unpopular, but short-lived. In 1734 a young Spanish prince, Charles of Bourbon, arrived in Naples to lay claim to the Kingdom of Naples, in which Sicily was included.

Bourbon period (1734–1860) The rule of Charles of Bourbon was a blessed interlude for the Sicilians, who were given many concessions—notably in taxation—by the progressive king. Unfortunately Charles succeeded to the throne of Spain in 1759 and the Kingdom of Naples was abandoned to his son, the feckless Ferdinand IV.

Ferdinand was not interested in government and delegated the affairs of state to his wife, Maria Carolina. The centre of Ferdinand's world was the Neapolitan court, and his only visits to Sicily were in forced circumstances during the Napoleonic Wars.

The first occasion was in 1799. Ferdinand, who at the prompting of Maria Carolina had made an alliance with Britain against Napoleon, was further persuaded to attack France. In a swift reprisal, the French occupied Naples, and Ferdinand and his queen fled to Palermo. (It is interesting to record that the royal couple sailed to Sicily in Nelson's flagship, the *Vanguard*, in the company of Sir William Hamilton, the British Ambassador to Naples, and his wife the famous Lady Emma.)

After six months the French were driven out of Naples and the Bourbon court restored. In 1806, however, the French were back with Joseph Bonaparte, who had been given the Kingdom of Naples by his brother Napoleon. Again Ferdinand was forced to take refuge in Sicily and it was not until 1815, after the fall of Napoleon, that he was restored as King Ferdinand I of the Two Sicilies.

During the Napoleonic Wars the British had exerted an increasing influence in Sicily. In exchange for their protection Ferdinand had granted them a military foothold on the east coast, and the commander-in-chief of the British forces, Lord Bentinck, was able to impose a British-type constitution on a highly unrepresentative parliament of nobles. After the departure of the British Ferdinand, who had a great following among the Sicilian aristocracy, suspended this constitution. This caused a popular revolt in Sicily, which Ferdinand put down with the aid of Austrian mercenaries.

Ferdinand died in 1825 and under the Bourbon kings who followed him Sicily suffered one of the worst periods of repression in its unhappy history. The most notorious king was Ferdinand II (1830–59) who held his throne by giving favours to the rich and by ruthlessly crushing his opponents. In 1848 he earned the name 'King Bomba' when he reduced Messina—in revolt against his rule —by a five-day naval bombardment. This tyranny not only pricked the conscience of

Baroque façade, Syracuse Cathedral

the European nations but gave a focus to the movement known as the *Risorgimento*, whose aim was the unification of Italy. In 1860 an unsuccessful rising in Palermo prompted Giuseppe Garibaldi, the military leader of the movement, to set sail for Sicily from Genoa with the famous 'Thousand', the spearhead of the campaign.

Unification of Italy and Kingdom of Savoy (1860–1946) On 11 May 1860 the Thousand effected a successful landing at Marsala on the west coast of Sicily—with the discreet protection of those same British warships that 50 years previously had supported King Ferdinand. From Marsala the Thousand marched on Palermo, gathering *en route* the support of the Sicilian people, whose primary concern was their liberation from the detested Bourbons. Half-way to Palermo, at Calatafimi, the Garibaldini defeated a force of 3000 Neapolitans: a heroic battle which cleared the way to the capital. After three days of street fighting Palermo was taken and the defending Neapolitans departed with their fleet. The march continued along the north coast of Sicily and after a further victory

at Milazzo Garibaldi arrived at the Strait of Messina. Crossing to the mainland he marched north to Naples, which he entered in September. After the last decisive victory over the Neapolitans (Battle of the Volturno, 1 October) Naples, Sicily and Piedmont were united under Victor Emmanuel, King of Savoy.

The capture of Rome from the Papal forces (who were supported by the French) became the next target in the achievement of a Kingdom of Italy in fact as well as name. In 1862 Garibaldi returned to Sicily and with his famous cry *Roma o Morte!* (Rome or Death) drummed up Sicilian support for a march on Rome. His campaign was however thwarted by the Piedmontese, who feared the French repercussions of an attack on Rome. It was not until 1870, in fact, when the French troops had withdrawn to their own country to fight the Prussians, that Rome submitted and the unification of Italy was complete.

Although she was now part of a new independent state, Sicily reverted, ironically, to the status of a poor relation—no longer to Spain or Naples but to the industrial and commercial centres of central and northern Italy. She became, in fact, part of the underprivileged region known as the Mezzogiorno, which in addition to the accustomed ravages of a harsh climate and a mountainous terrain suffered the deprivation of much of its work force in a continuing emigration to the more prosperous parts of Italy and to other countries such as America and Australia. In this period the secret organization known as the Mafia rose to power in the island, particularly in the west in the region of Palermo. The depressed conditions here provided an ideal breeding ground for their criminal activities (bribery, extortion, selective killings) which led to their virtual control of the resources of the area.

In July 1943, during World War II, the Allies invaded Sicily in a massive sea-borne assault. The Americans, landing at Gela, concentrated their attack on the west of the island, while the British fought their way up the east coast. The German resistance, centred on Etna, broke when the Allied armies joined forces in the east. After the retreat of the Germans to the mainland the island was administered by the Allied powers, who were popular with the Sicilians. The Mafia, which had been outlawed by the Italian dictator Mussolini, was re-established in the west of Sicily, the Americans taking a tolerant view of the *mafiosi* who had assisted their invasion of the island.

It was a period that gave the Sicilians a new identity, a feeling of separateness from the rest of Italy which was realized after the war (1946) when the island was granted regional autonomy by the government of the new Italian Republic. (For the current economic situation, see p. 9.)

Statue of Garibaldi, Palermo

Practical information

TRAVEL
Air

Daily flights are available to Sicily by **Alitalia**. These flights are to Palermo or Catania via Rome or Milan, and the total flying time for either destination is 3 hrs 10 mins (allow approx. 1 hr for the connection).

Reduced **tourist excursion return fares** are available to Palermo or Catania. Fares vary according to season (summer Apr 1–Oct 31, winter Nov 1–Mar 31) and time of flight (day or night, mid-week or weekend). Validity 1 month, minimum stay 6 days.

International airports	*Distance from city*
Palermo Punta Raisi	32 km

(*buses every ½ hr from Piazza Politeama*)

Catania Fontanarossa	7 km

(*buses every ½ hr from Piazza Repubblica*)

Internal flights operate from Palermo to Trápani and Pantelleria, and from Trápani to Pantelleria and Lampedusa.

Timetables and details of fares may be obtained from the airline or travel agents.

Sea

There is no regular service from the UK to Sicily. The journey by sea must be made to Genoa, Livorno or Naples for connecting routes to Sicily. **All steamships include a car ferry service.**

The following is an outline of boat services available at the time of publication. For local sailings, more precise information is available from the agents of the navigation companies, which are usually situated in the harbour area. **Note: the frequency of services is subject to alteration.**

PALERMO

Steamship	*Grandi Traghetti*
To and from	Frequency
Genoa	3 times wkly
Livorno	3 times wkly
	Tirrenia Line
Naples	Daily
	Tirrenia also have less frequent sailings on the routes Naples/Catania/ Syracuse Malta/Syracuse/Catania Cagliari/Palermo Tunis/Palermo Tunis/Trapani

Agents in UK
Grandi Traghetti c/o Associated Oceanic Agencies, Eagle House, 109/110 Jermyn St, London SW1
Tirrenia Line c/o Sealink Travel Ltd, 52 Grosvenor Gdns, London SW1

MESSINA

Steamship	*Siremar*
To and from	Frequency
Naples	Twice wkly
(via Aeolian Is)	
Hydrofoil	*SNAV*
Reggio Calabria	Continuous
Ferry-boat (cars)	
Reggio Calabria	Continuous
Villa S. Giovanni	Continuous
(rail terminal)	

AEOLIAN IS.

Steamship	*Siremar*
To and from	Frequency
Naples	6 times wkly Apr–Sep
	Once wkly rest of year
Messina	3 times wkly Jun–Sep
	Twice wkly rest of year
Milazzo	Daily
Hydrofoil	*SNAV*
Naples	Daily 1 Jun–15 Oct
Messina	Twice daily 1 Jun–15 Oct
	SAS, Siremar
Milazzo	Daily
	SAS
Palermo/Cefalù	3 times wkly Jul–Sep
(Vulcano and	(day excursion)
(Lipari only)	

USTICA

Steamship	*Siremar*
To and from	Frequency
Palermo	Daily Jun–Sep
	6 times wkly rest of year

EGADI IS.

Steamship	*Siremar*
To and from	Frequency
Trápani	Daily
Hydrofoil	*Siremar*
Trápani	Daily Jun–Aug
	5 times wkly rest of year

PELAGIC IS.

Steamship	*Siremar*
To and from	Frequency
Porto Empedocle	Daily Apr–Oct
	5 times wkly rest of year

PANTELLERIA

Steamship	*Siremar*
To and from	Frequency
Trápani	Daily
Porto Empedocle	Once wkly
Mazara del Vallo	3 times wkly

Agencies in Sicily
Aliscafi (hydrofoil)

Messina	SNAV, Cortina del Porto Siremar, Alliatour, 144/6 Via Garibaldi
Milazzo	SAS, Molo L. Rizzo 14 Siremar, Largo dei Mille

Palermo	Siremar, Via F. Crispi 124
Cefalù	SAS, Agenzia Barbaro, Corso Ruggero
Trápani	Siremar, Via Amm. Staiti
Steamship	
(Siremar)	
Messina	Alliatour (agent) 144/6 Via Garibaldi
Milazzo	Largo dei Mille
Palermo	Via F. Crispi 124
Trápani	Molo Sanita
Porto Empedocle	Via Marullo 12
Mazara del Vallo	Via Molo G. Caito 47

Passenger tickets for boat services should be purchased at least half-an-hour before departure. Car drivers should arrive earlier.

Rail

The most direct route by rail from the UK to Sicily is via Calais and Rome. International trains connect with the daily services from Rome to Palermo or to Syracuse via Taormina and Catania. These are through services, crossing the Strait of Messina by ferry. Sleeping cars and/or couchettes are available on these services. (The journey from London to Palermo takes $43\frac{1}{2}$ hours.) Tickets issued in Britain have a validity of two months and journeys can be broken at intermediate stations. Tickets for these journeys on Italian State Railways are obtainable through local branches of Thos. Cook or CIT (England) Ltd, 10 Charles II Street, London SW1.

Internal services
Sicily has a comprehensive railway system with four different types of train:

Rapido These are the fastest trains, connecting the major towns. A supplement of 30% is charged and seats should be booked in advance

Espresso Long distance express trains
Diretto Trains stopping at most stations
Locale Trains stopping at all stations

One of the most interesting rail trips is the journey around Etna by the *Ferrovia Circumetnea* (p. 93).

Reductions
Fare reductions are offered to travellers on Italian State Railways in certain cases. These include families of four or more, children under 12, and parties of ten or more. There is also a special 'Travel at Will' ticket suitable for tourists who intend to travel extensively on Italian Railways. It is only obtainable outside Italy and allows unlimited travel on any Italian train. More details of these and other bargains may be obtained from authorized agencies.

Motoring

Motorists taking their own vehicles to Italy must carry:
1. Registration book

2. International insurance (Green Card)
3. UK driving licence with inserted translation (obtainable from Italian State Tourist Office, 201 Regent Street, London W1 or through the AA or RAC)

Car Ferries to Sicily
Motorists driving all the way to Sicily via the 'toe' of Italy will cross the Strait of Messina by car ferry from Villa S. Giovanni or Reggio Calabria to Messina.
Those who prefer not to drive the length of Italy can arrange to transport their car by ferry to Palermo from Genoa, Livorno or Naples. For details of services, see p. 17.
Price reductions Both Tirrenia Line and Grandi Traghetti offer reductions on their car ferry services. These are 50% on return tickets for cars with foreign registration, provided the visitor stays in Sicily a minimum of 7 days. These reductions do not apply in the high season (July–Aug).

Car-hire
Car-hire firms may be found in most of Sicily's large towns. The rates vary between companies, but there is little to choose between the 'Big Four'—Hertz, Avis, Maggiore and Europcar. A typical tariff for a small car (Fiat 126) would be:
Daily rate L6400
Weekly rate L37,500
Mileage L100 per km extra
Rate for unlimited mileage L126,000 per wk
Optional extra charges:
Collision damage waiver L3000 per day
Personal accident insurance L1200 per day
All car-hire charges are subject to a government tax (IVA) of 14%.

Motor-scooters are available for hire at most resorts and towns in Sicily.

Breakdown services
Breakdown services operated by the Automobile Club of Italy are available to motorists who break down in Sicily. To contact this service, telephone 116.
Drivers taking their own vehicles to Sicily are advised to take out special insurances through the AA or RAC to cover the cost of repairs and other expenses resulting from breakdown.

Roads

The roads in Sicily are extremely good, with the exception of some of those off the beaten track or in the poorer parts of the towns. There are three main categories:
Autostrada (motorway)
Rapid progress has been made in autostrada construction in recent years. The main routes now open are Messina–Catania (A18), Palermo–Catania (A19), Palermo–Trápani (A29) and Palermo–Mazara del Vallo (A29). The main route under construction is

the A20, linking Palermo–Messina via the north coast, which is now nearing completion.

Strada statale (state road)
These are the roads (abbreviated SS) linking the main towns of Sicily. They have a good surface and are usually 2-lane, with some stretches (*superstrada*) 4-lane.

Other roads
The standard of the side roads which connect the smaller towns and villages varies greatly. Landslips are not uncommon in Sicily and detours are occasionally necessary.

Road maps
The best road maps of Sicily are those published by the Touring Club Italiano. There are three separate maps, for the east, west and south of the island.

Buses and coaches

The major towns have good bus services, details of which may be obtained from the local tourist information office. It is useful to remember that the starting point for many town buses is the central railway station. There are also local bus services connecting the smaller towns and villages, though these are not the speediest form of transport.

For tourists not wishing to drive in Sicily, the coach services offering inclusive tours provide the best opportunities for sightseeing. The best service is the package tour by coach run by Europabus and CIT from Palermo, Catania or Taormina. These tours, which include guides and overnight accommodation, visit the most important places of interest and are of 4–8 days' duration. Further details of prices and itineraries are available from CIT.

Shorter (one day or half-day) guided excursions, run by CIT, are also available. Apply to local CIT office.

Taxis and cabs

Taxis are generally equipped with meters. If not, the fare for the journey should be agreed before setting out. The tariffs to and from the airports are official, and notices are posted to this effect, stating the exact fare. With metered journeys a 10% tip should be offered.

Fares for trips in horse-cabs (*carrozze*) should be agreed beforehand.

INCLUSIVE HOLIDAYS

A package tour including air flight, accommodation and food is the quickest and cheapest way of holidaying in Sicily. The airlines serving the island from the UK offer package holidays in association with travel agencies.

The varied range of holidays available includes resort holidays (return flight and accommodation), fly and drive (return flight and car hire), archaeological tours and special interest holidays. Details of tour operators' specialities are in the traveller's handbook available from the Italian State Tourist Office.

Exchange Travel Exchange House, Parker Rd, Hastings, Sussex offer hotel and self-catering holidays based on Taormina and Cefalu. A two-week holiday can include a one-week tour of the island and one week in a resort. Other tour operators specialising in Sicily are:

CIT 10 King Charles II St, London SW1
Club 18–30 100 Oxford St, London W1
Cosmos Tours 1 Bromley Common, Bromley, Kent
Enterprise Holidays PO Box 410, West London Terminal, Cromwell Rd, London SW7
Facts Travel 155 Upper Richmond Rd, London SW15
Furness Travel 148 Gloucester Rd North, Filton, Bristol
Hayes & Jarvis 6 Harriet St, London SW1
Horizon Ltd 214 Broad St, Birmingham
Intasun Leisure House 29/31 Elmfield Rd, Bromley, Kent
Rofe Travel 17 Princes Arcade, London SW1
Sicilian Holidays 4 Station Rd, Pangbourne, Berks
Small World 5 Garrick St, London WC2
Sovereign Holidays PO Box 410, West London Terminal, Cromwell Rd, London SW7
Sunvil Travel 88 Sheen Rd, Richmond, Surrey
Supertravel 22 Hans Place, London SW1
Swans Tours 329 Putney Bridge Rd, London SW15
Thomson Holidays Greater London House, Hampstead Rd, London NW1

Self-catering specialists:
Eurovillas 64 Church St, Coggeshall, Essex
Interhome 10 Sheen Rd, Richmond, Surrey
Perrymead Properties 55 Perrymead St, London SW6
also CIT, Sunvil, Swans and Thomson as above

ACCOMMODATION

Hotels

Hotel development is keeping pace with Sicily's growing popularity as a holiday island. The main towns and resorts have hotels of all grades, from 1st–4th class, and a choice of pensions (three classes). The De Luxe hotels are in Palermo (*Villa Igiea*) and Taormina (*San Domenico Palace*, *Mazzarò Sea Palace*).

Among the 1st class hotels the following are worth a mention:

Grande Albergo e delle Palme (Palermo) Strategically situated in the Via Roma in the centre of the city. Elegant hotel with relaxing 19th c. atmosphere.

Jolly (Palermo) Near the sea, in the Foro Italico—but with its own swimming pool.

Note: there are also Jolly Hotels in Agrigento, Catania, Piazza Armerina, Messina, Taormina and Syracuse.

Timeo (Taormina) Old-style hotel with elegant decor and excellent service. Perfectly situated by Greek theatre with view of Etna.

Grande Albergo delle Terme (Sciacca) Modern well-appointed hotel, with commanding views of the sea. Offers additional facility of thermal cures, for those with rheumatic and other complaints.

Villa Politi (Syracuse) In the north-east of the city, near the Latomia dei Capuccini. Old, quiet hotel with pleasant garden.

A point to watch with the resort hotels is that some of those graded as 2nd class have all the appointments of a 1st class hotel. Higher grading involves a higher rate of tax, and there is an obvious temptation to some proprietors to disqualify themselves from this status. It should not be assumed, therefore, that the 2nd class category is always inferior to the 1st class.

Prices vary considerably according to the class, season and location of the hotel. Full board in a 1st class pension in a popular resort, for example, can cost as much as in a 1st class hotel in a town. Prices now include the service charge and IVA at 9%.

A complete list of hotels in Sicily, with categories, facilities and prices, is published by the Sicilian Tourist Board and is available from ENIT at 201 Regent St, London W1. Bookings should be made through travel agents or hotel representatives.

Motels These are ideal for motoring tours, and for the one-night stop. Most of the motels in Sicily are run either by Agip or the motoring organisation ACI. They are listed in the hotel guide (see above).

Sea resorts and Tourist Villages

With its varied coastline and pleasant climate, Sicily offers a great choice of resorts, many of which have a year-round season. Tourist Villages are usually located by the sea and offer accommodation in bungalows or apartments, with shops and restaurants, and sport and recreational facilities.

Sicily's main sea resorts (those with Tourist Villages marked with asterisk):

Agrigento Province
San Leone, Sciacca

Caltanissetta Province
Gela

Catania Province
Acireale, Riviera dei Ciclopi, *Capo Molini, *Aci Trezza, *Catania, La Plaja

Messina Province
*Patti, *Castroreale Terme, *S. Marina, *Milazzo, Lido di Mortelle, Contesse, Maregrosso, *S. Margherita, Lípari

Palermo Province
*Terrasini, Cinisi, Isola delle Fémmine, *Sferracavallo, Mondello, Acquasanta, Romagnolo, *Aspra, Vetrana, Términi Imerese, *Cefalù (Club Mediterranée), Ustica

Ragusa Province
*Marina di Ragusa, *Marina di Modica, Pozzallo

Syracuse Province
Agnone Bagni, *Syracuse, *Penisola della Maddalena (Villagio Turístico), Fontane Bianche

Taormina
Mazzarò, Spisone, Giardini

Trápani Province
Lido di San Giuliano, *Favignana

A full list of Tourist Villages, with details of season, facilities etc., is available from ENIT (Italian State Tourist Office, 201 Regent Street, London W1).

Villas and flats

A list of agencies offering villas and flats to let is available from ENIT, as above.

Alberghi Diurni (Day Hotels)

These are not, strictly speaking, hotels, but temporary resting-places for travellers *en route* to other destinations. They are found only in the large towns, in or near the main railway station. Open during the day (6 am-midnight) they are provided with bathrooms, rest-rooms, laundry and other services.

Hill resorts

There are many resorts at different altitudes for those who prefer a more refreshing climate during the heat of the summer. The Etna region has a number of hotels and villas which provide a suitable base for exploring Sicily's most fascinating landscape.

There are Tourist Villages at Érice (La Pineta) and at Lake Pergusa near Etna. The resort of S. Martino delle Scale provides a cool retreat from Palermo, which has the island's highest summer temperature.

Watering places

Sicily is extremely rich in thermal phenomena. These include mineral springs, sweating grottoes, and sulphur baths, all of which are renowned for their curative and therapeutic properties.

The most important spas are at Acireale, Ali Terme, Castroreale Terme, Sciacca and Términi Imerese. Also at Sciacca are the natural steam and sweating caves of Monte San Calogero. Visitors to the islands of Vulcano and Panarea will enjoy bathing in the thermally heated sea.

Camping

Sicily has official camp sites at most of the major resorts. These are listed in the publication *Campeggio in Italia*, published by the

the TCI, Corso Italia, Milan (L5000). Some of the sites are run by TCI themselves: these have fixed tents, restaurants etc.

An abridged list of sites with location map (free of charge) and the publication *Guida Camping d'Italia* (L5000) are issued by the Federazione Italiana del Campeggio, Casella Postale 649, 50100 Firenze, or from ENIT in London when available. The leaflet *Sicilia Camping* is available from tourist offices in Sicily.

Youth hostels

These are known as 'Alberghi per la Gioventu' and accept YHA members. There are only two in Sicily, at Castroreale and Lipari. Details from YHA, 29 John Adam St, London WC2.

There are also student hostels 'Casa dello Studente' in Catania and Messina.

BEACHES

All the sea resorts listed above have good beaches. As the choice of resort often depends on the type of beach, however, further research will be necessary. Mondello, for example, has a wide sandy beach: Taormina, a series of small but very attractive shingle beaches. Away from the resorts there are many fine wayside beaches, particularly on the south-west and south-east coasts. Some are in close proximity to archaeological sites, which is a convenient way of satisfying two objectives. At Eloro the rocky promontory conceals a pleasant sandy beach. The white beach at Eraclea Minoa, screened by pine trees, stretches along a gently curving bay. Selinunte has the beach at Marinella. Another fine beach backed by low cliffs and guarded by a medieval castle, is at Falconara, west of Gela.

The north coast, with its high cliffs and railway line, makes access to remote beaches difficult. There is, however, an easy approach to Cefalù and other resorts.

FOOD AND DRINK

The **food** of Sicily is like that of Italy, with the emphasis on *pasta*. There are, however, regional specialities, and it is worth going to local restaurants to sample these.

One of the favourites is *pasta con sarde*, in which either spaghetti or macaroni is served with a dressing of sardines. Pasta is served with fish as a common practice in coastal towns and villages. Among the meat dishes, *involtini alla Siciliana* is particularly recommended. These are slices of meat—usually veal—which are rolled around a filling of salami, ham, cheese, breadcrumbs and onion and baked. Another popular dish is *caponata*, a delicious *ratatouille* of olives, aubergines and other vegetables.

Fish is plentiful in Sicily, and in the tunny season one will be amazed by the size of these great fish as they are cut up on the fishmongers' slabs. No opportunity should be missed to sample the swordfish, *spada*. This is usually cut in slices and grilled.

The variety of fruit in Sicily is bewildering. In a fixed price menu, the fruit course may consist of one apple or pear. If dining *a la carte*, however, one can expect a whole bowl of mouth-watering cherries, plums, medlar-fruit, peaches or grapes, depending on the season. *Note:* a fixed price menu does not usually include the service charge.

If you don't mind standing up to eat, try a *bar-pasticceria*, where you can have an early morning cup of coffee and freshly-baked rolls (*panini*), croissants (*cornetti*) or any of a grand variety of cakes and macaroons. Remember to pay as you go in—and then hand the receipt to the barman who actually takes your order.

At places marked *Tavola Calda* (i.e. 'hot table') a large choice of ready-prepared hot or cold dishes is available, either for eating on the spot (standing or sitting) or for taking away. Pasta, pizzas, salads, various batter-cooked rice and savoury balls (*arancini*) and meat dishes are usually on display.

The ice-cream known to English people as *Cassata Siciliana* is not often found—instead the real Sicilian *cassata* turns out to be a form of cake with candied fruits and marzipan. Sicilian ice-creams are eaten in large quantities and their flavours include *nocciola* (hazel-nut), *mandorla* (almond), *pistacchio*, *zuppa inglese* (with added candied fruit), and *torrone* (another delicious mixture). An odd habit is that of eating ice-cream or cream-filled rolls for breakfast (*briosce con gelato, con panna*).

Sicily is also famous for its cakes and confectionery. The *cassate* already mentioned are in the category of a craft, which the confectioners of Palermo learned from the Arabs. So too are the marzipan fruits, painted in natural colours, and the *confetti*, the sugar almonds which are popular sweetmeats at weddings.

Good food in Sicily is quite expensive and if one is not staying 'full pension' in an hotel, it is better to limit oneself to one good meal a day in the evening. There are many places where breakfast and a very adequate midday snack can be enjoyed.

The **drink** most readily associated with Sicily is *Marsala* wine, from the region around the town of that name in western Sicily. This is an amber-coloured dessert wine. Other famous dessert wines, with their places of origin, are *Moscato* (Syracuse and Noto) and *Malvasia* (Lipari). Among the table wines to be recommended are *Zucco*, *Corvo* and *Regaleali* (Palermo) and *Faro* (Messina) and the varied wines of the Etna region.

The light imported beer and local mineral waters are good alternatives to the wines.

RESTAURANTS

The main Sicilian towns have a wide range of restaurants, from the luxury category to the simple *trattoria*. Some restaurants offer a 'Menu Turistico' at a fixed price. Service charges vary from 5–20% depending on the category and location of the restaurant. Prices are subject to an additional 9% IVA. Some good Sicilian restaurants, with reasonable prices:

Palermo
Al Ficodindia da Pedro Via Emerico Amari
Peppino Piazza Castelnuovo
Al Cassaro Via Isnello
'A Cuccagna Via Principe Belmonte
Pappagallo Via Principe Granatelli
Pizzeria Piazza Bellini (ideal for lunch)
Spano (on the sea-front, south of the city, at Romagnolo. Excellent sea-food)

Messina
Borgia Via dei Mille
Lisi Via Maddalena
Donna Giovanni Via Risorgimento
at Ganzirri   at Mortelle
Borgia   *Sporting*

Taormina
Chez Angelo Corso Umberto
Ciclope Corso Umberto
Myosotis Corso Umberto
at Mazzarò
Il Pescatore

Catania
La Fazenda Viale 20 Settembre
Pagano Via de Roberto
Turi Finocchiaro Via Cestai
Rio Corso Italia
Alba Via Pacini

Syracuse
Minerva Piazza Duomo
Darsena Riva Garibaldi
Santoro Viale Rizzo
Bandiera Via Eritrea

Agrigento
La Caprice Via Panoramica

Lípari
Filippino Piazza Municipio

FOLK ART

The souvenir shops of Sicily's resorts give the visitor a taste of the island's long tradition of popular crafts. Prominently displayed are the most celebrated symbols of that tradition: the marionettes and hand-painted carts. Though mass-produced for the tourist trade, it can be said that these souvenirs have done something to maintain a live interest in Sicily's folk art. The marionette shows, after all, can hardly compete with television: the carts, which for practical purposes have been supplanted by the three-wheeler and the van, are now only seen on festive occasions.

Medieval legend provides a linking theme for both these nostalgic expressions of a vanishing culture. The **Sicilian carts** are decorated with scenes from the age of the paladins, those Frankish knights who went in pursuit of fair maidens and infidels with equal relish. The theme is often varied by a painting of a scene from Sicilian history. The heroic exploits of that great slayer of Saracens, Count Roger, make a popular subject: so too the Sicilian Vespers and the march of Garibaldi and the Thousand. At the back of the gift shop, if one searches diligently, one may find bits of the painted sides and tailboard of a genuine Sicilian cart, or those fine wrought-iron arabesques and miniature figures also used as ornaments. Though vastly overpriced these make slightly more authentic souvenirs.

Those who would like to see a Sicilian cart being manufactured are recommended to go to the factories of the *Figli di D. Monteleone*, 18 Via G. Ingrassia, Palermo, or *Ducato*, 22 Via Sanfratello, Bagheria.

The **opera dei pupi** (marionette theatre) dramatises the same legends of the age of chivalry, with those French Galahads, Orlando and Rinaldo, as the stock characters. When they are not duelling for the hand of the fair Angelica, the two heroes are doing battle with the Moorish infidels: a grand drama played out on the tiny stage of the *Teatrino* under the expert guidance of the puppet-player (*puparo*) and his assistants. Most of Sicily's large cities have marionette theatres. They are usually located in a side street, in a small room with seating for fifty or so people. The *opera* is a family business. If he is lucky, the *puparo* will have a strapping teenage son to help him operate the marionettes (in a full suit of armour a marionette three feet high can weigh as much as 30 lbs). His wife will take the money and show people to their seats and his daughter—ideally, a compliant eight-year-old—will play the barrel-organ.

Inevitably, the intimate appeal of the marionette theatre has lost ground to the different forms of mass entertainment. But among the Sicilians there is still a hard-core of support,

Sicilian cart, Palermo

The best examples of Sicilian folk art may be seen in the G. Pitre Ethnographical Museum, in the Parco della Favorita, Palermo.

LANGUAGE

The Sicilian dialect is virtually a language in its own right. It does not have the same ancestry as modern Italian, i.e. the long Latin tradition of the mainland. Its basis is the Low Latin spoken in Italy in the early Middle Ages, with an infusion of Greek from the Byzantine period and Arabic from the later period of Arab rule. There are also words of French and Spanish origin, from the Norman and Aragonese periods. The study of such a complex vernacular is not recommended for the ordinary holidaymaker. Although Italian is readily understood by most Sicilians, the Sicilian dialect is difficult for Italian speakers. For the foreigner, the interest of Sicilian lies mainly in the origin of place names. A good example is Punta Raisi, the shoulder of land which has given its name to Palermo's airport. 'Punta' is the Italian for 'point'. 'Raisi' on the other hand is a Sicilian word of Arabic origin meaning 'captain of a fishing vessel'. Hence 'Fisherman's Point'. Another interesting Arabic word is 'Kal'at' (corrupted to *calta* or *calata*) meaning 'fortress' which appears as the prefix of a number of town-names such as Caltagirone, Calatafimi, etc.

English, French or German are spoken to some degree in most of the hotels.

FESTIVALS

On any day in the year it is certain that at least one of Sicily's towns will be engaged in a religious or cultural festival. The cultural events range from Palermo's six-month opera season to the performances of classical theatre at Syracuse; the religious events from Holy Week to the feast days of individual saints. The latter give an intimate view of the devotion of the people to their local saint, brought to a climax when the elaborate bier containing the saint's relics is paraded through the streets of the town or village.

Religious and Traditional

Jan 6	**Piana degli Albanesi** Epiphany. Celebrated throughout Sicily but with particularly colourful ceremony here, according to the Byzantine rite. The women of the town wear their traditional Albanian costumes
Feb (1st week)	**Agrigento** Almond Blossom and Folklore Festival in the Valley of the Temples
Feb 3-5	**Catania** Festival of St Agatha

consolidated by the companies who are prepared to travel with their shows, offering 'spettacolini per i bambini a domicilio'. For the tourist, the strongest persuasion lies in his own curiosity. This will be quickly satisfied by half-an-hour or so of crashing swords and armour, rolling Saracen heads, pounding feet and the bellowed dialogue, in raw Sicilian, of the *puparo*. No-one can emerge from the experience, however, without feeling they have enjoyed a little of the romance of Sicily.

The addresses of the local puppet theatres (Palermo has a choice of four good ones) may be obtained from the hotel or tourist office.

Pottery is another popular Sicilian craft. In Collesano the tradition of decorative glazed pottery is more than four centuries old, the most familiar products the 18th c. figurines in their perfect period costumes. Caltagirone has a similar tradition of fine ceramics, and on the north coast it is worth stopping for pottery at S. Stefano di Camastra. **Embroidery** flourishes in Palermo, where traditional costumes (notably those worn by the women of Piana degli Albanesi) are made. **Hand-weaving** is found in the mountain towns of the Madonie range, particularly in Petralia Sottana and Petralia Soprana, where the carpets are worked with Byzantine and Arab patterns. The marionette theatres have encouraged the craft of **metal-working**, best seen in the Palermitan workshops which produce the armour of the paladins.

Sicilian marionette

Mar	**Acireale** Carnival **Taormina** 'Battle of Flowers'
Easter	Public Holiday. Sicily's major religious festival. Of particular note are the celebrations at **Marsala** (Maundy Thursday Procession) **Trápani** (Good Friday Procession of the Stations of the Cross) and at **Piana degli Albanesi**
May 1	Public Holiday. Labour day
May	**Taormina** Rally of Sicilian costumes and carts
May 10	**Trecastagni** Festival of Sts Alfio, Filadelfo and Cerimo, with pilgrimage to sanctuary
Jun 3	**Messina** Festival of the Madonna della Lettera, protectress of the city
Jul 11–15	**Palermo** Festival of St Rosalia, Palermo's patron saint
Aug 15–17	**Piazza Armerina** *Palio dei Normanni*. Processions in medieval costume
Aug	**Petralia Sottana** *Cavalcata degli Sposi* and *Ballo della Cordella* (Nuptial Procession and Dance of the Ribbon). Traditional events performed in local costumes
Aug 14	**Messina** Procession of the Giants. Two great figures, representing a Moorish prince (Grigone) and his lady (Mata) are carried round the city during the Feast of the Assumption
Sep 4	**Palermo** Pilgrimage of St Rosalia (up Monte Pellegrino)
Sep 8	**Tíndari** Pilgrimage of the Black Madonna
Nov 1–2	Public Holiday. *Ogni Santi* (All Saints). Rituals in honour of the dead
Dec 13	**Syracuse** Festival of the Santuzza
Christmas	

Arts

Dec–May	**Palermo** Opera season (Teatro Massimo)
Feb–Apr	**Catania** Opera season (Teatro Bellini)
Mar–May	**Palermo** International Drama Festival
May–Jun	**Syracuse** Season of Greek plays performed in the Greek theatre
Jun–Jul	**Syracuse** International Ballet Festival
Jul	**Trápani** Music Festival (Villa Margherita)
Jul–Aug	**Messina, Taormina** International Film Festival
Jul–Aug	**Segesta** Greek theatre
Jul–Aug	**Tíndari** Greek theatre
Aug	**Taormina** International Music Festival

SPORT

Sicily's resorts have excellent facilities for water sports, including skin-diving, surfing, water-skiing and underwater swimming. Underwater fishing is also popular, particularly in the Aeolian islands and off the coasts of Palermo, Messina, Catania and Syracuse. No licence is required and the best season is from March–May and September–October. Mt. Etna and the Madonie Mountains are popular locations for winter sports. The ski lift at the Rifugio Sapienza on Etna can be reached in one hour from Catania. Similarly, the ski centres at Piano Zucchi and Piano della Battaglia in the Madonie may be quickly reached from Palermo.

CLIMATE

Sicily has an equable climate: neither too hot in summer nor too cold in winter. The average temperature of the hottest month (July) is 84°F (29°C) and of the coldest month (January) 52°F (11°C). The wettest months are March and October.

On Etna, snow falls early in the autumn and persists till late spring, and at all times of the year it can be chilly on the higher parts of the volcano.

Spring and autumn are the best seasons to visit Sicily.

CURRENCY, BANKS AND SHOPS

The monetary unit is the Italian Lira. Notes are for 500, 1000, 2000, 5000, 10,000, 20,000, 50,000 and 100,000 Lire. Coins in general circulation are of 50, 100 and 200 Lire. In shops, in lieu of small change, you may be offered sweets or chewing gum!

Banks give a fair rate of exchange but can be frustratingly slow in serving customers. They are usually open on weekday mornings (08.30–13.30). Hotels may be willing to exchange travellers' cheques.

Shops are open from 08.30/09.00–13.00 and from 15.30/16.00–19.30/20.00 (closed on Sundays).

WEIGHTS AND MEASURES

The metric system is in use. Some approximate equivalents:

1 litre	1.76 pints
20 litres	4.3 gallons
1 kilo	2.2 pounds
1 etto	3.5 ounces
1 metre	39 inches
1 kilometre	0.62 miles

A quick method of converting kilometres to miles is useful for UK motorists uncertain of distances. The method is to divide the distance by half and add the first digit if the distance is 10km or more. Thus 24km is about 14 miles $(12+2)$.

MUSEUMS AND MONUMENTS

Opening times Museums in Sicily are generally open mornings only (09.00–14.00 weekdays, 09.00–13.00 Sundays and holidays). Most museums, with one or two exceptions, are closed on Mondays.

Admission charges, where they are imposed, are very low. There is no charge on Sundays or holidays. Last tickets are usually issued $\frac{1}{2}$ hr before closing.

Archaeological sites are usually open from 09.00–1 hr before sunset, although the less visited ones are often closed from 13.00–15.30. All sites are closed on Mondays.

The prehistoric caves at Addaura, Lévanzo and Favignana may only be visited by special permission of the Soprintendente alle Antichità in Palermo.

Museum cards These allow foreign visitors free admission to museums. They are obtainable, with a list of all the State-owned museums in Sicily, from the CIT, RAC or Barclays Bank. Price: 40p.

Churches are usually open in the mornings and shut at 1 pm, opening again later in the afternoon or evening. To gain access to derelict churches, one must ask a local person for the key. (A small gratuity should be offered.)

GUIDE AND REFERENCE BOOKS

Official guide books to the major museums and monuments, published by the Ministero della Pubblica Istruzione, are available from custodians.

The most comprehensive Italian guide to Sicily is the Touring Club Italiano's *Sicilia,* in the *Guida d'Italia* series.

An excellent guide book to *Palermo,* by Giuseppe Bellafiore, is published in English by the Azienda Autonoma di Turismo.

Other books of special interest to visitors:

Archaeology

Sicily Before the Greeks by Bernabò Brea (Thames & Hudson, 1957)

*Sicily: An Archaeological Guide by Margaret Guido (Faber & Faber, 1967)

History

A History of Sicily Published in 3 vols:
  *Ancient Sicily by M. I. Finley
  Medieval Sicily by D. Mack Smith
  Modern Sicily by D. Mack Smith
  (Chatto & Windus, 1968–9)

The Normans in the South: 1016–1130
by John Julius Norwich (Longmans, 1967)

The Kingdom in the Sun: 1130–1194
by John Julius Norwich (Longmans, 1970.

*Also as Faber paperback 1976)

The Sicilian Vespers by Steven Runciman (Cambridge University Press 1958)

Travel

Italian Journey by J. W. Goethe (reprinted by Collins, 1962)

Spring in Sicily by Peter Quennell (Weidenfeld & Nicolson, 1952)

The Golden Honeycomb by Vincent Cronin (Hart-Davis, 1959)

Sicily, the Garden of the Mediterranean by Francis M. Guercio (Faber & Faber, 1968)

Sicily by P. Sebilleau (Kaye & Ward, 1968)

The Barrier and the Bridge: Historic Sicily by Alfonso Lowe (Geoffrey Bles, 1972)

Sicily (Islands Series) by Russell King (David & Charles, 1973)

Sicily by Anthony Pereira (Batsford, 1972)

*Sicilian Carousel by Lawrence Durrell (Faber & Faber, 1977, also as a Penguin, 1978)

Fiction

*The Leopard by Giuseppe di Lampedusa (Collins, 1960, also in Fontana paperback)

Two Stories and a Memory by Giuseppe di Lampedusa (Collins, 1962, also as a Penguin, 1966)

Dolci

The following books by Danilo Dolci are published in English by MacGibbon & Kee:

The Outlaws of Partinico (1960)

To Feed the Hungry (1960, also as a Penguin under title *Poverty in Sicily,* 1966)

Waste (1963)

Fire Under the Ashes The Life of Danilo Dolci by James MacNeish (Hodder & Stoughton, 1965)

*Indicates in print at the time of this edition

TOURIST INFORMATION

Information on all aspects of travel to Sicily is available from ENIT (Italian State Tourist Office), 201 Regent Street, London W1.

In Sicily, tourist offices are run by two different bodies. *Provincial Tourist Boards* are the responsibility of EPT (Ente Provinciale per il Turismo) and *Local Tourist Boards*—the tourist offices of the individual towns—are run by the Azienda Autonoma di Cura Soggiorno e Turismo.

The location of tourist information offices open to visitors is shown on the maps of the main towns in the Gazetteer section.

Exploring Sicily

Any tour of Sicily should begin at Pantálica, on that shoulder of earth between the dizzy deep gorges where an ancient king once stood and gazed at his realm. His name, we may imagine, was Hyblon, King of the Sicels. His kingdom, a large part of eastern Sicily, stretched far beyond the limits of his gaze. This was before those rival bands of Greeks had arrived, to divide the spoils of a beautiful new territory and to deliver them to history: that blissful, timeless space before Sicily felt the first concussion of civilization. This space and timelessness are still there, suspended in the gorges with their rock-cut tombs. And the view enjoyed by that ancient king is unchanged.

Unfortunately Pantálica is some way inland (the east coast, from which its first settlers were driven by the Sicel invasion, is 20 km distant) and only a helicopter could make it a starting point. Where else, more accessible, can we find Sicily's prehistory? A cave in Monte Pellegrino (Addaura) has incised drawings of the late Palaeolithic period, but these may only be seen with special permission. The Aeolian Islands have Neolithic and Bronze Age sites, but one needs two or three days to visit them. Easier to reach is Bronze-Age Thapsos, on its windswept penin-sula north of Syracuse. But standing there now, with the shoreward view of oil refineries, one can hardly feel time standing still. It is better, perhaps, to come to terms with the great era of civilization that produced these wonders and go southwards to Syracuse, capital of **Greek** Sicily.

Although Naxos, the first Greek colony, was founded earlier, Syracuse is the inevitable introduction to a tour of ancient Sicily. The fascination of its Greek and Roman ruins, described elsewhere, goes deeper even than the dark, mysterious stone quarries among which they are set, and the delights of its little island, the ancient Ortygia, should be savoured at leisure.

For the motorist Syracuse is the perfect base for visiting other ancient sites in the area, including Pantálica and Akrai inland and Thapsos and Megara Hyblaea on the coast to the north. But then there is a problem. To continue the Greek story, one must go to Agrigento, the great rival of Syracuse. Which route to follow—the southern way through the lovely Val di Noto, joining the coast at Gela, or the way inland through the mountain ranges of the Iblei and Erei? The same problem applies, of course, to the journey from Agrigento to Syracuse, and it can only be resolved by one of those decisions that are sent to try all car travellers abroad who have freedom of movement but not of time. The choice is between the primitive, but never hostile country of Sicily's interior, linked with the historical attractions of Piazza Armerina and Enna, and the gentler southern route with the charming Baroque towns of Noto, Módica and Ragusa.

Whatever the approach (and there is now, additionally, a fast *super-strada* route from Palermo) Agrigento is an incomparable reward, with its superb row of Greek temples on their proud barren ridge, waiting for the sun to rise—and set—on their golden columns. West of Agrigento two more sites show the cleverness of the Greeks at picking their view. Inevitably Eraclea Minoa's white beaches and headlands exercise a greater appeal than her excavations, at least to the non-specialist. At Selinunte the acropolis is a low hill between two rivers, overlooking the sea. A perfect site for everything—except defence. The ravages of war and earthquakes have left little of the ancient city but a jig-saw of tumbled stone. To the east, however, the great temples are triumphant. Ruined but massive, inspiring awe of a different kind, but no less powerful, than that which created them.

And what of Segesta, that delicious image of ancient Greece in Sicily's interior? Among the many literary travellers to this site, whose responses would make an anthology of admiration, Guy de Maupassant's is surely the most telling: 'The Temple of Segesta appears to have been posed by a man of genius who had revealed to him the only site where it might be fittingly placed; where it alone, in its solitude, animates the immensity of the landscape, giving life to the scene and rendering it divinely beautiful.'

Despite their long tenure of occupation (both had colonies in Sicily for more than 500 years—or at least as long as the Greeks) the Carthaginians and the Romans made a lesser impression on the island, both in terms of their culture and their architecture. Of Carthage's colonies, in fact, we have only the scant ruins on Motya, originally a settlement of the **Phoenicians**. This tiny island, just off the coast north of Marsala, seems as impregnable now (it is privately owned, and there are no regular boat services) as in the days of Dionysius.

Of the **Roman** and **Hellenistic** periods the legacy is far greater, but with the exception of domestic architecture this is mainly confined to adaptations to Greek buildings. Apart from Syracuse, with its magnificent Roman amphitheatre, the best evidence of Roman influence may be seen at Tíndari and Taormina. At Tíndari the monumental propylaeum or 'basilica' (or as much of it as the modern reconstruction will concede) is Roman: so too the alterations to the Greek theatre. At Taormina the theatre is largely Roman, superimposed on the Greek original, but the reputation of this as the most photographed ruin in Sicily must be attributed to the magnificent view of Mount Etna, framed by the broken backdrop of the scene-building.

One cannot fully estimate the Roman legacy to Sicily—or for that matter, the Carthaginian or Greek—until the last archaeologist has hung up his shovel. Recalling that miraculous discovery (1950–60) of forty mosaic floors in the Roman villa at Piazza Armerina, one can only wonder what treasures lie in store.

The generous record of Sicily's ancient civilization enhances the desolation of the period between the Romans and the Normans, 700 years that left little imprint, other than cultural, of their passing. The Byzantine monuments were destroyed by the Barbarians and Saracens, and the catacombs of Syracuse are the only significant relic of the early

Christians. The Saracens, in turn, felt the weight of the Norman heel. This, happily, was only in the act of conquest, and **Norman** Sicily—a truly enlightened place—saw the fostering of both the earlier cultures, manifest in the architecture and decoration of her medieval palaces and churches.

For the explorer on foot, Palermo offers innumerable pleasures. Nothing on the grand scale that clamours for attention, but rather pleasures unlocked, like a casket of jewels. The interior of the Cappella Palatina, with its golden mosaics and Saracenic ceiling; the Sala di Re Ruggero in the Norman palace; the interior of the Martorana church where the Byzantine mosaicists applied themselves so gracefully to the smaller scale. Intimate, too, are the little Arabo-Norman churches of San Cataldo and St John of the Hermits.

More commanding is Monreale, where the proudest achievement of Norman art in Sicily awaits our enduring admiration. The cathedral, poised on its foothill above Palermo, offers the city's most pleasant short excursion: a twenty-minute drive with a matchless reward in that great hall of glowing mosaic where the sunlight plays its captivating tricks and the giant presence of Christ, given magisterial form in the mosaic of the apse, creates an unfathomable stillness.

Along the coast, only 74 km from Palermo, the splendour of Monreale finds an echo in the cathedral of Cefalù. This little fishing port, for all the exploitation of recent years, has managed to keep its integrity. For this we must thank nature, in the shape of the headland on which the old part of the town stands, and the great rock which towers behind it. This sheer cliff stands guard over Roger's church, founded by the Norman king as a thank-offering for a safe landing after a stormy voyage.

The explorers of Norman Sicily can test their skills further in a search for the little rustic churches, tucked almost forgetfully in the fold of a hill, the side of a river valley, in various remote corners of the island. Thus did the Normans reclaim the island for Christianity, marking out their new territory with churches, many of them built to commemorate a victory over the Saracens. In tracking down these churches, which are often no more than a short diversion from the coast road, one can discover something of the delights of the Sicilian countryside. The little-used side roads can be a blessed refuge from the *strade statali*, and the flowers that abound at the roadside and in the fields, especially in spring and early summer, are a rare pleasure. Happily, in these days of superhighways and global travel the adventure of searching, in our own time, for an image of the 12th century (one may choose here the lovely old church of SS. Pietro and Paolo, on the Fiumara Agro, north of Taormina) is still open to us.

13th-century architecture assumed a military bias with the rule of 'Stupor Mundi', the **Emperor Frederick II**. A defensive mentality was inevitable in a ruler whose empire stretched from Sicily to the German states: in Sicily it is best displayed in the massive Castello Ursino in Catania, the Castello Maniace in Syracuse and the Castello Lombardo on the heights of Enna. Frederick did much travelling in what was, after all, his native island: in his wake the castles sprang up to command the terrain. Their relics—often little more than a crumbled tower on an isolated hill-top—remain to remind us of his impregnable spirit.

Although the Renaissance had little impact on Sicily, the **Aragonese** rule saw the beginning of the patronage that was to typify the period. Rich families—many of them French or Spanish—built their own convents, palaces and churches, creating an architectural style that may be broadly termed as Sicilian Gothic. In their buildings the Chiaramonte family (originally Clermont) created their own unique compound of Norman and Gothic decoration, best seen in the portal of the Convent of S. Spirito in Agrigento (late 13th century) and the Palazzo Chiaramonte in Palermo (early 14th century). A century later, Taormina's aristocracy built their fairy-tale palaces, fancifully decorated with black and white lava, which are unlike any other buildings of the period in Sicily. This 'Taorminan Gothic' is best seen in the Palazzo Corvaia and the Palazzo S. Stefano.

In the late 15th century, under the **Spanish Viceroys**, a new style—the Catalan Gothic—introduced Renaissance forms into the architecture of churches and palaces. The best examples are in Palermo (Church of S. Maria della Catena, Palazzo Abbatellis, Palazzo Aiutamicristo). Here one may make the first reference to painting and sculpture, up to this time neglected arts in Sicily. Apart from the work of the Norman stone-masons in the doorways and cloisters of Monreale and Cefalù, there is little record of figure sculpture in Sicily before the arrival of Francesco Laurana and Domenico Gagini from northern Italy. Between them

Laurana and his pupil, Domenico's son, Antonello, founded the Sicilian school of Renaissance sculpture. Their work and that of their followers (notably the enduring line of the Gagini) may be seen in churches throughout the island. Laurana's masterpiece, the *Bust of Eleanora of Aragon*, is in the Palazzo Abbatellis, Palermo.

Sicily's only native-born painter of any significance was Antonello da Messina (1430–79). Although active for a period in Messina and Palermo, this great artist, who introduced the Flemish technique of oil-painting to Italy, spent much of his time in the capitals of Italian art, where he was much admired. Little of his work survives, and Palermo and Messina each have only one major painting (*Annunciation*, Palazzo Abbatellis, Palermo, and *Madonna with Sts. Gregory and Benedict*, Museo Nazionale, Messina). Other works are in Cefalù and Syracuse.

An important painter working in Sicily at the beginning of the 17th century was Caravaggio, who spent a brief period here during his exile from Rome. Unfortunately there is little of his work to be seen, one painting (*Nativity with St Lawrence and St Francis*) having been stolen from the Oratory of S. Lorenzo in Palermo and another, the *Burial of St Lucy*, having been removed after the partial collapse of the church of S. Lucia in Syracuse (since restored). Now the only examples of his work (*Resurrection* and *Adoration of the Shepherds*) are in Messina, in the Museo Nazionale.

Palazzo Corvaia, Taormina

One can find consolation, perhaps, in the work of another visitor to Sicily, Anthony Van Dyck, whose *St Domenic and the Patronesses of Palermo* may be seen in the Oratory of S. Domenico in Palermo. Van Dyck greatly influenced the work of his contemporary Pietro Novelli (1603–47) who must rank as Sicily's greatest native-born painter after Antonello da Messina. Novelli's work may be seen in many churches throughout the island and in most of the major museums.

The architecture of 17th and 18th century Sicily was Baroque, and although Sicilian architects were employed the Spanish influence was strong. Apart from Palermo, the best examples of Baroque are in the Etna and Val di Noto regions. Devastated by the 1693 earthquake, the towns of these regions were reconstructed by order of the Spanish Viceroys. Surprisingly, although they share the same 18th century character, the towns of the two regions look quite different. The buildings of Catania and Acireale, incorporating the dark lava stone of Etna, contrast strongly with the much lighter buildings of the Val di Noto region to the south. Here the locally quarried golden stone gives the Baroque a touch of airiness and warmth which even the most forceful denigrator of the style must find appealing. After the eclipse of Taormina, trampled by the tourists, there can be no doubt that Noto and Ragusa are now the most charming towns in Sicily, set in some of the island's loveliest and most varied landscape. A visit to this 'Spanish' region of Sicily—with its isolated and attractive coastline to the south—offers another experience of the island's fascinating diversity.

The destructive forces of nature are not only a part of Sicily's history but an ever-present reality, as witnessed by the recent earthquake in the south-west (1968) and the eruption of Etna (1979). Against such a background of disaster the work of restoration in the the island can only be applauded, with a special bouquet for the resuscitators of the little Norman churches which are so much a feature of the countryside.

The positive attitude of the Central Government towards Sicily's artistic heritage has been shown by the allocation of funds by the *Cassa per il Mezzogiorno* to the restoration of her monuments. The only criticism which must be offered—by the observant visitor who travels more than once to the island—is the evident slowness of the work. Progress on the Palazzo Zisa in Palermo has been subject to continual delays and one wonders when, if ever, a start will be made on the Favara, that other intriguing pleasure palace on the outskirts of Palermo.

Concern for the Norman period must not divert attention from the Sicilian Gothic or Baroque. Here one can cite, for the 14th century, the pressing case of the Palazzo Montalto in Syracuse, and for the 17th–18th the church of S. Maria di Valverde in Palermo. These buildings are in urgent need of proper restoration. It would be unfortunate if, having survived earthquakes, volcanic eruptions and Allied bombs, they succumb finally to neglect.

Road maps

The following road maps divide Sicily into three areas. The traveller with a car and at least two weeks' holiday will enjoy a circular tour, starting at either Messina, Palermo or Catania, depending on his point of arrival. In this circular tour there are a number of diversionary routes to places of interest and alternative routes which cut corners to save time. The A19 autostrada, connecting Palermo–Catania in two hours, offers a fast alternative to the SS192/121, but has strategic exits (e.g. to Enna). There is also an autostrada from Palermo to Mazara del Vallo (A29) with a branch to Trápani. These roads are state-built and therefore not subject to tolls. The other autostrada routes, from Messina–Catania (A18) and from Messina to the A19 link (the A20, not yet completed) are privately built and subject to tolls.

The plan is ultimately to link all the major towns in Sicily either by autostrada routes or by improved state roads. It is impossible to reflect all these rapid changes in the following maps, but routes in process of construction at the time of publication are shown with broken lines. These maps are intended only as a guide for the traveller to the major points of interest, and motorists are recommended to use them in conjunction with an up-to-date touring map of the Island (see Maps, p. 19).

All place names listed in the Gazetteer are shown on the maps.

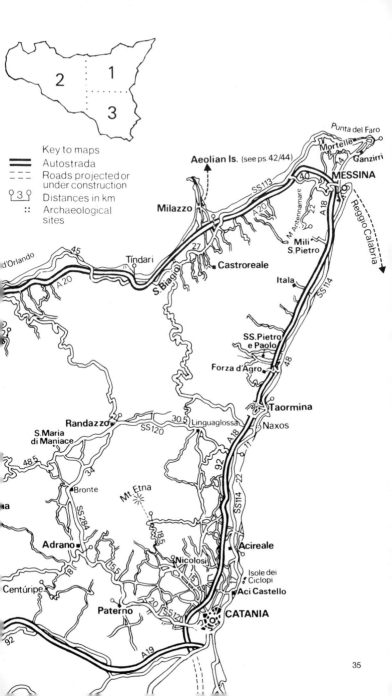

Key to maps

═══	Autostrada
---	Roads projected or under construction
⊖ 3 ⊖	Distances in km
∷	Archaeological sites

1
2
3

Punta del Faro

Mortella

Ganzirri

Aeolian Is. (see ps. 42/44)

SS113

40

MESSINA

Milazzo

A20

M Antennamare

22

A18

Reggio Calabria

45

d'Orlando

Tíndari

27

S.Biagio

Castroreale

Mili S.Pietro

Itala

A20

SS114

SS.Pietro e Paolo

48

Forza d'Agro

Randazzo

30.5

Linguaglossa

Taormina

S.Maria di Maniace

SS120

Naxos

48.5

34

92

11

22

SS114

A18

Bronte

Mt Etna

18.5

SS284

Acireale

Adrano

15.5

15

Nicolosi

Isole dei Ciclopi

Centúripe

18

Aci Castello

20

Paterno

SS121

CATANIA

92

A19

35

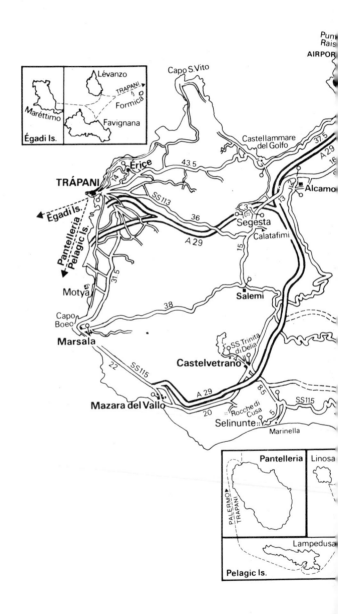

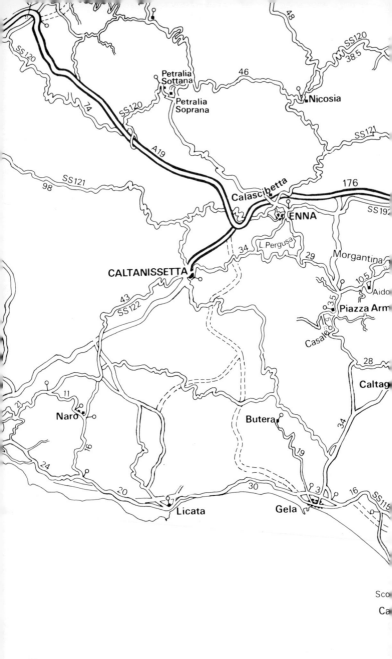

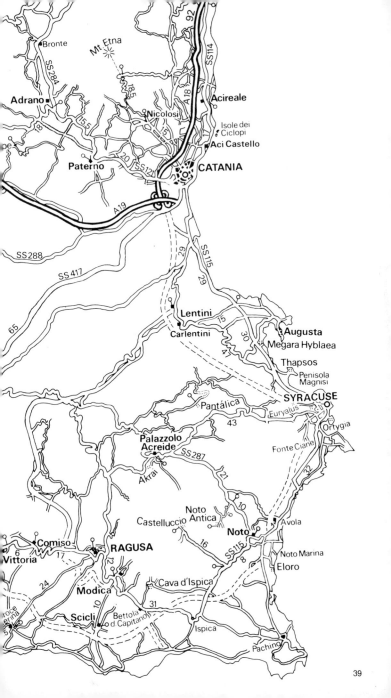

Gazetteer

This Gazetteer contains information on the location, history and main features of the places of interest in Sicily. Information about hotels, restaurants, etc. will be found in the Practical Information section.

Where possible, museum opening times are shown, but as these are continually subject to change, note should be made of the general rule (see Museums and Monuments, p. 25).

Altitudes shown are for places 500 m or more above sea level. Distances are to the nearest half-kilometre.

Populations (approximate) are for islands and for towns of more than 50,000 inhabitants.

Note: The abbreviation 'S.' before the name of a saint is short for 'Santo' or 'San' before a male name and 'Santa' before a female name. 'SS.' is for the plural 'Santi'. It is useful to remember this when asking for directions.

Aci Castello Town on east coast, 9km north of Catania (SS114, A18).
The coast here is characterized by the rocky debris of ancient volcanic eruptions. On a blunt rock projecting into the sea stands a Norman **castle** built in 1076. During the rule of Frederick II of Aragon this castle was occupied by a rebel admiral, Roger di Lauria, but was subsequently recaptured by the king, whose only way to reach the castle was to build a special tower to the height of the rock. No admittance, unfortunately, to modern besiegers.

Acireale Town on east coast, 17km north of Catania (SS114, A18).
The town, bypassed by the SS 114, is worth a short diversion. Built on a site occupied since ancient times, Acireale owes its name partly to mythology (Acis was a young Sicilian herdsman who became a victim of the jealousy of the monster Polyphemus) and partly to the Spanish king, Philip IV, who during the period of the Viceroys made the town a direct subject of the crown, giving it the affix 'reale'. This was in 1642: in 1693 the town was severely damaged by the earthquake which destroyed Catania and other towns. The architecture of its historic buildings is accordingly a compendium of original fabric and reconstruction.
The most important buildings are in the short stretch of the town centre between the Piazza Duomo and the Piazza Vigo. On the east side of the Piazza Duomo stands the **Cathedral** which incorporates in a more recent façade of mixed styles an impressive marble *portal* from the pre-earthquake building, with fine statues by Blandamonte (1668). To the south

the **Palazzo Communale** is another 17th c. building, and further south, in the Piazza Vigo, is the impressive church of **S. Sebastiano**, whose main feature, the elaborate façade, was originally constructed in the first half of the 17th c. and restored in 1705. The balustrade with its ten statues by G. B. Marino was added in 1754. On the opposite side of the square is the elegant 19th c. **Palazzo Pennisi**, which contains a fine collection of Sicel and Greek coins (viewed by application only). Other places of interest in Acireale are the **Pinacoteca Zelantea** (Via Marchese di S. Giuliano) which incorporates an art gallery and library, and the **Terme** (sulphur baths) by the station.

Addaura Prehistoric caves on north side of Monte Pellegrino near Palermo, with Upper Palaeolithic incised drawings. (For access see Museums and Monuments, p. 25.)

Adrano Town on west flank of Etna, 35km from Catania, on circum-Etna route.
The founder of *Adranon*, the first settlement here, was Dionysius I. Remains of the **Greek walls** lie to the south of the town but should only be pursued by the enthusiast as they are barely distinguishable from the later walls, also of lava, built over the surrounding terrain. In the centre of the town is the Norman **castle**, built in the 11th c. by Count Roger. It contains a small but very interesting **museum** (hours 09.00-13.00 & 15.30-17.00; Sun and hol 09.00-13.00; closed Mon) with varied finds from local sites. These include Early Bronze Age pottery (Castellucian) and bronzes from Mendolito, the Sicel settlement near Adrano.

Next to the castle is the **Chiesa Madre**, originally Norman but now undergoing a dubious bit of reconstruction. Inside, the antique columns of the nave are thought to have been preserved from a Greek temple. Dominating the Via Roma to the east of the castle is the long façade of the former Monastery of **S. Lucia**, founded in the 12th c. The present building dates from the end of the 16th c., with the third floor modern. In the centre of the façade is the 18th c. church of S. Lucia.

Aeolian Islands (Isole Eolie) Group of

seven islands (the largest in an archipelago of small islands) off the north-east coast of Sicily.

Traditionally the Aeolian Is. were the home of the winds, under the stewardship of Aeolus who smoothed the passage of Odysseus through these waters and who gave the wandering hero a bag of adverse winds, with the instruction that he was on no account to open them. Inevitably the curiosity of the sailors became too great: the bag was opened and Odysseus was blown off-course. These islands have many attractions for the traveller. Their main interest is their volcanic origin, manifested by the northernmost of the group, Stromboli, which is still an active volcano, and by the thermal features found in many of the others, notably Vulcano. To the historian and archaeologist, however, the fascination lies in the origins of their settlement, which can be traced back as far as c. 4000 BC. Excavations in recent years in several of the islands have revealed a more comprehensive picture of the development and relationship of successive prehistoric cultures than in any other part of Sicily, a picture which is expertly presented to the visitor in the Museum of Lìpari. Adding to the special appeal of these islands is the amazing variety of their landscape and the colours of their rocks and beaches, and the opportunities for water-sports, boating and under-water fishing which are seemingly inexhaustible. For a description of the individual islands, see below. **For details of boat services, see p. 17.**

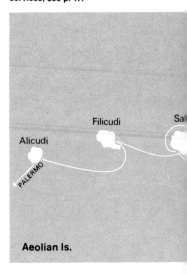

Aeolian Is.

Milazzo harbour, departure point for the Aeolian Is.

Lípari (pop. 12,000 area 37.6 sq km) Principal island of the Aeolian group.

Lípari is the most fertile of the islands, with small farms scattered over the hills behind the town, but despite this and the success of its malmsey wine and pumice industries, Lípari does little more than hold its own economically. Its attractions however—as a holiday centre for the Aeolian Is.—have not been overlooked by the tour operators. An improving boat service to the islands, from Naples, Messina, Milazzo and other ports is an indication of their growing popularity, for both day-trippers and long-term visitors.

History Evidence of settlement begins with the Neolithic period (4th millenium BC) when the main industry was the mining of obsidian, a volcanic glass found in greatest concentration around Monte S. Angelo. The obsidian, used for making tools which required a cutting edge, was in great demand throughout the Mediterranean for about 2000 years, until the Copper Age. The discovery of metal reduced the need for obsidian, but the improvement in navigation and expansion of trade that came with the Bronze Age guaranteed a place on the map for Lípari and the other Aeolian islands, which as ports-of-call developed trading contacts between western Europe and the cultures of Greece and the Aegean.

In the 13th c. BC, the influences were nearer at hand: the Ausonian tribe from southern Italy, under their leader Liparos, conquered the islands, the beginning of a 400-year link between Lípari and Italy. Vestiges of this occupation have been found on the acropolis of Lípari and evidence that the ancient village was eventually destroyed—probably by pirates—in 850 BC.

The island submerged into oblivion until 580 BC, when a party of Greeks—beaten off by the Carthaginians in an attack on the west coast of Sicily—arrived here as refugees, and stayed as colonists. In this period the Liparians, so often the victims of piracy, tried their own hand at this profitable pursuit, concentrating on the trade routes running up the west side of southern Italy (then part of Magna Graecia) via the Strait of

Messina. Their success was such that they were able to dedicate their spoils to the Oracle at Delphi. Lípari remained in Greek hands until the First Punic War, when the Carthaginians, who had taken possession of the islands, surrendered them to the Romans (252 BC). Lípari became an important naval station under the Romans and was contested during the war between Octavian and Sextus Pompey. Its history continued thereafter to be guided by its position, but the assaults on the island were largely those of pirates. In 1544 marauders sacked the town of Lípari and the inhabitants were carried off as slaves to Turkey. The town was later restored by the Emperor Charles V.

Lípari The capital of Lípari Island, situated in a sheltered bay on the east coast. This bay is divided in two by the projecting headland which was the acropolis of the ancient Lípari, the citadel of the medieval period. On the north side of the citadel, where the boats come in from Sicily and the mainland, is the long fisherman's quay, otherwise known as the *Marina Lunga*, with its line of flat-fronted, pastel-tinted houses. To the south is the *Marina Corta*, a smaller bay where the fishing-boats are almost stacked on to the small sandy beaches and where the people of Lípari gather in lively throngs in the summer evenings, to talk about the day and eye the promenading visitors. This is a lively corner at any time: during the day there is a great deal of activity on the landing-stage, as boats are loaded with the island's products. The **acropolis** (or citadel) on the great rock of lava with its cladding of 16th c. fortifications, dominates the view. The easiest way up is from the north side, through a gateway at the top of an inclined approach: the steeper, but more direct ascent is via a flight of steps which leads from the main street of the town up to the cathedral.

The **Cathedral** which crowns the citadel was built in 1654 by the Spanish on Norman foundations. Elsewhere this might be an historic building: on this site, the ancient acropolis of Lípari, it is overshadowed by the history that has gone before it. Opposite the cathedral lie excavations, to a depth of 9 m, which present a record of the settlement of this site from as far back as Neolithic times. These excavations, the work of Dr Bernabò Brea (former Superintendent of Antiquities for Eastern Sicily) and Madeleine Cavalier have contributed greatly to our knowledge of Mediterranean prehistory.

For a clearer understanding of these different cultures a visit should be made to the **Aeolian Museum** (Museo Aeoliano). This museum, also the work of Dr Brea and Mme Cavalier, houses one of the most important archaeological collections in the Mediterranean area, comprising material collected from this site and from others in the smaller islands.

In July and August this museum has special hours, from 09.00–14.00 and 15.30–18.00, open Mon a.m. For the rest of the year it follows the opening times of other museums (see p.25).

The collection is divided between three different buildings. To the south of the cathedral (in the Bishop's Palace) the arrangement is on two floors. Relics here are from the Acropolis of Lípari, each phase displayed separately.

Upstairs *Rooms 1–6* Neolithic to Early Bronze Age. Note the incised 'Stentinello' ware (*Room 1*) from the most ancient Neolithic settlement (4th millenium BC) found also in eastern Sicily. The pottery in *Room 6* of the Capo Graziano (1800–1400 BC) and Milazzese (1400–1250 BC) cultures includes imported ware from Greece.

Downstairs *Rooms 7–9* Late Bronze Age to Iron Age (Ausonian culture). *Room 10* Greek, Hellenistic and Roman periods.

Another section of the museum (opposite) comprising *Rooms 11–15* is devoted to material from the smaller islands: Filicudi (the Capo Graziano culture) and Panarea and Salina (Milazzese culture). It is very interesting to note in this Bronze Age pottery the Greek style of decoration, showing the influence of trade with Mycenae and the Aegean islands.

To the north of the cathedral is the third part of the museum, in a modern building, which contains material from the Iron Age and from the Greek, Hellenistic and Roman periods.

Ground floor *Rooms 16–17* Finds from the necropoli of Milazzo from the 14th–6th c. BC including reconstructions of the necropolises of three different periods. *Rooms 18–19* Sarcophagi from Lipari and reconstruction of Early Iron Age necropolis of Piazza Monfalcone (1125–1050 BC).

First floor Here in *Rooms 20–24* are displayed finds from the Greek and Roman necropolises of Lipari (from the 'Diana' quarter behind the port). The best of these objects are from the 4th c. BC. *Room 22*, entered first, has some fine funerary vases, including red figure kraters from S. Italy and the interesting multi-coloured pottery of the 'Lipari Painter'. The most enchanting objects recovered from this quarter are the *theatrical masks* and terracotta *figures of comic actors* (*Rooms 20, 24*). *Room 23*, devoted to the Hellenistic and Roman periods, includes jewellery and glassware. *Room 25* has a reconstruction of the necropolis of Lipari.

Room 26 (ground floor) has underwater finds, including amphorae and anchors.

On the seaward side of the museum lies a small garden and belvedere, with an arrangement of *sarcophagi* from the necropolis of the 'Diana' quarter (late 5th–4th c. BC).

Excursions from Lípari

The landscape of Lípari, which seems to encapsulate on a tiny scale that of its mother island Sicily, offers many pleasing car excursions and walks for those who have a little time for exploration. A circular tour of the island is now possible by car, and it is recommended that the visitor starts from the more spectacular western side. Once out of Lípari the road climbs rapidly to the belvedere near the village of *Quattrocchi* (3.5 km). Here one should stop to take in the sublime view to the south. The rocks breaking the surface of the sea like short daggers are the *Faraglioni*, and the island sprawling its bulk over the blue stillness beyond its Vulcano, with the grey-edged crater of Vulcanello in the foreground. (A side road below this point leads down to the top of a track which in turn leads down to the sea: an arduous descent rewarded by a quiet beach.)

After 5 km, a side road leads west to the *Terme di S. Calogero* (Baths of S. Calogero) where there are hot springs. Since ancient times these waters, the active evidence of Lípari's volcanic origins, have been used for cures. Near the spring is a hot-air grotto or 'stufa' used by the Romans, and at the end of the road a thermal establishment (open Jul 1–Sep 30).

Returning to the main road, the journey continues via *Pianoconte*, site of Copper and Bronze Age discoveries to the nearby village of *Varesana*. From here one can climb in 20 min. to the summit of *Monte S. Angelo* (594 m) the highest point of the island. This is an extinct volcano, and from here it is possible to see the craters of several others, also the contrasting effusions of pumice and obsidian.

The road continues 5 km to *Quattropani*, which offers a fine view of Salina, Filicudi and Alicudi. It then descends to *Aquacalda* (5 km) and continues 2 km to *Porticello* on the east coast from where one can enjoy the spectacle of the towering white pumice quarries. The pumice, which is a volcanic deposit, covers about a fifth of the island and is one of her most important exports.

At *Canneto*, a further 3 km, one can take a side road (2 km) to *Lami*, from which a $\frac{1}{2}$-hr climb affords a view from *Mt Pelato* (476 m) of the *Campo Bianco*, a field of white pumice, and the obsidian outflows. At Canneto is the *Spiaggia Bianca* (White Beach) popular with tourists. The return to Lípari can be made by the high road (5 km) or via the tunnel (3 km). Total distance 26 km.

Boat trips

Perhaps the best way of appreciating the geological diversity of Lípari is to take a trip around the island by boat. In this way one can enjoy a close-up view of grottoes, coves and cliffs of sheer rock, imbued with an extraordinary range of volcanic coloration. Boats are also available for trips to Vulcano and other islands.

View of the Faraglioni and Vulcano from Lípari

Vulcano (pop. 400 area 21 sq km) Island 1km south of Lípari.

Vulcano offers an adventurous destination for a short boat excursion from Lípari. (It can also be reached directly from Sicily by steamship or hydrofoil services—see page 17.) As its name suggests, the island is a volcanic creation and consists in fact of a group of volcanoes, erupting at different times from the sea bed, which have joined together. The most recent addition was *Vulcanello* (123m) which erupted from the sea in the 2nd c. BC and now forms a protruberance on the north-east coast. The southern part of the island is largely occupied by the *Piano*, a plain resulting from the infilling of an extinct crater. To the south of this is the highest point in the island, another extinct crater (Monte Aria 500m). The *Gran Cratere* (391m) overlooking the main port, is the only volcano on the island that can be described as in any way active. Its last eruption was in 1890, since when there have been emissions of smoke and occasionally liquid sulphur.

The strongest evidence of the island's volcanic origins is in the area around the main port, *Porto di Levante*. The earth here is covered by a white deposit of chalk and silica, and there are continual emissions of a sulphurous vapour from the fumaroles— the crevices in the volcanic cone. For those who can overcome their antipathy to the smell of sulphur, there are hot mud pools, immersion in which is supposed to be beneficial to rheumatism sufferers and the like. Alternatively, the afflicted can bathe in the warm waters of the *Baia di Levante* to the north of the port. The sea close to the beach is heated by submarine vapour, which creates a series of hot bubbling pools in the water. A warning to the unwary: do not go on the beach without shoes!

Excursions from Porto di Levante
On foot The *Gran Cratere* can be reached in one hour. The climb, though strenuous, offers a further look at fumaroles in action and a magnificent view at the crater's rim. More accessible is *Vulcanello*, only $\frac{1}{2}$ hour to the north. The *Baia di Ponente*, with its small harbour and beach of black sand, is also quickly reached across the neck of the Vulcanello peninsula.
By boat The most popular boat excursion is to the *Grotto del Cavallo* (Horse Grotto) on the west side of the island.

Salina (pop. 3000 area 26.8 sq km) Island 4km north-west of Lípari.

After Lípari, this is the most populated of the Aeolian Is. It is also the most fertile, with a vigorous grape production and exports of malmsey wine and raisins. The main feature of the island is the twin peaks of its volcanoes, now extinct. The one on the east, the *Monte Fossa delle Felci* (962m) is the highest point of the Aeolian Is., and the climb to the top is rewarded by a magnificent view of the group.

There are several villages on the island and three main harbours: *Santa Marina*, *Malfa* and *Rinella*, the latter a popular centre for under-water fishing. There are some remains of the Roman period at *Santa Marina* and to the north, on the way to the *Capo Faro* lighthouse, a village of the Milazzese period (1400–1270 BC).

Panarea (pop. 500 area 3.4 sq km) Island 14km north-east of Lípari.

This tiny island, the nucleus of a smaller archipelago within the Aeolian group, has a special significance in the history of Bronze Age culture in the Mediterranean. On the south side of the island is a promontory which takes its name, *Punta Milazzese*, from the culture predominant in these islands at the time. Here is the site of a 14th c. BC village, consisting of a complex of oval-shaped huts whose walls have been revealed in outline by the 1948 excavations. The Mycenaean pottery found here, the evidence of commerce with the Greek world, is on display in the Aeolian Museum on Lípari. Despite its small size, Panarea rises to a height of 420m at the peak of *Pizzo del Corvo*. It also has its share of volcanic activity with fumaroles in the north and hot springs on the east, in the village of *San Pietro*. Exploring a group of islets within a

Sulphur bath, Vulcano

group of islands might seem a slight refinement: but one of the greatest pleasures of a visit to Panarea is a journey by boat around the island and among the rocky islets to the east, which reveal in detail the dramatic geology of this volcanic region. The largest of these, *Basiluzzo*, is also of interest to the archaeologist. Now uninhabited, it was once occupied by the Romans, as may be seen from the vestiges of their architecture in different parts of the island.

Stromboli (pop. 900 area 12.6 sq km) Island 35 km north-east of Lípari.

This is the northernmost of the Aeolian Is. Steamship and hydrofoil services are available from Lípari and Sicily and there is also a steamship service from Naples (summer only).

Like the other islands in the group Stromboli is volcanic in origin, but has a special claim to fame in being the only one that is a fully active volcano, with frequent emissions of lava. The island is in fact the top of a volcanic cone, rising 2200 m from the sea bed. (The height from sea-level to the rim of the crater is 924 m.) Eruptions occur every hour or so, and take the form of emissions of vapour and hot ash, with the occasional flow of lava. From a boat, cruising round the island, the spectacle is thrilling—if not a little daunting. The crater is so shaped that the lava always flows in a concentrated stream down the west side of the cone—the *Sciara del Fuoco*. The direction of the flow is so predictable that there is no threat to the two villages on the island, which between them muster a population of 900. In contrast to the almost sheer west side, with its precipices of dark jagged tufa, the east side of Stromboli has gentler, vine-covered slopes.

Stromboli, the principal village and harbour, comprises the hamlets of *S. Vincenzo* and *S. Bartolo*, with churches of the same name. There are a few hotels and pensions. The tourist information office is at *Ficogrande*, on the coast between the two hamlets.

Excursions from Stromboli

On foot The approach to the *crater* is from *S. Bartolo*. A climb to the *Semaforo* (look-out rock) takes two hours, following a path and then markers. Another hour is necessary to reach the crater.

By boat Trips are arranged to *Strombolicchio*, a huge castle-shaped rock of basalt 2 km from Stromboli, and to *Ginostra*, the tiny village on the south side of the island.

Filicudi (pop. 300 area 9.5 sq km) Island 27 km west of Lípari.

The two main features of this island are the peak of the extinct volcano the *Fossa Felci* (773 m) and the *Capo Graziano* peninsula which is the site of the Early Bronze Age culture (pre-1400 BC) preceding that of the Milazzese. Excavations are still in progress

on this and other sites. The rocky coastline of Filicudi, with its grottoes, basalt rocks, and vine-covered slopes, makes an enjoyable boat excursion (from *Filicudi Porto*).

Alicudi (pop. 200 area 5.2 sq km) Island 47 km west of Lípari.

This island is the tip of a volcanic cone, long extinct, rising to a height of 675 m. The people of this remote island are dependent on fishing for their livelihood. Sheep are grazed on the more gradual eastern side of the island.

Agrigento (pop. 52,000) Town on south-west coast famous for its group of ancient Greek temples, built in the 5th c. BC. These are situated on a broad ridge to the south of the town, 2 km from the sea, the site popularly known as the 'Valley of the Temples'. The town itself is built on a rocky hill, the site of the ancient acropolis.

History Agrigento has had four names. The modern name, the Arabic name (Girgenti) and the Roman name (Agrigentum) derive from the original Greek name *Akragas*. The colony was founded in 581 BC by the citizens of Gela, 77 km to the east. In addition to the Geloans, many of the colonists were from Rhodes—the Greek island which had originally colonized Gela. The site chosen was a hill to the north of the confluence of two rivers, the Akragas and Hypsas (now the San Biagio and Sant'Anna). The ancient city, which developed trading contacts with the African coastal settlements, grew rapidly and gradually extended down towards the sea. Its southernmost limit was the fortified ridge on which the great temples were built, linked by further fortifications to the acropolis hill. The city's most notorious tyrant, Phalaris (565–549 BC) is credited with the construction of these defences: he is also discredited by a legend which one assumes, by its very enormity, to have little basis in fact. It was said that this tyrant's method of disposing of his enemies was to put them inside a great bronze bull and light fires under it: their cries, as they roasted to death, gave the impression of the bull roaring.

A more admirable tyrant was Theron, who ruled Akragas from 488–472 BC. This was the period in which the Carthaginians presented their first great threat to the Sicilian Greeks and the period in which, correspondingly, the Greek cities of Akragas and Syracuse forged their strongest alliance. The basis of this alliance was the friendship between Theron and Gelon of Syracuse, consolidated by the marriage of Gelon to Theron's daughter. Together the two leaders defeated the Carthaginians at Himera, a town on the north coast which was, in fact, a dependency of Akragas. The Greek victory served to draw a line at this point (i.e. from Himera to Akragas) against further Carthaginian advances for another 70 years. This line was

Akragas' sphere of influence and she simultaneously controlled territory stretching along an 80 km coastline, from Phintias (modern Licata) in the east to Heraclea Minoa in the west.

The city's wealth derived from the produce of a fertile hinterland, and her prestige from successes at the Olympic Games. Most of the trophies were won at the chariot-races, and Akragas became famous for its breed of race-horses. Second only to Syracuse in political power, she rivalled her sister city in artistic achievement. Like Syracuse she attracted the poets who had migrated from Greece, among them Pindar who described Akragas as the 'most beautiful of mortal cities'. A native of Akragas was the scientist-philosopher Empedocles, who flourished, like Pindar, in the middle of the 5th c. BC. This was also the golden age of the city's architecture, when most of the great Doric temples, including the spectacular but unfinished Temple of Zeus, were built.

After the deaths of Theron and Gelon the alliance between Akragas and Syracuse weakened and finally fractured in warfare. Syracuse got the upper hand and Akragas wisely submitted, retiring to a neutral prosperity in the no-man's land between Syracuse and Carthage. She offered no help to Syracuse during the Athenian siege (415–413 BC): similarly, Syracuse refrained from assisting Akragas when the Carthaginians renewed their threat in the west and eventually captured the city (406 BC).

The Carthaginians held Akragas until 340 BC, when Timoleon of Syracuse arrived with his army to reclaim it for the Greeks. Timoleon gave orders for the city's restoration, which started it on a new period of prosperity. During the rule of Timoleon's successor Agathocles, Akragas maintained a strongly independent line, and went as far as forming a league against the Syracusan tyrant when he was away campaigning against Carthage. This did not, however, put Akragas on the side of Carthage. She ended up fighting two separate wars, against both Syracuse and Carthage, wars which Akragas was not strong enough to pursue with any real hope of success. After the dramatic—but short-lived—conquest of Sicily by the Greek king Pyrrhus, Akragas was forced into an alliance with Carthage, which was maintained until the capture of the city by the Romans (261 BC). Carthage later won the city back, but in 210 BC, after it had changed hands several times, Akragas finally became Roman Agrigentum.

Its status diminished thereafter to that of a minor provincial town and it dwindled in size, the buildings receding to the area of the acropolis on which the Greeks built their first settlement and where the modern town now stands. The ridge on which the Greek temples had been built became the cemetery

Agrigento

Walking tour

1 Piazza Vittorio Emanuele
2 Convent of S. Spirito
3 S. Giuseppe
4 S. Maria dei Greci
5 Cathedral
6 Tourist Information Office

of the Roman and Byzantine population. Apart from this and some ruins of the Hellenistic period near the museum, little remains of the Roman town, its masonry having been pillaged for the building of Porto Empedocle. In 827 AD the town was taken by the Saracens who held it until the arrival of the Normans under Count Roger (1087).

The modern town stretches along the site of the ancient acropolis, from Monte Camico in the west (on whose summit the cathedral stands) to the area below the Rupe Atenea (Rock of Athena) to the east. The conformation of the land has been much obscured by the modern tower blocks which seem to be marching inexorably down to the sea: from the Valley of the Temples, however, the area of the town can still be seen as confined to the heights on which it was originally built. The centre of the town is the huge Piazza Vittorio Emanuele, into which all the main roads lead (from Palermo, Sciacca and Enna).

Walking tour Though the description of 'Girgenti' by a 19th c. traveller as being as 'foul and foetid as the face of nature is fair and smiling,' strikes a chord with the contemporary visitor, a brief exploration of the old town will bring rewards.

The starting point (see map) is the Via Atenea, which runs off the west side of the Piazza Vittorio Emanuele. From the north side of this street a series of steep and twisting alleys lead up to the less accessible corners of Agrigento, which seem, in this present-day scramble for 'development', sadly neglected. After 200 m the Via Porcello, right, and the Salita S. Spirito lead to the

Convent of **S. Spirito**, founded in the late 13th c. This convent, tucked away in a courtyard between unsympathetic modern buildings, suffered serious damage in World War II: happily restoration work has preserved it as Agrigento's finest medieval building. The doorway of the church survives on the left of the façade: the entrance to the cloister is on the right.

Passing through this entrance and into the **cloister** one can admire, on the east side, one of the most perfect examples of Chiaramontine architecture in the façade of the *chapter house* and *refectory*, with its beautifully moulded doors and double windows.

This delightful rendering of Sicily's native Gothic style is particularly appropriate here. S. Spirito was founded by the devout Marchisia Chiaramonte, a member of the illustrious family who owned much of Sicily in the 13th and 14th c. and who gave their name to the decorative style employed in the architecture of their palaces and in other buildings of the period.

The fine vaulted rooms may be viewed by the visitor, although the refectory, which now houses the Biblioteca (Public Library) is closed in the afternoons. On the first floor is the *great hall* of the convent, now used for concerts. To the left of the chapter house, in the north-east corner of the cloister, is a small *chapel*, also Chiaramontine in style.

The interior of the **church**, to the north of the cloister, was largely remodelled in the Baroque style in the early 17th c. and has a fine series of altar *stuccoes* attributed to Serpotta.

The Via S. Spirito and Via Fodera lead back to the Via Atenea which should be followed to the Piazza Pirandello. To the south of this square a *belvedere* affords a view of the dramatic landscape between Agrigento and the sea, including the Valley of the Temples. A steep alley (Via Bac-Bac) by the church of S. Giuseppe leads to a flight of steps running north from the Piazza Lena. From here a series of steps lead up to the church of **S. Maria dei Greci**.

The interest of this 13th c. church lies in its site. In the 5th c. BC a Doric temple was built here on the acropolis of Theron's city, dedicated, it is thought, to Athena. By descending a flight of steps to the left of the church it is possible to see the remains of this temple in an underground passage: part of the stereobate and the bases of six columns. Inside the church, which was founded on the site of the temple in the 5th c. AD, one can see the insides of the columns—now flattened—in the wall on either side. Behind the altar is part of the old altar of the temple.

Continuing northwards, the visitor will reach the Via Duomo which leads west to the **Cathedral**. Massive in construction, and dominating the town from its highest point, this is now one of the saddest buildings in Sicily.

Built in the 14th c. on a foundation of the 12th c. Norman bishop San Gerlando, the cathedral was badly shaken by an earth movement in 1966, which did considerable structural damage. The cathedral has since been closed, and it is uncertain whether any restoration is now practicable. Apart from the cracks in its fabric, the sense of ruin is enhanced by the awkwardness of the building.

Convent of S. Spirito

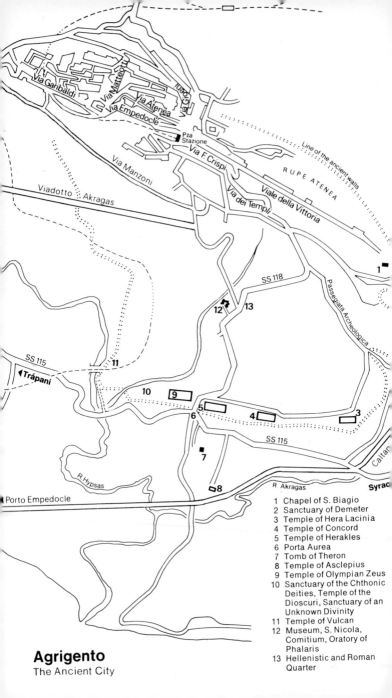

Agrigento
The Ancient City

1 Chapel of S. Biagio
2 Sanctuary of Demeter
3 Temple of Hera Lacinia
4 Temple of Concord
5 Temple of Herakles
6 Porta Aurea
7 Tomb of Theron
8 Temple of Asclepius
9 Temple of Olympian Zeus
10 Sanctuary of the Chthonic
   Deities, Temple of the
   Dioscuri, Sanctuary of an
   Unknown Divinity
11 Temple of Vulcan
12 Museum, S. Nicola,
   Comitium, Oratory of
   Phalaris
13 Hellenistic and Roman
   Quarter

The campanile, which dates from the 15th c., is unfinished, and presents the curious puzzle of two rows of Catalan-Gothic blind arcades on the south face, surmounted by a balconied window with Arabo-Norman decoration. The Baroque façade of the cathedral provides another contrast.

Many alterations were made to the cathedral in the 17th c., particularly to the interior: but much of this work was subsequently removed to reveal the original walls and pillars of the 14th c. building. This enlightened restoration makes the present dilapidation of the cathedral particularly tragic, and it is equally unfortunate that the Diocesan Museum on the north side of the square in front of the church, has also been closed. Some of the treasures from this museum, and from the cathedral itself, are now housed in the new Museo Nazionale in the lower archaeological zone.

Tour of the ancient city If the visitor is looking for inspiration rather than perspiration, the tour of Agrigento's archaeological zone should not be too hastily undertaken. At least a full day should be allowed for an adequate coverage of all the sites, and half a day if the Museum and Valley of the Temples are the only objectives. The tour should be made by car, stopping at selected points. (Visitors without a car or personal transport will be able to take a Bus No. 8 or 9 from the Piazza Stazione, which will drop them at the Museum or at the Porta Aurea for the Valley of the Temples.) Before setting out some study should be made of the plan of the ancient city (map, opposite) taking particular note of the layout of the walls and the position of the gates. It will be noticed that the walls closely followed the natural contours of the land: to the north the acropolis and the arc of the Rupe Atenea (Rock of Athena), to the

west and east the heights overlooking the valleys of the ancient Akragas and Hypsas Rivers, and to the south the ridge on which the great temples were built. The area between the ridge and the slopes of the Rupe Atenea was once occupied by a large part of Greek Akragas: current excavations are now revealing the elaborate layout of the Hellenistic and Roman city which overlaid it.

Note A point to remember for those visiting the Valley of the Temples is that they are best seen at sunrise or sunset, when the softer light brings out the lovely warm colour of the sandstone.

Chapel of S. Biagio This is the first stop on the comprehensive tour of the antiquities (those wishing to do a briefer tour should concentrate on the Museum and the Valley of the Temples). The chapel is reached by a road running off to the left from the SS118, about 1km south of the town. This road brings the visitor to a car parking area from which a path leads up to the chapel, perched on the east flank of the Rupe Atenea. The chapel is otherwise known as the Temple of Demeter; the roof, apsidal east end and interior being Norman adaptations of a building that in fact belongs to the early 5th c. BC. The temple was probably built by Theron as the centrepiece of a sacred precinct dedicated to the Chthonic deities (Demeter and Persephone). It was a simple structure consisting of a *cella* and a *pronaos* with two columns *in antis*, and had no peristyle. Part of the foundations of the temple can be seen at the east end of the chapel (exterior) and part of its *cella* is incorporated in the walls.

Rock Sanctuary of Demeter This mysterious shrine lies half-way down the cliff below the Chapel of S. Biagio, and is reached by a path and steps (a guide is available to conduct visitors to the site). The ruins provide an interesting study of the religious practices of the ancient Greeks and of their particular devotion to the cult of Demeter and Persephone, the mother-and-daughter divinities who were so closely identified with the fruitfulness of the earth.

The sanctuary comprises two adjoining buildings and behind them two caves hollowed out of the rock, in which the offerings to the divinities were placed. It will be noted that the sanctuary lies outside the walls of the ancient city, unlike the later Temple of Demeter, built on the rock above, which is inside the walls. A sanctuary existed here, in fact, at least two centuries before the foundation of the Greek colony of Akragas (581 BC). Evidence for this is in the dating of the terracotta votive offerings (8th–5th c. BC) found when the sacred caves were excavated, which shows that the sanctuary was in use for about four centuries. The earlier worshippers were the pre-Greek peoples of western Sicily, the Sicans: it was their corn-

Cathedral, Agrigento

goddess which became, later on, the Greek Demeter. The immediate objects of veneration were the earth and water: the greatest desire their happy union which would, of course, bring forth the crops. The deep, dark caves made the earth seem more accessible, if more frightening; the water ran naturally and abundantly down the hillside, as it still does today.

The function of the buildings, which are of different dates, is not certain. The long building to the rear, which opens on to the cave entrances, is thought to be an early temple or vestibule (c. 7th c. BC). In front of it is an enclosure with a number of water troughs for the ablutions of the worshippers. This is a much later addition (c. 4th c. BC) and its date suggests that it was not associated with the sacred caves, which by that time had been abandoned, but was in use as a *nymphaeum* (shrine of the water nymphs). The troughs were fed with water by an intricate system of pipes leading through a third cave to the right of the sacred caves.

The view from the sanctuary, down the scrub and oleander-covered slopes to the valley of the S. Biagio River (the ancient Akragas) is particularly fine.

Returning to the SS118 the visitor has a choice of routes. This choice will depend on the time of day. If for example it is early morning you might prefer to see the Valley of the Temples first to avoid exploring it in the midday heat—a time more suited to the cool interior of the Museum. If it is the afternoon, however, the reverse order is recommended, starting with the Museum and completing the tour at sunset with the temples. (Before making final plans it is best to check the opening times of the Museum.) The tour described follows a clockwise direction, starting with the Valley of the Temples. To reach the temples, the next turning on the left should be taken, leaving the SS118. This is the Passeggiata Archeologica, a route specially constructed for the enjoyment of the antiquities. Passing the walls of Akragas on the left, the visitor comes eventually to the first of the great Greek temples, standing proudly on its rampart of rock at the south-eastern corner of the ancient city.

Temple of Hera Lacinia (Temple of Juno) The name of this temple is imaginary, as no evidence exists for its identification with the Queen of the Gods. Its dedication to a supreme deity can be assumed however from the long altar running parallel to the east end, on which animals were offered in sacrifice. The temple was built between 460 and 440 BC in the Doric style, with 6 columns at either end and 13 on each side. After an earthquake had shattered them 25 of these columns were re-erected in the 18th c. Looking at them carefully one can see the traces of an earlier disaster: the reddy-pink

discoloration from the burning of the temple in 406 BC, when the Carthaginians sacked the town. Another, more serious, defacement is continuing to this day: the steady erosion of the sandstone of the columns by the action of the wind.

The temple has the traditional lay-out of the classical period, with the *pronaos* preceding the *cella* and an *opisthodomos* to the rear. Inside the *pronaos*, on either side of the entrance to the *cella*, a stairway was built into the stonework, giving access to the roof.

To the west of the temple, following the line of the ridge, are substantial remains of the ancient wall of the city, which was partly cut out of the rock. Immediately below the temple is an ancient entrance to the city (*Gate 3*). The structure of this gate, and the inside of the wall, has been much altered by the hollowing out of tombs in the Byzantine period. Following the Via dei Templi the visitor will reach, after 500 m, the finest and best preserved Greek temple in Sicily.

Temple of Hera Lacinia

Temple of Concord Here is the glory of the Valley of the Temples, the most complete record of the classical achievement in Greek Sicily. To find a building so intact, amid so many ruins, is a refreshment and a pleasure, enhanced by the purity of its concept. The name, however unrelated to the true dedication of the temple, seems wholly appropriate. The temple, built between 450 and 440 BC, owes its preservation largely to its conversion into a church in the 6th c. AD. Happily, this conversion did not greatly alter the structure of the temple. The spaces between the columns were filled in, to make the outer walls of the church, but these fillings were subsequently removed in the 18th c. when the temple was restored to its original form. A more radical alteration was the cutting of six arched openings in each of the side walls of the *cella*. With the filled-in outer walls, this created an interior with a nave and two aisles, similar to that of the converted Temple of Athena in Ortygia (now the cathedral of Syracuse). A further alteration was the removal of the wall between the *cella* and the *opisthodomos* to make a larger nave. (Note also the carved niches in the walls and the tomb recesses cut in the pavements of the portico.)

In studying this attractive temple one cannot help recalling that it was built at the same time as the Parthenon in Athens. Although it is smaller than the mother temple (6 × 13 columns as opposed to 8 × 17) and does not enjoy such a commanding site, it is no less of an achievement, combining all those visual subtleties that distinguish the ultimate refinement of the Doric order. The tapering of the columns and the manner in which they lean inwards slightly to give lightness and balance to the heavy masonry are devices that are difficult to appreciate, merging as they do in the graceful unity of the whole structure. All that is missing from this temple is sculpture, but perhaps that is a fortunate omission as it would hardly have withstood the ravages of wind and weather which have so deeply pitted the soft stone of

the building. It is certain, however, that the temple was highly decorated (like most of the ancient Greek temples) with white stucco as a basis to emphasise the architectural forms. The pediments, and the plain metopes on the inner and outer frieze, were probably painted with mythological scenes. The identity of the temple's deity has not, unfortunately, been revealed—the name 'Concord' (*Concordia*) being taken from a Latin inscription found on the site.

Excavations to the west of the Temple of Concord have revealed a large number of tombs, showing that this area was one of the principal burial places of the city in the Roman, early Christian and Byzantine periods. To the north of the road, and passing beneath it, is an early Christian *catacomb*, with tomb niches cut out of the rock at different levels. To the south of the road lies the garden of the Villa Aurea, in which there are further early Christian and Byzantine tombs and two interesting *hypogea* (underground burial vaults) which are adaptations of ancient cisterns. Below the walls at this

point lies the most extensive burial ground of all, the *Roman cemetery* (named Giambertoni) which stretches along the foot of the hill as far as the Porta Aurea (*Gate 4*).

Temple of Herakles (Temple of Hercules) Further on, just before the Porta Aurea, are the tumbled remains of the earliest of the major temples of the Greek city, built in the late 6th c. BC. The attribution of this temple was suggested by a reference in Cicero's description of the city, in which he mentions a Temple of Hercules near the *agora*, which contained a prized statue of the god. Like the Temple of Hera, this temple has traces of fire on its stonework from the Carthaginian assault. It was subsequently restored by the Romans, only to be destroyed later on by an earthquake. The temple was partially restored in 1924, when eight of the columns of the southern colonnade were re-erected by the English archaeologist Sir Alexander Hardcastle.

The stylobate is built up from the ground on the north side, where there is a steep slope to the road, and had eight steps at the west end. A feature of this temple, copied by the builders of the two other temples to the east, was the incorporation of a stairway in the piers on either side of the entrance to the *cella*. This led up to an attic, and it is a matter for conjecture how the architect was able to construct a roof to span the extremely wide *cella* of this temple, half as wide again as that of the Temple of Concord.

Immediately to the west lies the **Porta Aurea** (*Gate 4*) which was the main entrance to the ancient city. It is now the main entrance from the south to the modern city, and the original gateway has disappeared under the asphalt of the SS118. A short diversionary walk may be made from here to the **Tomb of Theron**, which is not, as the name suggests, the resting-place of the great tyrant of Akragas but an unidentified tomb of the Roman period (*c*. 75 BC). It is an odd little building consisting of a square podium and an upper part resembling a temple in miniature, with a curious mixture of Doric and Ionic features.

Going east along the SS115 a turning to the right leads in $\frac{1}{2}$ km to the interesting **Temple of Asclepius**. (This is a long walk on a hot day and transport is recommended.) No building of the period could express more individuality than this small Doric temple, dedicated to the God of Healing, which was built in the late 5th c. BC. The site, close to the River S. Biagio and a medicinal spring, was unsuitable for building, and a solid base had to be constructed with deep foundations. On this a temple with solid walls was erected, the front (east end) with an opening divided by two columns (*in antis*) and the rear (west end) closed, with two engaged columns giving the effect of an entrance to an *opisthodomos*. The latter room was, in fact, omitted from this temple, and only a *pronaos* and a *cella* were incorporated. The most interesting survival is the pier at the entrance to the *cella*, which stands proud from the ruin like a small tower. It is possible to climb to the top of the pier by the stairway inside it.

Temple of Herakles

Western archaeological zone (Hours: 09.00– 1 hr before sunset. Entrance free) This area lies to the north-west of the Porta Aurea. The car park by the entrance covers part of the ancient *agora* of the city, which has only been partly excavated. Inside the entrance is a long *altar* (54·50 × 17·50 m) associated with the Temple of Olympian Zeus to the west. The foundation blocks of the altar platform have been exposed by the pillaging of stone that took place at this site in the 18th c. To the south-east of the temple are unrelated ruins of different periods, including walls of Roman and Byzantine dwellings and the base of a small *archaic temple* with *cella* divided by piers.

Temple of Olympian Zeus (Olympieion) Had this temple been completed it would have been one of the wonders of the ancient world. Certainly its scale puts it in the same class as the legendary Temple of Diana at Ephesus, and one can only deplore its loss to the ravages of Carthaginians, earthquakes and stone-robbers. Only the foundations and some of the fallen masonry remain, but this gives sufficient idea of its extraordinary dimensions.

A degree of mystery surrounds the origin of this temple. From the founding of the colony in 582 BC there would certainly have been a plan to build a temple to Zeus, and as the city increased in size and splendour the pressure to embark on such a prestigious undertaking would have increased. There is historical evidence that the Carthaginians captured at the battle of Himera in 480 BC were put to work on the temple, and this may be the date of its foundation: the unusual style of the temple, however, makes dating very difficult.

The dimensions of the temple are 112·60 × 56·30 m, which makes it larger than any other Greek temple in either Greece or Magna Graecia. This was by no means the only difference. Instead of the conventional peripteral form, i.e. with surrounding colonnade, the temple was enclosed by a wall with Doric half-columns set along it at intervals (7 at either end, 14 at the sides). Walling between columns is also found in Temple F at Selinunte, but the comparison ends here. At Selinunte the columns retained their complete rounded form: in the Temple of Zeus the columns were round on the outside of the building but backed by square pilasters on the inside. Another extraordinary innovation was the use of *Telamones*, or Atlas figures as a decorative support for the architrave. These giant statues, forerunners of the Caryatids on the later classical temples, were set in openings in the walls between columns, their arms raised to give the effect of carrying the weight of the entablature. Each figure, 7·65 m high, was made out of huge blocks of stone and covered with plaster (a cast of one of destroyed it. Much of the stonework—further shattered by earthquakes—was finally removed from the site in the 18th c. for the construction of the nearby harbour at Porto Empedocle.

The area to the west of the temple, still under excavation, is very confusing, containing as it does the archaeological debris of at least 1000 years. The area mainly comprises the site of the ancient **Sanctuary of the Chthonic Deities**, a sacred precinct dedicated to the earth-goddesses Demeter and Persephone. Like the other Sanctuary of Demeter already described, this site pre-dates the founding of the Greek colony and is probably Sicel in origin. Excavations have shown, however, that it was in use as a sacred area for much longer than the Rock Sanctuary—probably until Roman times.

The precinct is bounded on the east by the narrow and indented entrance of *Gate 5*, and to the south by a well preserved stretch of the city wall. Inside the precinct, or *temenos*, are the remains of a number of shrines and altars. The remains of four temples can also be seen on the site. Most conspicuous is the **Temple of the Dioscuri** (Castor and Pollux), a building of the early 5th c. BC which has had four columns and part of the entablature and pediment restored (1836). How much of the material belongs to the original building is uncertain, and it is not now considered an authentic reconstruction. To the south of this temple is the stylobate of a larger temple building, with an associated altar to the east. To the north of the Temple of the Dioscuri are

Temple of the Dioscuri

Stones showing U-cuts for hauling

these figures lies in the middle of the *cella*).

The temple was entered from the east, the entrance being between the columns at either end of the façade. The interior of the temple was divided into three parts (a *cella* and two side aisles) by two rows of square pillars, joined together by a screen wall. The temple was built on massive foundations 6m in depth (best viewed on the north side) but unfortunately nothing of the temple itself remains standing. We cannot be sure how far it was completed, but after at least 70 years of labour it must have been largely built by 406 BC when the Carthaginians

the foundations of two other *temples* of the mid and late 6th c. BC. These were unfinished, the construction of the later temple slightly overlapping that of the earlier. West of these is one of the most interesting survivals of the sanctuary: a *circular altar* used for sacrifices. The construction consists of two circles of stones, joined by four arms. This allowed four animals to be sacrificed together, their blood running into the centre of the altar (*bothros*). Beside this altar is another *square altar*, on which the sacrifices were burnt (note the reddening of the stone from the fire).

Telamone

Circular altar

To the west, within an enclosing wall, lies another sacred area, the **Sanctuary of an Unknown Divinity**. This has its own shrines and a circular altar, but there is little for the visitor to see.

Temple of Vulcan (Hephaestus) Two reconstructed columns stand as a landmark to this ruin, situated in the south-west corner of the city wall. The best approach is from the SS115, $\frac{1}{2}$ km west of the Porta Aurea. Before reaching the river bridge, turn off to the right. A track leads to the railway bridge: beneath the arches steps lead up to the temple. There are few remains on the site. The temple, built in the late 5th c. BC on the site of an earlier archaic temple, had 6 × 13 columns and incorporated Ionic elements—a rarity in Sicilian temple architecture. The enthusiast who has come this far will probably wish to continue along the wall of the ancient city until it completes its circle (with intermittent breaks) to the north. Three more fortified entrances (*Gates 6–8*) may be seen on this route.

Returning to the city by the SS115, a turning to the left leads to the new **Archaeological Museum** (Museo Nazionale Archeologico) which is now the main repository of the city's archaeological and historical treasures. (For opening times, see p. 25.)

The design of this very modern museum, though imaginative, lacks a sense of direction. The map at the entrance suggests a logical route, but it is difficult for the visitor to carry this in his head. Clearer directional signs and labelling of showcases would be helpful, as there is nothing more infuriating than to see interesting exhibits confusingly arranged. The collection, which includes material from the old Civic Museum in the town, and from the temporarily closed Diocesan Museum, is encyclopedic, and is most simply described by a list of the rooms with some of their most important exhibits.

Room 1 Plan of the ancient city. *Room 2* Prehistoric material and early Greek finds from sites east of Agrigento, immediately preceding the foundation of Akragas in 581 BC. *Room 3* contains, in a series of upright display cases, the vases from the old Museo Civico (6th–3rd c. BC). *Room 4* has examples of lion's-head water spouts from the roofs of various temples. *Room 5*, over the basement well, is devoted to finds from the Greek sanctuaries of Akragas, of the classical and Hellenistic periods. These

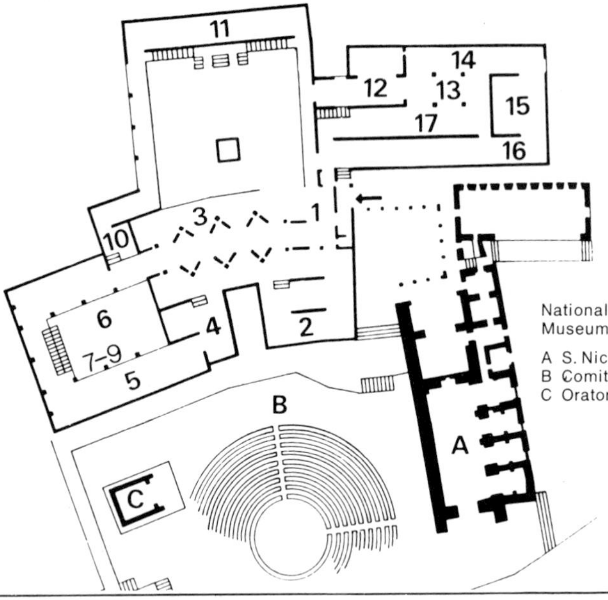

National Archaeological
Museum, Agrigento

A S. Nicola
B Comitium
C Oratory of Phalaris

include heads of *kouroi*, goddesses, votive figurines and the moulds from which they were made.

Room 6, the basement well, contains a reconstruction of the Temple of Zeus and a magnificent *Telamone*—one of the giant figures which supported the eaves. In a niche are the heads of three more *Telamones*. The three rooms leading off the basement well, which may be closed, are: *Room 7*, finds from the residential area of the ancient city; *Room 8*, inscriptions; *Room 9*, coins.

Returning to the upper level, *Room 10* has examples of Greek sculpture, including a fine marble *ephebe* (*c*. 470 BC). A corridor leads on to *Room 11* with material from the necropolises of various temples including sarcophagi. *Rooms 12* and *13* share material from prehistoric sites around Agrigento and *Room 14* is a topographical exhibition of the province of Agrigento. *Room 15* has material from Gela, notably a magnificent red-figure *krater* (5th c. BC) representing a battle of the Amazons. *Room 16* is the topographical section devoted to Nisseno, *Room 17* to Caltanissetta.

The museum is also temporarily housing the most important treasures of the Museo Diocesano, damaged by a landslip in 1966.

Next to the museum is the bizarre yet attractive little church of **S. Nicola**. This church, built in the 13th c., has the extraordinary combination of a Gothic doorway in

its west front and on either side a massive pier topped by a Doric cornice. This classical detail, together with the monumental construction of the church, can be attributed to the use of stones from a nearby ruin of the Roman period.

The cornice is repeated inside the church, running along the walls. It was originally a kind of gallery, and it is interesting to note the doorway in the south wall above the cornice which connected this upper level to the convent. The interior of the church, which underwent reconstruction in the 14th and 15th c., has a single nave and ogival vault, with supporting ribs. The north and south sides have blind arcades: to the south, the arches open into chapels.

The second chapel on the right contains the fine marble **Sarcophagus of Phaedra**, originally in the Cathedral. This was found near Agrigento in the 18th c. and is a Roman work of the 2nd c. AD. The carvings show scenes from the mythological tale of Phaedra and Hippolytus. On the front, Hippolytus, about to go on a hunt, learns of the love of his stepmother Phaedra (note the message in his left hand, and the diminutive nurse who has delivered it). The scenes at the ends of the sarcophagus show Phaedra's grief at her rejection by Hippolytus and Hippolytus' tragic death, thrown out of his chariot by the wrath of Poseidon. On the reverse is an unfinished scene depicting the fateful boar hunt.

The end chapel on the right (interior and exterior) combines arches of many different styles, which give a good idea of the varied history of this church. At the east end of the church, behind an arcaded wall with 16th c. frescoes, is the original apse, now closed and used for concerts.

Little now remains of the convent which originally adjoined the church. Most of it has been rebuilt or incorporated in the new museum, and one cannot help but wonder however, a double window in the 13th c. Chiaramonte style survives.

To the west of S. Nicola is the strange little **Comitium**, an assembly place of the 2nd c. BC shaped like a small theatre. This interesting survival of the Hellenistic city, not yet fully explained, was uncovered by the site-clearing for the approach road to the new museum, and one cannot help but wonder what further archaeological finds this rich area will bring forth.

To the north of the Comitium is the monumental tomb of a Roman lady, misleadingly known as the **Oratory of Phalaris**. This tomb, built in the 2nd c. BC is slightly earlier than the Tomb of Theron and has a similar design: the replica of a classical temple standing on a rectangular podium. In the Middle Ages it was converted into a chapel. In place of the porticoed entrance an arched doorway was constructed, and the interior vaulted: additionally a small pointed window was opened in the wall. The interior of the base of the

tomb has now been removed and an entrance opened on the west side.

Hellenistic and Roman Quarter On the opposite side of the road to the museum are the excavated streets of an area of Agrigentum, inhabited from the 2nd c. BC to the 5th c. AD, which is a fragment of the great urban development covering the shelf of land between the Rupe Atenea and the Valley of the Temples. So far four streets have been revealed. These are side streets, or *cardines*, which run off the main street (*decumanus*) now lying beneath the modern SS118. The houses were built of sandstone and many of them were highly decorated, as can be seen from the traces of frescoes on walls and the surviving floor mosaics. Most of the latter are geometric in style, and the best are those that are covered, at the north end of the site.

Rupe Atenea Another pleasant walk may be made along the Rupe Atenea, which is reached via the Piazza Vittorio Emanuele. The road leading to the summit of the rock (signposted) lies opposite the Post Office. One can easily follow the ridge as far as the north wall of the Psychiatric Hospital: the goat-footed can then continue along the ridge under the lee of the hospital's west wall, arriving eventually at the Chapel of S. Biagio. The fun of this is reserved for those who wish to follow the *line* of the ancient walls (there are no actual remains of these on this stretch).

Comitium and Oratory of Phalaris

Akrai see **Palazzolo Acréide**

Álcamo Town 48km west of Palermo, by-passed by SS113 (A29).

Founded by Frederick II in 1233, Álcamo possesses the remains of a 14th c. castle and a number of churches decorated by artists whose work is familiar elsewhere in Sicily: Antonello Gagini, Pietro Novelli, Giacomo Serpotta and Borremans. These churches may be found on or near the long main street of the town (Corso 6 Aprile) which crosses it from east to west.

Starting from the east the churches are: **S. Francesco d'Assisi** (17th c.) containing statues of *St Mark* and *Mary Magdalen* by Antonello Gagini; the 18th c. **Badia Nuova** (Via Caruso) with stuccoes by Serpotta and a painting of *St Benedict* by Novelli; **SS. Cosma e Damiano** (also 18th c., annexed to the monastery of S. Chiara) with work by Serpotta, Andrea Carrera and Borremans; the **Badia Grande** (Via Rossotti) with paintings by Novelli; the **Chiesa Matrice** or **Assunta** (Piazza 4 Novembre) with frescoes by Borremans and sculptures by Gagini; finally, in the Piazza Ciullo at the west end of the Corso, the church of **S. Oliva** with a fine statue of the saint by Antonello Gagini and a painting (high altar) by Novelli.

To the south of the town, on a height (Monte Bonifato, 825m) stands the chapel of the **Madonna dell'Alto** and the remains of a medieval **castle**. This was the site of the Saracenic fortress of *Alcamuk* which gave its name to the town. This vantage point offers one of the finest views of the Gulf of Castellammare.

Alicudi Island see **Aeolian Is.**

Altofonte Town 12km south-west of Palermo on road to Piana degli Albanesi.

The other name of this town, Parco, reminds us that this was one of the retreats of Roger II, the site of the hunting-lodge built by the Norman king on this belvedere overlooking the great royal park which stretched all the way from Palermo. A ghost of the Royal **chapel** (later incorporated in a monastery) remains. It may be entered through the main church in the Piazza Umberto. Restoration has been thorough and one can appreciate the form rather than the fabric of the original. Note the cupola, raised on its small tower at the east end, and the little gallery at the west end. The view from the north side of the church, of Roger's former domain, is spectacular.

Augusta Town and seaport on east coast of Sicily.

The peninsula on which Augusta is built is in fact a small island connected to the mainland by a bridge. There the similarity with Ortygia ends. There is little recorded history for Augusta: although the coast round here was settled by Megarians from Greece, the main settlement, Megara Hyblaea, was to the south, and it is a matter for conjecture that Augusta was a dependancy, *Xiphonia*. Its site, however, commended itself for military use and it was developed as a fortress-post by the Emperòr Frederick II. The Aragonese developed it further, and it was from here that the fleet of the Holy League set sail to defeat the Turks at the Battle of Lepanto (1571).

Some of the fortifications from these periods have survived: in the town, a **castle** founded by the Emperor Frederick II, and on the tip of the peninsula and in the Porto Megarese, 16th c. **forts**. Another castle (1548) commands a little bay to the north of Augusta (7·5km) at **Brucoli**. This is thought to be the site of the ancient *Trotilon*, one of the earliest (pre-Megarian) Greek settlements in Sicily.

Bagheria Town 14km east of Palermo (A19). Originally the country retreat of the rich Palermitans in the 18th and 19th c., Bagheria is now a bustling market town at the heart of an area rich in vineyards and citrus plantations. Diminished as they are by the encroachments of modern building, the villas of that privileged minority are still worth discovering, if only for a glimpse of Lampedusa's Sicily.

The best starting point for a walking visit is the Piazza Garibaldi, off the Corso Umberto I. In a corner are the entrance gates to the **Villa Palagonia**. The villa is private property, with a small entrance fee (Hours: 09.00–12.30 & 17.00–19.00 or 15.00–17.00 in winter). Built in 1715 by Tommaso Napoli, this villa is a parody of the Baroque of the last period of Spanish rule, symbolised by the rather menacing eagle surmounting the pediment. The eagle is a foretaste of greater eccentricities: passing through the central arch one finds oneself in a courtyard enclosed by high walls topped by a procession of extraordinary figures.

These are the *sculture grottesche* described with some distaste by Goethe in his *Italian Journey*: dragons, monkeys, dwarves with giant heads, animal-human hybrids. Such monsters belong to the heights of a Gothic cathedral, not the garden wall of a Baroque palace. The story of their creation is suitably bizarre. Ferdinand, the Prince of Palagonia, who dreamed them up, was a hunchback whose revenge on his wife's lovers was to make deformed caricatures of them, so alarming that the 18th c. traveller Brydone records that '. . . the seeing of them by women with child is said to have been attended with very unfortunate circumstances, several living monsters have been brought forth in the neighbourhood.' The vengeful prince carried his mania to the

Villa Palagonia, Bagheria

inside of the palace, decorating the rooms in a similar manner with grotesque figures, and building mirrors into the walls, doors and ceilings to lend a distorted image to his visitors. The villa is still privately owned by members of the prince's family: they do not however live there and the building is in a very poor state of repair, though scheduled for preservation.

On the opposite side of the Corso Umberto I, the Via Trabia leads to the gates of another palace built by Napoli, the **Villa Valguarnera**. Here the architecture is a little more restrained, with the statues of Marabitti adding a more classical touch. Another palace worth visiting on the west side of the town is the **Villa Butera** (1658) which incorporates a 'Certosa' (Carthusian monastery)—a collection of wax figures in Carthusian habits.

Baida see **Palermo** (Excursions)

Basiluzzo Island see **Aeolian Is.**, Panarea

Butera Town 22 km north of Gela, built on a pinnacle of rock between two valleys.

A natural fortress, this rock was occupied in prehistoric times. The present town dates from the Saracenic and Norman periods and retains, at the summit, an 11th c. Norman **castle** in good state of preservation. To the north of the town in the *Piano della Fiera*, recent excavations have revealed a Siculo-Greek necropolis. Contents of tombs from the 7th–3rd c. BC may be seen in the Gela museum.

Cáccamo (521 m) Town set high in coastal range east of Palermo, reached by turning off A19 at Términi Imerese (10 km) or from Términi Imerese (SS113, 12 km).

The traveller shunning the beaten track will enjoy the steep but traffic-free drive to this old hill town, with its magnificent views of the northern coastline.

Castle On a high bastion of rock, overlooking the town and the valley of the River S. Leonardo, is one of the largest and most complete medieval castles in Sicily, dating in part from the 12th c. Until recently the home of the Dukes of Cáccamo, this castle is now the property of the Region of Sicily. It is unfortunate that such a fine building—complete with story-book towers and battlements —should be so long *in restauro* and inaccessible to visitors.

Elsewhere in the town, in a small square set in the hillside below the Corso Umberto I is the church of **S. Giorgio**, founded by the Normans but reconstructed in 1614.

Calascibetta (878 m) Town 7 km from Enna (SS290, A19).

Situated on a height slightly lower than that of Enna, Calascibetta has the aspect—like its larger neighbour—of a medieval hill town. It is more familiar, perhaps, as part of the view to be enjoyed from Enna, but visitors to the smaller town will find that it preserves more of the character of the middle ages than Enna with its sprouting office blocks. Its origin, in fact, is shown in its name, from the Arabic *Kalat-Scibet*.

Above: Caltabellotta   Right: Cáccamo

Calatafimi Town 34km west of Trápani which gave its name to the battle between the Garibaldini and the Bourbon army on 15 May 1860. This was the major engagement in the campaign of the 'Thousand' and cleared the way for their march on Palermo. A monument stands on a hill overlooking the site of the battle, 4km to the south of the town. This is reached by a turning off the main road (*Ossario*).

Caltabellotta (758m) Town 22km northeast of Sciacca.

For those with time for the diversion, this is one of the pleasantest excursions to be made from the coast. The route is from the junction of the main coastal road (SS115) with the SS188b to S. Margherita di Belice. Leaving Sciacca on this road, a turning is shortly made to the right. The road to Caltabellotta is beautiful, through countryside that builds in a rhythm of hills and pastureland, broken increasingly by a *staccato* of rock, to the heights on which the little town balances. The precariousness of the site is evident in the damage caused by the 1968 earthquake: the effect of which is most apparent at the highest point of the town. Here, in forlorn isolation, stands the **Chiesa Madre**, badly damaged by the earthquake and now shut. The church founded by Count Roger after his defeat of the Saracens (1090) now presents a sorry sight: the original portal, with its pointed arch, is severely damaged, and much of the stonework has collapsed. Mounting the rock behind the church, however, one finds compensation for the disaster in the magnificent view. The terraced hillside

below makes a *cavea* for a spectacular amphitheatre of rock: beyond lies a panorama of mountains and river valleys. A still grander view may be had from the pinnacle rock (Monte Castello, 949m, reached by steps from the town) where cling the scant remains of a Norman castle.

Caltagirone (608m) Town 65km east of Enna.

Its commanding site—the present town is built over three hills—brought settlement to Caltagirone as far back as the Neolithic period: rock-cut tombs discovered locally are similar to those at the vast necropolis of Pantálica. Its name, and traditional nicknames, are descriptive of the town and its history. *Kalat* and *gerun* are Arabic for 'castle' and 'caves'. 'Regina dei Monti' and 'Faenza di Sicilia' are the nicknames, the first referring to the site of the town, the second to its most famous industry, ceramics. The tradition began with Sicel pottery and refined, in the time of the Arabs, into the beautiful majolica which can be seen in the form of tiles and other ornamentation on the buildings of the town. The finest example of this work may be seen in the **Museo della Ceramica** (Via Roma). The old parts of Caltagirone owe their 18th c. character to the earthquake which destroyed the town in 1693: many of the fine buildings of this period were subsequently lost in the heavy bombing of World War II.

At the centre of the town is the Piazza Umberto I, with the 18th c. **Banco di Sicilia** building, the 19th c. **Cathedral** and (adjacent) the **Corte Capitaniale** with a fine 17th c.

façade by the Gagini. To the east is the Piazza Municipio, dominated by the 19th c. Baroque-style **Palazzo Municipio**. From here the Via Luigi Sturzo leads past the churches of the **Rosario** and **Salvatore** (both containing sculpture by the Gagini) to the church of **S. Giorgio**, one of the first buildings to be reconstructed after the 1693 earthquake. It contains a 15th c. Flemish painting of the *Trinity*, believed to be the work of Roger van der Weyden. Returning to the Piazza Municipio one can ascend by a great flight of steps (Scala della S. Maria del Monte) to the church of that name. This is one of the hills of Caltagirone: worth the climb for the view.

Elsewhere in the town (Viale Principessa Maria, by the railway station) is the 15th c. church of **S. Maria di Gesù**, with a statue of the *Madonna of the Chain* by Antonello Gagini.

Caltanissetta (pop. 65,000) Provincial capital (A19).

The unattractive modern aspect of this town seems in conflict with the ancient origin of its name. The Saracens, who were here, added the prefix *Kalat* (castle) to the name of an early settlement (originally Sican, later Greek) called *Nissa*, on the summit of M. Gibel Gabel. (Keen students of the period may like to visit the site, 4 km to the south of the town, turning off the SS191. Another site belonging to the same period—7th-4th c. BC —is at *Sabucina*, 6 km to the north-east of the town, turning off the SS122.)

The town itself holds little of historical or architectural interest for the visitor. What might appeal has all but been lost to the ravages of earthquake, war damage or neglect. The 17th c. **Cathedral** (Piazza Garibaldi) lost much of its ceiling—painted by Borremans—in the last war. Damage was also done to the cupola, choir and transept, all of which have subsequently been restored. To the left of the cathedral, the Via Giannone, the Via S. Domenico and the Via Angeli lead to the church of **S. Maria degli Angeli**. This church, which adjoins a convent, was built in the 14th c. and retains a beautiful Gothic west door. It is otherwise ruined, and now fronted by a brickyard. Beyond the church, on a steep, oddly-shaped rock, are the sparse remains of the **Castello di Pietrarossa**, once upon a time the home of Frederick III of Aragon and now the relic of an earthquake.

Elsewhere in the town (in the Via Colajanni near the railway station) a small **museum** houses objects recovered in recent excavations at the local sites mentioned above.

From the SS122, about 2.5 km outside Caltanissetta, a turning to the left leads to the **Badia di S. Spirito**. Here is one of those rare survivals in Sicily—a totally Norman church. Founded by Count Roger and his wife

Adelasia in the 11th c., this church has a single aisle with three apses. Between the north and central apse, an engraved stone records the consecration of the church in 1153—much later than its foundation. Over the central apse is a fresco of the 15th c. At the west end of the church is a 12th c. font.

Camarina Ancient site on south coast, 35 km south-west of Ragusa.

This was an important colony of Syracuse, founded in 598 BC, which had to struggle to hold its own in its rather isolated position, nearer to Syracuse's rival Gela than to Syracuse itself. Its history was one of shifting alliances and it was destroyed and rebuilt several times before its abandonment in the Roman period.

The approach to Camarina is either from S. Croce Camerina, 24 km south-west of Ragusa (take track to left 10.5 km west of village and continue 2 km to headland) or from Gela (after 16 km turn off SS115 at 'Zona Archaeologica' sign to Kamarina. After 23 km take coast road from Scoglitti). On the headland to the east of the village lie the remains of the ancient city).

At the summit is the *antiquarium* which

Hunting scene, Casale

stands on the site of the *Temple of Athena* (5th c. BC) lying in a sacred area defined on the west by the traces of a wall. To the west lie the ruins of the Hellenistic-Roman city. At the sea's edge, one can appreciate the full beauty of the site, with the prospect of a sandy beach and steep cliffs. The objects recovered from Camarina in recent excavations may be seen at the museums of Ragusa and Syracuse.

Carlentini see Lentini

Casale Ancient site 5 km south-west of Piazza Armerina at the foot of Monte Mangone. (Hours 09.00–1 hr before sunset.) This **Roman villa** of the 3rd c. AD, with 40 mosaic pavements, stands as the most exciting post-war discovery in the archaeology of Sicily, and one of the finest relics of the Roman age. Its situation, on the side of a wooded hill in the remote interior of the island, gives it an isolated character which makes a visit here one of the most pleasurable experiences of a Sicilian tour. Although the existence of ruins was known on this site from the 18th c., systematic exploration was not carried out until 1950. The work is still in progress, but the main complex of buildings that comprises the villa has now been fully excavated and covered with an opaque perspex roof.

History The history and function of the villa has been largely gleaned from the study of its mosaics. The *Adventus Imperator* mosaic at the entrance (*tablinum*), the appearance of an imperial figure in the hunting scene (main corridor) with identifying features, the hairstyles and insignia of other figures, and the series depicting the Labours of Hercules (*triclinium*) all serve to relate the villa to the Emperor Maximianus Herculius (Maximian), whose patron and divine protector was Hercules. The emphasis on wild animals and hunting parties in the mosaics, and the natural setting of the villa—in an area that abounded with game in ancient times—suggest its use as a hunting lodge.

There is no direct evidence that the villa was the home of Maximian but the scale and splendour of the building indicate that its owner was of the highest rank, and there is a further clue in the hunting scene in the main corridor, already mentioned: the landscape depicted here is African, as are the

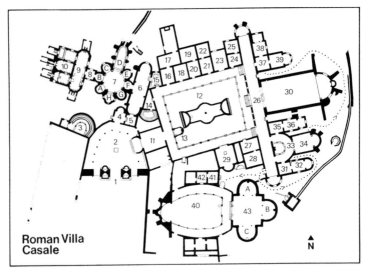

**Roman Villa
Casale**

N

animals: lions, elephants and leopards. As
co-emperor with Diocletian in the period of
the division of the imperial power (Tetrarchy),
Maximian was largely responsible for Spain,
Gaul and North Africa, and it is almost certain that the mosaics were the work of artists
imported from the African provinces. The
period of Maximian's rule (286–305 AD) and
of his African campaigns (297–298 AD) provides a date for the commencement of the
mosaics: but the scale of the work is such
that it is unlikely that they were finished
before the advent of Constantine and the
recognition of Christianity. In the light of this
it is interesting to consider these mosaics as
one of the last great works of pagan art in
civilized Europe: perhaps even a final,
spirited protest against the new religion.

Apart from the mosaic floors, little remains
of the villa, which was buried by a landslide
in the middle ages. A few architectural fragments and statues were recovered, and
parts of the wall reconstructed. The plan of
the villa is very complicated and can best be
described as comprising four groups of
buildings with a monumental entrance. The
first group, to the north of the entrance, is the
baths; the second, the central peristyle with
the private chambers leading off it; the third,
the rooms to the east of the main corridor
including the hall of the basilica; the fourth,
the *xystus* or open court with rooms leading
off, including the large *triclinium* (dining-
room). Most of the rooms (there are 50) have
mosaic pavements, and to be sure of seeing
them all it is recommended that the visitor
follows the route described, which has been

determined by the arrangement of stairs,
walkways and exits. The basis of the illustrated plan is that published in the official
guide, prepared by Prof. G. Gentili, the
supervisor of the excavations. (This guide
is obtainable from the custodian.)

Tour of the villa (see plan) The monumental
entrance (**1**) consists of a wide central opening and two smaller openings, flanked by
columns. Set into the gateway on either side
of the main entrance are a double set of
basins, rectangular on the outside and circular on the inside. It is assumed that these
basins, which served as *nymphaea* (fountains sacred to the nymphs) received their
water supply from a reservoir in a chamber
built over the entrance. The *entrance atrium*
(**2**) retains part of its original floor, and some
of the columns of the portico, which have
been reconstructed. To the right a flight of
three steps leads to the peristyle, the large
central court of the building. This was the
official entrance to the villa itself, and it is
interesting to note the stone bench for
waiting guests.

To the west of the atrium lies the *large
latrine* (**3**). The semi-circular row of seats
has disappeared, but there are some traces
of the original pavement.

Before entering the villa, it is most practical to see the **baths**, which lie on the
north side of the atrium. They are entered
via a small shrine, the *Chapel of the Thermae*
(**4**) with a floor of geometric design. This
would have contained, in the apse, a statue
of Venus. The next room (**5**) is the *Vestibule
of the Thermae* with a similar decorative

floor. This vestibule leads into the main entrance hall of the baths (**6**) whose floor can be seen later in the tour.

Adjoining the hall, to the west, is the *frigidarium* (**7**). This room, octagonal in shape, was a cold bath. The mosaic here shows a marvellous miscellany of sea creatures, nereids, tritons and centaurs, disporting themselves around the central figure of Oceanus. Particularly charming are the cupid fishermen in their boats. Off each side of this octagonal room is a separate chamber. Two of them (B and F) were vestibules; another two (D and H) were plunge baths and the remaining four (A, C, E and G) were used for undressing or simply resting. With the exception of A and E the mosaics in these chambers are either fragmentary or non-existent. The mosaic in A shows a girl taking off her robe assisted by maids, and that in E her counterpart, a man who has just emerged from the bath, wrapped in a towel, being offered his clothes by servants.

To the west of the frigidarium is the *Chamber of the 'Unctiones'* (**8**) which takes its identity from the mosaic portraying a bather being rubbed with oil by a servant (note the oil-flask and the strigil, used for scraping off the oil, in the hand of the figure to the right). This room was used for anointing and massage after the bath. From this point there is no convenient access to the remaining rooms of the baths, the *tepidaria* (**9**) and the *caldaria* (**10**). The pavements here have largely disappeared, exposing the hollow spaces under the floors through which the hot air from the furnaces circulated.

Returning to the atrium, we now approach the main entrance of the villa. Going up the steps, we enter the *tablinum* (**11**), a vestibule that has in its floor the *Adventus* mosaic, a fragmentary scene depicting a ritual welcome for the emperor. We can appreciate in this room the function of the modern shelter built over the site, which serves not only to preserve the colours of the mosaics from the bright sunshine but to create the impression for the visitor that he is inside a building. Although the tablinum gives access to the portico of the *peristyle* (**12**) it is not possible to walk around the portico at this point. We can however admire the mosaic floor of the little *shrine* (**13**, possibly covered) set between two of the columns of the portico (note the *hedera* or ivy leaf in the centre, the symbol of Herculius) and the mosaic floor of the portico itself. The design of this floor, which runs around the four sides of the peristyle, appears at first glance a formal sequence of decorative borders and medallions: then we see, in the medallions, the humorous portraits of animals, a prodigious Noah's Ark procession that introduces us to the down-to-earth world of the Romans at play—a world dominated by the delights of nature. From the west portico of the peristyle an opening leads into a triangular chamber from which one can view the *small latrine* (**14**) with a mosaic of wild animals and birds. Through an opening in its east wall one can now view the main hall of the baths, the *Hall of the Circus* (**6**). The pavement here has an impressive scene depicting the sequence of a Roman chariot race, probably in the Circus Maximus in Rome. The contest is between four teams each distinguished by a colour: green, red, blue and white. Starting at the northern end of the mosaic (to the right) and following the course of the race, the sequence begins with two charioteers with attendants, preparing for the race. Then, at the start of the race, four chariots are shown galloping out from the *carceres* (starting boxes). The race is shown in progress around the arena with its central *spina*, the long division with its triple-columned *meta* (turning post) at either end. One chariot is shown overtaking another: further on, at the turn, there is a collision between two others. Finally a chariot of the green faction has beaten a red chariot to the finishing line and is being heralded by a trumpeter. Beside the trumpeter is a magistrate in a toga, about to present the palm of victory. Incidental to the actual race are the figures of the judges, on horseback, supporters of the competing factions, on foot, and spectators.

Another room associated with the baths is the *trapezoid vestibule* (**15**) between the baths and the peristyle. The bench around the walls, and the subject of the mosaic, indicate that this was used as a waiting room for the baths. The mosaic depicts a family group on their way to the baths: a woman who is probably mistress of the house and of the imperial family, accompanied by her children—a boy and a girl—and two servants. This mosaic provides one of the most definitive references for the dating of the villa. The woman's hairstyle and the treatment of her features are typical of the Tetrarchy (late 3rd c. AD).

Continuing towards the central corridor to the east, a group of seven rooms (**16–22**) can be viewed. These were the private rooms of the villa and were used as bedchambers or sitting-rooms. The mosaic pavements of these rooms were damaged by alterations carried out by the Normans. **16**, **17** and **18** have overall geometric patterns, **20** has disappeared and **19**—a dancing scene—is fragmentary. The *Hall of the Seasons* (**21**) is an interesting combination of geometrical and figurative work with the busts of the four Seasons and related animals depicted in medallions in a framework of stars and interlinking hexagons. The floor of **22** is purely figurative: a lively scene of *Cupids Fishing*. They are employing every conceivable means to catch the fish: nets, baskets, tridents, fishing-lines. One determined cupid has even jumped into the water and seized a fish by the tail. The Roman pavilion in the

background of this mosaic provides an interesting architectural detail.

A larger room to the east (**23**) contains the mosaic of the *Small Hunting Scene*, which in a strip cartoon treatment tells the story of a typical day's hunting, such as would be enjoyed by the Emperor Maximian. The topmost frieze shows hunters and hounds setting out for a day's sport: on the right they have started a fox. The next scene, below, shows hunters paying homage to an image of Diana, Goddess of the Hunt. Below her altar is a sacrificial fire on which one of the hunters is about to scatter incense. The two hunters approaching from the left are carrying a boar, caught in a net slung on a pole: to the right another man holds a hare he has just killed with a spear. Other methods of capturing and killing animals are shown below. Most interesting are the two hunters standing on either side of the tree at the third level. They are in pursuit of birds and carry on their backs bundles of reeds covered with sticky bird-lime. One of them also has a falcon perched on his shoulder. Other scenes of the chase show a fox pursued by hounds and then speared by a hunter on horseback; a stag-hunt in which three stags are being driven into a net; and a boar-hunt in which the boar, having apparently got the better of its pursuers, is about to be felled in a rather cowardly fashion by a rock thrown from above. At the centre of this great pageant of the chase is the culminating scene: the open-air banquet of the successful hunters.

Two further chambers with geometrical mosaics and some traces of wall decoration (**24** and **25**) lie to the east. Then the climax of the visit to Casale is reached: the magnificent *Long Corridor* with the *Great Hunting Scene* (**26**). The purpose of this corridor was to separate the private rooms of the villa from the hall of the basilica, which was used for official receptions. The corridor is 4.5 m

wide and 60 m long, running the full width of the villa, and its entire area is covered by mosaic—a vast panorama depicting with vigour and assurance the eternal contest between man and beast.

The action takes place on two continents separated by the sea: on the left Armenia, the Roman province in Western Asia, on the right Africa. The heavy undulations in the pavement, resulting from earth movements, give the landscape an extra dimension: it seems that all the wonders of the Roman Empire are unrolling at our feet. In the apse at the left end of the corridor is the figure representing *Armenia*, which is unfortunately damaged. In the apse at the right end is the figure of *Africa*, with an elephant and a tiger at her feet.

Across both continents the hunters advance, some pursuing animals, some—having caught them—manhandling them on to the boats which will transport them to Italy. Among the animals thus captured are ostriches, tigers and antelopes, an elephant being driven unceremoniously up a gangplank, a magnificent buffalo pulled along by several men, and a rhinoceros being coaxed out of a marsh. In the background the activities of lions and leopards attacking antelope and other prey seem almost a diversion: perhaps we are being told that man is not the only predator. But this is hardly a defence for our brave hunters. Most of the animals are being taken alive, and one need hardly guess at their fate. Wild animal fights remained, up to the 6th c. AD, one of the most popular events in the Roman arena.

A comprehensive description of the mosaic is impossible here, but three details are of particular interest. The first offers a fairly exact reference to the dating of the mosaic. Next to the scene of the rhinoceros is a group of three men, supervising the operations. The central figure has been identified by his costume and general appearance as the Emperor Maximian: supporting evidence is in the ivy leaf symbol on the shoulder of the officer to his right, the insignia of the members of his personal legion, the Herculiani. This then, is the lord of Casale, presented on the familiar territory of his African provinces—a happy reminder, in the seclusion and remoteness of his country villa, of the vaster domains of imperial power. Two other details at the far (south) end of the corridor tell us something of the men who created this vast and complex mosaic. A mounted hunter who has seized an armful of cubs from a tigress and is fleeing up the gangplank of the boat has inadvertently dropped one. The tigress, in angry pursuit, pauses to recover it. This moment of pathos suggests that the sympathies of the artists were, if only in this incident, on the side of the beast. But what is this menacing creature beyond, which surely has no place in the fauna of Africa? A winged

Left: Cupids Fishing   Right: Figure of Africa

griffon, straddling a cage from which peers the frightened face of a man. Is this the ultimate Nemesis for man the hunter?

From the corridor a stairway descends to the south portico of the peristyle. Immediately on the left is a chamber (**27**) with a geometric mosaic and part of the wall intact, with traces of frescoes. (The walls of the adjacent rooms are also partially preserved.) This is a vestibule to a room which contains the most popular, if not the most accomplished mosaic at Casale, in the *Chamber of the Maidens* (**28**). This mosaic was overlaid at a later date on the original pavement, which would account for the difference in style between it and the earlier mosaics. The subject is an athletic contest, the competitors nine rather elongated female gymnasts. They are wearing bathing costumes in the modern style and all but two are engaged in a variety of athletic activities. The exceptions are the girl in the centre of the bottom row, who has just been presented with a crown and a palm leaf of victory, and the girl next to her on the left who is being similarly honoured. The prize-giver—maiden No 10—is without doubt the most attractive, wrapped rather carelessly in her golden robe. A small cubicle separates the two last-mentioned rooms from a *diaeta* or dining-room (**29**) with an apsidal end and small fountain in the middle of the floor. The mosaic here is fragmentary, but quite fascinating. It is a companion piece to that in another *diaeta* (**34**) featuring the poet Arion. Here the hero of the piece is Orpheus, who sits on a rock in a perfect woodland setting, surrounded by a multitude of animals drawn by the enchanting strains of his lyre. The observation of nature is acute: the artists do not omit even the lowly lizard and the snail.

On the west side of the corridor, and raised above it, is the great hall of the *basilica* (**30**)

which served as an audience chamber and reception room for the emperor. It was approached directly through the entrance atrium and the peristyle via the central stairway leading from the east portico of the peristyle. In the apse at the far end of this hall stood the emperor's throne. Only fragments of the marble floor of this hall survive. On either side of the basilica are chambers with mosaic floors, probably the private apartments of the emperor and his family.

To view the first group one must leave the villa by the exit at the south apse of the long corridor and re-enter it from the east (see plan).

In **31**, the *Vestibule of the Small Circus*, we have the children's equivalent to the *Circus Maximus* mosaic (6). In this delightful composition four chariots compete, each drawn by two birds and driven by a child. The children's chariots have the same colours as the factions in the senior race (even the birds have matching plumage) and the same faction—green—is the winner. The adjacent room (**32**) has in its apse a mosaic of two maidens seated below a tree which bears the now familiar ivy leaf (*hedera*), the symbol of the Emperor Maximian. In its main chamber the participants in a Greek theatrical contest are shown in three separate friezes: musicians, comedians and tragedians.

33 is the semi-circular atrium of a further group of rooms. The mosaic here is of *Cupids Fishing*. Extending from this atrium is **34**, a large *diaeta* (dining room) with an apse and floor mosaic which though badly damaged is one of the most interesting in the villa. The subject is the rescue of the lyric poet Arion (an actual historical figure of the 7th c. BC) who, cast in the sea by a villainous ship's crew on his way from Sicily to Corinth (here fables take over) was saved by music-loving dolphins. He is shown here after his

rescue on the crest of a wave, playing his lyre surrounded by a fantastic and no doubt admiring assembly of sea-creatures. The *Vestibule of Eros and Pan* (**35**) to the north of the atrium, shows a contest between the God of Love and the God of the Forests, with an umpire on the left, behind whom are a satyr and Maenads. The figures to the right are thought to represent members of the imperial family. In the background, under a table set with vases of palm leaves, are bags of prize money. The next room the *Cubicle of Children Hunting* (**36**) has a recess in which the mosaic shows, on three levels, children gathering flowers. In the main part of the chamber children are shown—again on three levels—in pursuit of a miscellany of small creatures, including a hare, a duck, a cock, a buzzard, a peacock and a goat. In a couple of episodes (second level) the youthful hunters seem to be getting the worst of their encounters.

To view the three rooms to the north of the basilica it is necessary to go round its exterior and re-enter the villa from the other side. The *Vestibule of Polyphemus* (**37**) contains a mosaic representing a famous scene in Homer's Odyssey, when the one-eyed giant Polyphemus (Cyclops)—the man-eating monster who lived in a cave on the south-west coast of Sicily—is about to be given a drink of wine by his prisoner Odysseus, who later blinds him. The double room of **38** combines, in the geometrical design of its floor, a figurative scene of children playing, a series of female theatrical masks and female personifications of the seasons, and, as a centrepiece, a touching *Erotic Scene*. The apsidal chamber of **39** is called, appropriately, the *Cubicle of Fruit*.

To view the last group of buildings one walks around the east side of the villa and re-enters by the south apse of the long corridor. To the west lies the *xystus* (**40**), an open court which was used for walking and conversation. This had a portico on three sides and a fountain in the centre. The plan is ovoid, with one end rounded and the other straight. Parts of the walls and floor mosaics survive, the latter a design of acanthus leaves and animals. To the north of the xystus are three small rooms, two with mosaics. These show *Cupids Harvesting Grapes* (**41**) and *Wine Pressing* (**42**). The last room on the tour is the great dining-room or *triclinium* (**43**), approached by a flight of steps from the *xystus*. The mosaics in this room and in the three apses leading off it are among the finest examples of the art of mosaic in the pagan world, full of drama and vitality. The mythography is more aggressive here than elsewhere at Casale: the celebration of Hercules the climactic tribute to the Emperor Maximianus Herculius. In the main chamber we can see extracts from ten of the *Labours of Hercules* which most interestingly do not include the figure of Hercules himself. The student of mythology will be able to identify the mares of Diomedes, with their riders shot by Hercules' arrows; the dragon Ladon that guarded the Golden Fruit of the Hesperides; the pitchfork and the river used to clean out the Augean stables; the Cretan Bull; the Erymanthian Boar; the Cerynian Hind; the Hydra with its dog-like body and nine snakes' heads; the three-bodied warrior Geryon; the three-headed dog Cerberus.

In the north apse (**A**) stands the immortal hero himself with his leopard skin around his neck. Around him are symbols of his exploits and various deities, among them Zeus who is crowning him with a laurel wreath. In the east apse (**B**) are the contorted muscular figures of *Five Giants*, the victims of Hercules' arrows. In the south apse (**C**) another legendary figure dominates the scene. This is *Lycurgus*, the insane king of Thrace, encountered by Dionysus during the wine-god's travels in Greece. Here the king is trying to kill the Maenad Ambrosia, a follower of Dionysus, with a double-headed axe. In self-defence his victim is turning into a vine.

Victorious gymnast, Casale

Castelbuono Town 14km south of road junction on SS113 9km east of Cefalù (A20). The town grew up around the castle built by the Ventimiglia princes of the early 14th c., becoming the seat of this illustrious and powerful family. In the main square (Piazza Margherita) is the 14th c. **Matrice Vecchia** with a Renaissance portico and—inside—a number of fine works of the 15th and 16th c., including a *polyptych* (high altar), a beautiful marble *ciborium* (Cappella del Sacramento), statues and frescoes. The Via S. Anna leads from here, through an arch, to the open space at the highest point of the town dominated by the great square keep, with towers at each corner, that survives from the old **castle**. On the first floor is the *chapel of S. Anna* with stuccoes by the brothers Giacomo and Giuseppe Serpotta: for the present both this chapel and the castle are closed for restoration.

Castelluccio Ancient site reached from junction on SS115 8km west of Noto. After 13km a right turn leads to the site (3km). This Bronze Age village (18th–15th c. BC), occupying the summit of an isolated hill, was excavated by Orsi. It has given its name to the most important Early Bronze Age culture in south-east Sicily. About 200 rock-cut tombs were found in the area, many with pottery. The door slabs from these tombs, examples of which may be seen in the Syracuse Museum, bear the only stone carving of the prehistoric period found in Sicily.

Castelvetrano Town 42km east of Marsala (SS115), at the centre of the wine-producing region of Sicily (A29).
The town has some interesting churches. Between the Piazza Umberto I and the Piazza Garibaldi stands the 16th c. **Chiesa Madre** with its unusual crenellation, detached campanile and fine Renaissance doorway. To the south of the Chiesa Madre the Via Bonsignore leads to the Piazza Regina Margherita in which stands the church of **S. Domenico** with rich decoration in stucco by Antonio Ferraro (1577) and the church of **S. Giovanni Battista** with a statue of the saint by Antonello Gagini (1522). One interesting work of art exists outside the churches of Castelvetrano: in the **Municipio**, opposite the Chiesa Madre, is a fine 5th c. BC bronze statue of a youth, the *Ephebe of Selinunte*.
SS Trinità di Delia This little Norman church, one of the few surviving in Sicily, is reached by a road to the west of Castelvetrano, which runs as far as the Lago Trinità (5km). (On this road, note the prefabricted houses built to accommodate the victims of the 1968 earthquake.) Before descending to the lake, keep a sharp eye open for a track going off to the left. This leads to a private house in whose grounds the church—originally a private chapel—stands.

The **church**, which in plan is Greek cross-in-square, has been perfectly restored, retaining the central cupola, triple apse and exterior arcading. It is now a mausoleum, with the tombs of the brothers Saporito who owned the church and were responsible for its restoration.

Castroreale Town 8km south of Barcellona Pozzo di Gotto, near Milazzo (A20). The name is Spanish for 'royal castle' and refers to the castle built here by Frederick II of Aragon (1324) as his personal residence. As one would expect from its appeal to the Royal imagination, the town is superbly situated, on a height (394m) overlooking the valley of the Longano and the foothills of the Peloritani, with the sea and Aeolian Islands in the distance. The view can best be enjoyed from two points: from the wide terrace beside the Chiesa Matrice and from the tower of Frederick's castle.
The churches of Castroreale are well endowed with works of art from the 16th and 17th c. The ubiquitous Antonello Gagini is represented by a *St Catherine* (**Chiesa Matrice**) an *Annunciation* (**S. Agata**) and the *Tomb of Geronimo Rosso* (**Ş. Maria di Gesù**). From the Corso Umberto I, opposite the Chiesa Matrice, steps lead up to the cylindrical **tower** which is all that remains of Frederick's castle. The tower is now enclosed by a youth hostel, but access is permitted and one may climb to the top.

Catania (pop. 370,000) Sicily's second largest city situated on the east coast below Mount Etna (A18, A19).

The 'Milan of Sicily' is a good description for this bustling, traffic-ridden city with its stately centre and expanding suburbs: a city whose inherent resilience is evident in its survival of numerous earthquakes and volcanic eruptions. The great mountain which has dominated the back-cloth and the history of the city since its earliest foundation continues to impose its inescapable presence, whether in the grey lava-stone used in the buildings and pavements or in the great sulphur refineries to the south of the city. By contrast, the sea, which has also played its part in the history of Catania, is almost invisible. In the congested heart of the city one can forget that the Porto Vecchio is only ten minutes' walk and that Catania is one of Italy's principal seaports, the outlet not only of her industrial region but of the fertile corn-growing area of the Plain of Catania.

The antagonism between the two rival cities reached its climax when the people of Katane offered their city as a base for the Athenians (415 BC) prior to their attack on Syracuse. When the Syracusans subsequently defeated the Athenians their tyrant, Dionysius I, pursued a campaign of revenge against the invaders' allies. In 403 BC Katane was again captured and this time her people were sold into slavery.

Later on, when Dionysius suffered a reverse in his war against Carthage (defeat by Himilco's fleet off the Isole dei Ciclopi) he could do nothing to prevent the Carthaginians occupying Katane, which was again to be used as a launching-point for an attack on Syracuse. Himilco's siege was, however, a failure, and Syracuse regained control of Greek Sicily. Katane returned to a succession of tyrannies, broken only by the arrival in 339 BC of the reforming Timoleon of Corinth.

In 263 BC the Romans captured the city and

History Catania (ancient *Katane*) was founded in 729 BC by the Greeks who had settled Naxos to the north. These Greeks, who were Ionians from Chalkis, were suspicious of the Dorian Greeks and were anxious to establish their colonies before Syracuse became dominant. Like the other Greek cities Katane was ruled by tyrants, the most famous of them Charondas who drew up a constitution and a code of laws which were emulated by the other Ionian colonies in Sicily and elsewhere. In the face of Syracusan expansionism Katane could not hope however to maintain its independence. In 476 BC Hieron I of Syracuse took the city, exiled the inhabitants to the other Ionian colony of Leontinoi (Lentini) and resettled it with Dorians. He renamed the city 'Aetna' and made his son its king. Fifteen years later however, in 461 BC, the exiles returned and recaptured the city.

renamed it Catina which later became Catania. The city took the side of Augustus during his war with Sextus Pompey, and in recognition of this was awarded the status of a Roman *colonia*. This meant that the people of the city were granted the privileges of Roman citizenship, and were able to enjoy the prosperity and security of life in a protected seaport of the Roman Republic.

Catania is indebted to her patron saint, Agatha, for its place in the history of the early Christian church in Sicily. St Agatha suffered a peculiarly excruciating martyrdom here (203 AD) and the city subsequently received recognition as a bishopric. The city's first cathedral, dedicated to St Agatha, was built by the Normans but later destroyed by an earthquake (1169). This earthquake, which ruined the entire city, was the first of the series of natural and man-made disasters which beset Catania for the

Piazza Duomo, Catania

next 500 years. In 1194 the city was sacked by the Holy Roman Emperor Henry VI, as part of the campaign of suppression attending his claim to the Kingdom of Sicily. Later on his son Frederick II repeated the exercise, building the great Castello Ursino to intimidate his subjects. In 1669 the city was buried by the lava of Mount Etna in the volcano's worst-ever eruption: in 1693 it succumbed to the great earthquake which devastated most of the east coast of Sicily. The old part of Catania belongs to the 18th c.: happily this too was not destroyed when the British fought the Germans for the city in 1943.

The town Modern Catania is not an easy acquaintance, particularly for those who come by car and have to tackle its traffic and the intricacies of its one-way system for the first time. It is, however, a lively prosperous city with an airport and a motorway link with Messina (A18). With the joining of the Catania–Palermo autostrada (A19), Catania is now on the map as one of Italy's leading industrial and business centres. The attraction of Catania, perhaps, lies in its easy communications: midway between the resorts of Taormina and Syracuse and within easy access of Mount Etna. The road to the foot of Etna's cone leads, in fact, directly from the heart of the city: the Via Etnea.

Walking tour (see map) Starting point: **Piazza Duomo**. This square contains the essence of the city's 18th c. character, and is largely the work of the architect G. Battista Vaccarini, who did so much to remodel Catania after the disastrous 1693 earthquake. Apart from the façade of the cathedral he was responsible for the elegant **Municipio** on the north side of the square and the delightful **Elephant Fountain** in the middle. This fountain was erected in 1736 and its centrepiece is an elephant made of lava and supporting an obelisk, a relic of the Roman city.

Cathedral Founded by Roger I, Count of Sicily, in 1092, the cathedral has twice been destroyed, by the earthquakes of 1169 and 1693. The present building dates from the 18th c., and the façade by Vaccarini (1736) incorporates granite columns recovered from the Roman theatre. The main part of the original Norman building to survive is the east end, with its three apses of volcanic lava. These are best viewed from the exterior of the cathedral, from the courtyard of the bishop's palace. This may be reached from the Via Vittorio Emanuele, passing along the north side of the cathedral (note, en route, the fine 16th c. north door, a survival from the second cathedral).

Interior Against the second pier of the south aisle of the cathedral is the tomb of Bellini (1801–35), the operatic composer who was a native of Catania. Although the interior of the cathedral is Baroque, there are Norman survivals. Apart from the three apses, there are restored windows and traces of the original masonry and columns in the walls of the transepts. Between the columns of the nave may be seen the bases of the columns and part of the foundation of the original cathedral. The Capella del Crocifisso (north transept) and the Capella della Vergine (south transept) have fine 16th c. doorways. The latter chapel contains the tombs of the members of the House of Aragon who ruled Sicily in the 14th c. On the right, in a Roman sarcophagus, are the remains of Frederick II of Aragon (d. 1337), two of his successors Louis I (d. 1355) and Frederick III (d. 1377) and other members of the royal family. Opposite is the tomb of Constance, wife of Frederick III.

The choir has finely-carved stalls (1588) with scenes of the life and death of St Agatha. To the right of the choir is the Capella di S. Agata. This contains a marble altarpiece with a group depicting the saint's coronation and, to the left, a treasury containing relics. On the right side of the chapel is the magnificent tomb of the Viceroy Fernandez d'Acuña (d. 1494) with a fine sculpture of the kneeling nobleman, attended by a page.

The sacristy (off north transept) has an interesting fresco (1675) showing the destruction of Catania by the eruption of Etna (1669).

At the south-east corner of the Piazza Duomo is the 18th c. **Porta Uzeda**, which leads to the public gardens and the Porto Vecchio. At the south-west corner the **Fountain of Amenano** (1867), named after one of Catania's rivers, stands at the entrance to a side-street running down to the fish and meat markets. The former market, the 'Pescheria', tucked under the railway arches by the church of S. Maria del'Indirizzo, provides one of the most amusing and colourful diversions of a walking tour of Catania.

The tour leads northwards from the Piazza Duomo up the **Via Etnea**. This is Catania's main street and is the most direct route out of the city to Mount Etna. On a clear day, the great cone can be seen in the distance at the apex of the long thoroughfare: a thrilling sight which must have prompted the writers who in the 18th c. described this as the finest street in Europe. It had then been newly built, after the devastating earthquake of 1693, and the homogeneity of its architecture has been well preserved. The finest buildings are those of the **University**, to the left of the Piazza dell' Universita. The courtyard here is the work of Vaccarini. Further on, to the left, is the **Collegiata** (collegiate church) with a fine concave façade, completed in 1768, and a royal chapel. The Via Antonio di Sangiuliano is crossed and the Via Etnea continues to the elongated Piazza Stesicoro.

Amphitheatre This ancient ruin, from the period of Augustus, occupies the west side of the square. It is only the northern end of a vast construction which now lies beneath the modern city. The arena (71m × 51m) was

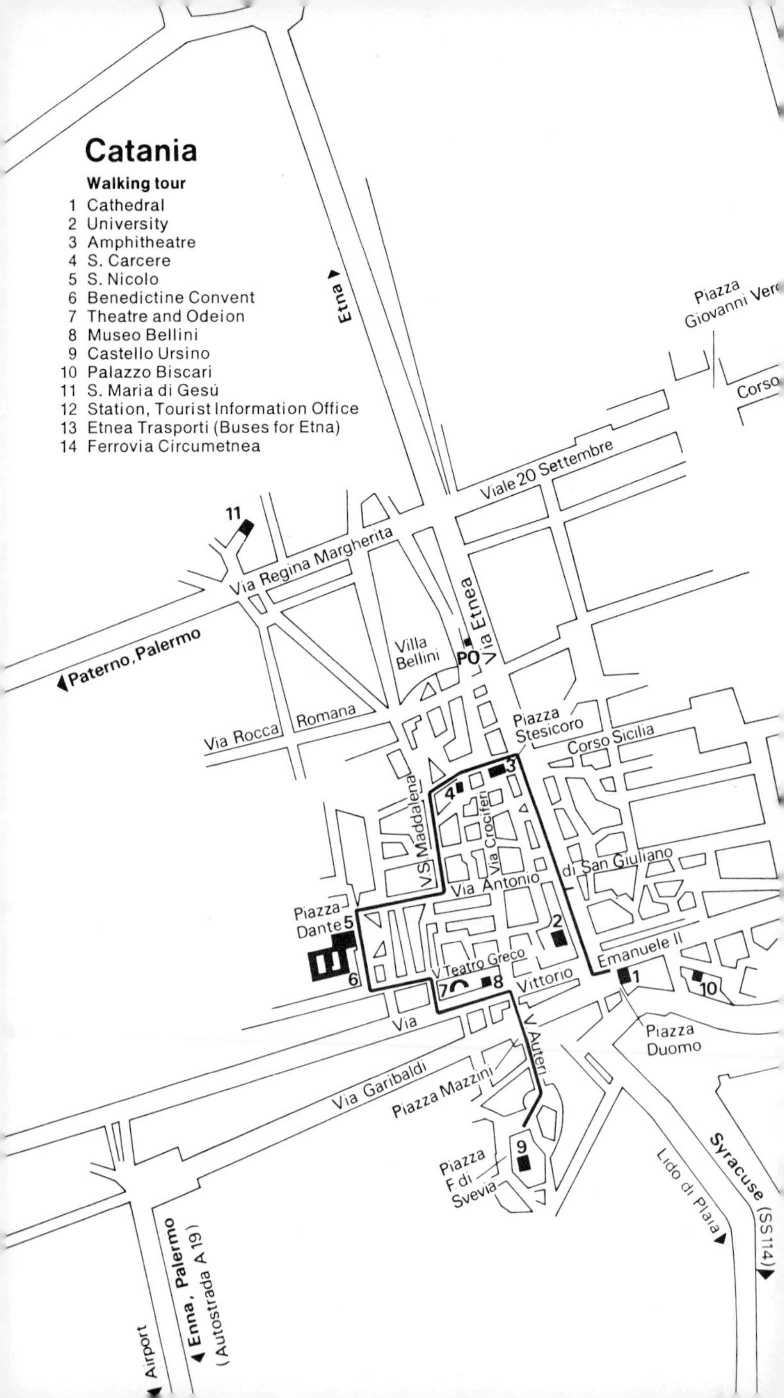

Catania

Walking tour

1 Cathedral
2 University
3 Amphitheatre
4 S. Carcere
5 S. Nicolo
6 Benedictine Convent
7 Theatre and Odeion
8 Museo Bellini
9 Castello Ursino
10 Palazzo Biscari
11 S. Maria di Gesú
12 Station, Tourist Information Office
13 Etnea Trasporti (Buses for Etna)
14 Ferrovia Circumetnea

Etna ▶

Piazza
Giovanni Vere

Corso

Viale 20 Settembre

11

Via Regina Margherita

Via Etnea

PO

Villa
Bellini

◀ Paterno, Palermo

Via Rocca Romana

Piazza
Stesicoro

Corso Sicilia

V.S. Maddalena

Via Crocifer

4 **3**

di San Giuliano

Via Antonio

Piazza
Dante **5**

2

Emanuele II

V Teatro Greco

7 **8**

6

Vittorio

1

10

Piazza
Duomo

Via

V. Auteri

Via Garibaldi

Piazza Mazzini

Syracuse

Lido di Plaia

Piazza
F di
Svevia

9

Airport

◀ Enna, Palermo
(Autostrada A 19)

(SS 114)

Messina (Autostrada A18.SS114)▶

Piazza Europa

14

Piazza della Stazione

12
13

Via S. Aprile

second only to the Colosseum in size and there was seating for up to 16,000 spectators. The amphitheatre was built with lava and faced with marble: unfortunately it has been so badly plundered that only the foundations, a section of the *cavea* and part of the lower corridor remain.

From the Piazza Stesicoro the Via dei Cappuccini leads westwards to the church of **S. Carcere**, overlooking a small square to the left. This church is built on the spot where St. Agatha was imprisoned before her martyrdom. Its portal (early 13th c.) was taken from ruins of the cathedral after the earthquake of 1693. The route returns southwards along the Via S. Maddalena. At the Via Antonio di Sangiuliano, turn right for the Piazza Dante, dominated by the huge unfinished church of **S. Nicolo**.

This is the largest, but surely the saddest church in Sicily, the columns of its front portico only half-erected. Work on the church, commenced in 1693, went on spasmodically for more than a century, but was finally abandoned through lack of funds. The *interior* of the church is as impressive as its dimensions would suggest: 145m long and 48m wide at the transept. Though barely decorated the church contains beautiful *choir-stalls* and a massive 18th c. *organ* with 2916 pipes. The *cupola*, one of the great landmarks of Catania, has an interior height of 62m.

Adjoining the church, to the south, is the former **Benedictine convent**, built in the early 18th c. This is the second largest convent building in Europe, and the lavishness of its endowment is attested by the elaborate Baroque decoration of its *façade*. Inside the convent are two fine *courtyards*, and one may freely enter the building to admire them. Perhaps *too* freely. The tragedy of this building has been its accessibility—both for piecemeal occupation and for the depradations of the aerosol vandals who have 'decorated' the vestibule. If only it could be cleaned up, this majestic convent would be one of the showplaces of Catania.

Further south, the Via Teatro Greco leads to two interesting buildings of the ancient city, where current excavation and restoration is creating much interest. From the Via Teatro Greco one has a rear view of the Roman

Benedictine convent, Catania   75

Odeion and the 'Greco-Roman' theatre, but to obtain access to these ruins one must proceed south down the Via S. Agostino to the Via Vittorio Emanuele (entrance at No. 272). The **theatre**, which is built of limestone and lava, is described as Greco-Roman and of the 1st c. BC. But for the sake of accuracy, this is a Roman structure which owes its Greekness purely to the site. This is, in fact, thought to be the site of the earlier Greek theatre where Alcibiades urged the Catanians to support the Athenians in their campaign against Syracuse (415 BC).

Much of the theatre is still covered by the ruins of later buildings and it is anticipated that further clearance will bring some interesting details to light. Excavation and restoration is being financed by the *Cassa per il Mezzogiorno* and the *Regione Siciliana*, and the major work to date has been in the clearing and partial reconstruction of the three corridors, or ambulatories, beneath the *cavea*. Excavation of the orchestra has not yet been carried out and one of the difficulties here is flooding by the waters of the Amenano, which runs beneath the city. These waters were evidently harnessed in Roman times for aquatic displays. An interesting discovery was made at the top of the theatre, where traces of steps showed that there was an upper level of seats, or balcony, similar to that constructed at the theatre of Taormina.

It is possible to walk along the restored upper corridor of the theatre to the adjacent **Odeion** to the west. This intimate little theatre was used for musical performances and recitations.

Continuing eastwards along the Via V. Emanuele the visitor will reach the Piazza S. Francesco d'Assisi. From the north of the square leads the **Via Crociferi**. Like the Via Etnea this street is a gallery of fine Baroque architecture, reminding us again

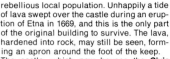

of the splendour of the 18th c. city. It is worth a diversion to admire the façade of the church of *S. Benedetto*, on the left. In the square is Bellini's house, in which the composer was born. This is now a museum (**Museo Bellini**). Crossing the Via Vittorio Emanuele, the Via della Lettera leads south to the **Piazza Mazzini**, an 18th c. square with a beautiful arcade (the columns are Roman). Such tranquil architecture cries out for tranquillity: unfortunately this graceful piazza, like the rest of Catania, has been thrown to the untender mercies of the motor-car. Continuing along the Via Auteri, and bearing right by the railway, the visitor reaches the Piazza Federico di Svevia.

Castello Ursino This great moated keep, with its massive round towers at each corner, was the centrepiece of the castle built here by Frederick II in 1239. Its construction had two purposes: first, to buttress Catania's seaward defences; second, to cow the

rebellious local population. Unhappily a tide of lava swept over the castle during an eruption of Etna in 1669, and this is the only part of the original building to survive. The lava, hardened into rock, may still be seen, forming an apron around the foot of the keep.

The castle, which now houses the **Civic Museum** (Museo Civico) is entered from the north (for opening times see p. 25). In the fine vaulted chambers are displayed a variety of treasures from private collections.

To the right of the entrance, *Rooms 1–6* contain relics from the Roman theatre and other sites of the Greek, Roman and Hellenistic periods in the Catania area. Most impressive are the Roman *Torso of an Emperor (Room 3)* and the Greek *Head of an Ephebe* from Lentini (500 BC) in *Room 4*.

In the event of *Room 6* being closed off for administrative purposes, it is necessary to return to the entrance. To the left of the entrance *Room 14* contains arms and armour of the 14th–18th c. The next two (*13 & 12*) contain 18th c. sculpture and the next (*11 & 10*) sculpture of the Medieval and Renaissance periods. *Room 9* has Greek and Roman funerary sculpture and *Room 7*, adjacent, has Roman busts and inscriptions. *Room 8*, which is in fact the tower leading off *Room 7*, contains a fascinating and intimate glimpse of the early Christian period, with its collection of enchanting small frescoes and funerary relics.

Three more floors contain further archaeological treasures and the city's art gallery with paintings from the 15th c. to the 18th c., including works by Antonello de Saliba, Pietro Novelli, Matthias Stomer and Simon de Wobrecht. The upper two floors are temporarily closed, but a good selection of these paintings is in the *Salone di Parlamento* (old Parliament chamber) at the top of the staircase on the south side of the courtyard.

Other places of interest in Catania

Palazzo Biscari To the east of the cathedral, in the Via Biscari, stands this fine 18th c. palace (admission to courtyard only).

S. Maria di Gesù Some distance to the northwest of the city centre (see map), this church should draw the followers of Antonello Gagini. Before entering the church to admire the work of the master, however, the visitor should pause to behold the quite beautiful marble lunette over the doorway, portraying the *Madonna, Child and Angels* by an unnamed sculptor. Inside the church, on the left, is the *Paterno chapel* with a *doorway* by Antonello Gagini (1519). The altarpiece of this chapel, a *Madonna with Sts. Catherine and Agatha*, is by Angelo di Chirico (1525). The group of the *Madonna with Angels* on the 2nd altar of the north aisle is also by Gagini.

For routes to Mt. Etna, see **Etna**

Castello Ursino, Catania   77

Cava d'Íspica Neolithic cave dwellings 14 km east of Modica. The best route to these caves for visitors driving on the SS115 is via the cross-roads at Bettola del Capitano, 7 km east of Modica or 11 km west of Ispica. Alternatively, a direct route may be taken from Rosolini (12 km).

These caves, which are partly natural, partly cut out of the rock, were used as cliff dwellings in the Neolithic period. They later became the 'grotte a forno' (beehive tombs) of the Sicel and Greek necropolises, and—in the Christian period—were adapted for use as catacombs. They are accessible by foot on either side of a valley.

Cefalù Town and seaport, 74 km east of Palermo (SS113, A20).

This is one of the most beautiful and unusually situated of Sicily's coastal towns, owing its name to the headland (Greek *kephale*, head) which rears above it.

History The date of the first settlement here is not clear, but it is thought that the ancient Sicels occupied the headland *c*. 9th c. BC. A harbour was subsequently built at the foot of the rock and a wall linking it with the fortifications above. Its friendly relations with the Carthaginian colonies to the west caused the ancient *Cephaloedium* to be subjugated by the Greek tyrants of Syracuse: first Dionysius, then Agathocles. It was subsequently conquered by the Romans (254 BC), the Saracens (9th c. AD) and the Normans (11th c. AD). It was the Normans who gave Cefalù its most impressive building, the graceful twin-towered cathedral that dominates the town from the top of its steep piazza.

The town In the 15 years since the arrival of the wattle paradise of the Club Mediterranée, Cefalù—which possesses, to the west, one of the best stretches of beach in the island—has become, with Taormina, the proving ground of Sicily's tourist boom. Fortunately the geography of the town is such that the old part, on its rocky promontory under the looming headland, is reasonably separated from the modern development of hotels and apartments which is building up behind it.

The old town is easy to explore on foot and even the **Rocca** (headland) presents few difficulties now that steps have been provided for the first part of the climb. The approach to the latter is from the Vicolo Saraceni, a steep alley on the right at the beginning of the Corso Ruggero.

The climb to the top, by steps and footpath, is little more than $\frac{1}{4}$ hour: one then continues through the ruins of medieval fortifications towards the northern extremity of the headland. Here are the remains of a mystery building, the so-called **Temple of Diana**. This is a prehistoric building of megalithic construction, built around a rock-cut cistern. Part of it is an addition of the 5th c. BC and

the two doorways incorporated in the structure, with lintels still in position, are classical. Vestiges of fortifications, including those of the earliest settlement, are scattered over this part of the headland. The highest point of the rock offers a magnificent view of the northern coastline.

Walking tour This can be commenced at the junction of the Corso Ruggero and the Via Umberto I (see map). The Corso Ruggero is the main street of the town, running through it to the sea wall on the north. On the corner of a street to the left—the Via G. Amendola—is the **Osterio Magno**, popularly identified as the palace of King Roger II. The only argument against this is the triple-arched window which survives—stylistically dated by some authorities to the end of the 13th c., more than a century after Roger's death. This would seem to corroborate the evidence that the palace was built by the Ventimiglia family, lords of Cefalù, in the early period of Spanish rule. Continuing along the Corso Ruggero one eventually reaches the Piazza Duomo.

Cathedral Founded by King Roger II in 1131, this building is a happy amalgam of the architecture and decoration of three centuries. It is one of the only three Norman cathedrals in Sicily, and its most outstanding features belong to that period: the twin towers, the apse, the mosaics.

The *west front* of the cathedral, the last part of the main building to be completed, belongs to 1240: note the two rows of blind arcades, the lower one intersecting, which lighten the façade and reduce the fortress-like severity of the building. A later addition (1471) is the *narthex*, with its elegant, triple-arched portico. Before entering the cathedral, the *east end* of the building should be viewed. This is reached by passing up the side street to the right and through a gateway to the footpath which leads up the slope behind the cathedral. From here one can appreciate the unusual form of the building: the long arm of the sanctuary, rounded off by the tall central apse; the two small side apses, the square projections of the transepts. Around the top of the building runs the same blind arcading as seen on the west front—a typical feature of Siculo-Norman architecture.

Interior The cathedral is entered through the west door, and the visitor will look spontaneously towards the apse, knowing that this is one of the few churches in Sicily containing mosaics of the Byzantine period, when this decorative art had reached its highest level of achievement. In the plain interior, currently being cleared of its Baroque decoration, the eye quickly focusses on the distant but commanding figure of the *Christ Pantocrator*, framed by the arch of the apse: but before studying this and the other mosaics the visitor should note the details of the architecture of the interior. The *nave* has

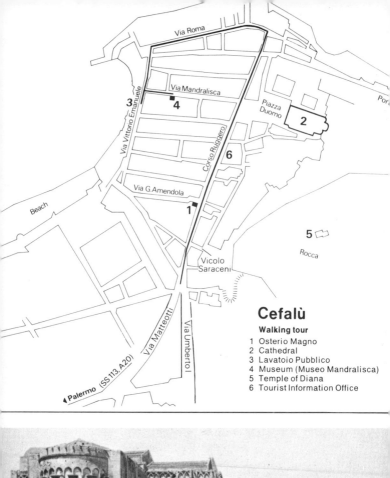

Via Roma

Via Mandralisca

4

Via Vittorio Emanuele

3

Corso Ruggero

Piazza Duomo

2

6

Via G.Amendola

1

Beach

Vicolo Saraceni

5 ⬭

Rocca

Por

Via Matteotti

Via Umberto I

◂Palermo (SS 113, A 20)

Cefalù

Walking tour

1 Osterio Magno
2 Cathedral
3 Lavatoio Pubblico
4 Museum (Museo Mandralisca)
5 Temple of Diana
6 Tourist Information Office

eight antique columns on either side, separating it from the aisles. The arches above these columns are slightly pointed: an Arabic touch. The *ceiling* is wooden and incorporates some of the original timbers, painted with Saracenic motifs (13th c.).

Passing through the great central arch between nave and crossing one can see that despite the associations of its decoration with the Greek and Muslim worlds the plan of this church is a Latin cross. The transepts are unusual: one with a wooden roof, the other with a ribbed vault. An arcaded gallery runs along the top of them. With so much restored of the original church, little Baroque decoration remains. There are now only vestiges in the choir and in the chapel to the north. This chapel contained a *Madonna* by Antonello Gagini, now in the north aisle. But it is the work of the Greek artists employed by Roger to decorate his cathedral that one has come to see: the beautiful **mosaics** in the apse and sanctuary that express, within the Byzantine discipline, an extraordinary vitality.

In the half-figure of *Christ*, composed within the conch of the apse, we have inherited one of the most skilfully-proportioned and dramatic representations of the Pantocrator in church art. The elongated face, large eyes and encircling halo give the head of Christ an extraordinary power, and the figure a life which finds further expression in the right hand raised in benediction, the left hand holding an open Bible with text in Greek and Latin ('I am the Light of the World' . . .). Below the *Christ* is the comparatively tiny but hardly less compelling *Madonna*, her hands raised in prayer. On either side of her are the *Archangels* and below, in two rows, the *Apostles*. A frieze along the bottom carries a Latin inscription recording the date of the mosaics: 1148. On either side of the presbytery are figures of patriarchs, prophets and saints: in the vault pairs of angels and six-winged cherubim and seraphim. Some of the latter mosaics are of a later date than those in the apse.

At the entrance to the choir (right) stood the bishop's throne: opposite, the King's. Other features of interest in this church are the 12th c. *font* (south aisle) and the **cloister** (entrance from north aisle) which has three galleries remaining, in process of restoration.

The tour of the old town should be continued northwards to the end of the Corso Ruggero. From here, turning left, the visitor will find a 16th c. **bastion** which offers a view, to the east, of the remains of the walls of ancient Cephaloedium. Retracing his footsteps to the Via Roma, the visitor should follow this street westwards to the old fishing port, which has retained its lovely staggered backdrop of medieval buildings. Behind these buildings lies the Via Vittorio Emanuele, from whence one can descend steps to the curious **Lavatoio Pubblico**, an early wash-house still used by the public. The basins have been excavated from a bed of rock, and the water piped in from underground channels. Opposite, the Via Mandralisca rises to the Piazza Duomo. At No. 13 is the **Museo Mandralisca** (Hours: 09.30–12.00 & 15.30–18.00, Sun & hol 09.30–12.30). The museum contains antiquities from Lípari and elsewhere and a fine red-figure *krater* of the 4th c. BC of local make. The lively scene depicted on the side, of a man selling tunny fish, has an obvious local inspiration. Also in this museum are 15th–18th c. paintings, including a fine *Portrait of an Unknown Man* (1470) by Antonello da Messina.

Excursions from Cefalù

Aeolian Is. From the port to the east of the town boat trips may be made from Lípari and Vulcano (details from the Tourist Information Office in Corso Umberto).

Gibilmanna (800 m) This resort, 14 km to the south of Cefalù, is a good place to stay for those wishing to explore the Madonie. For visitors, there is the beautifully situated *Sanctuary of Gibilmanna*, and one of the finest views in Sicily offered by the climb to the *Pizzo S. Angelo* (1081 m). The panorama from this peak embraces the Aeolian Is. and Ustica to the north and the mountains of the Madonie to the south. Another view, accessible by road, is from the nearby *observatory*.

Centúripe (733 m) Town 18 km west of Adrano in the Etna region.

Its site, overlooking the approach to the coast on the south-western flank of Etna, made Centúripe an imporant strategic settlement, notably in the Sicel, Hellenistic and Roman periods. Finds from the last two periods may be seen in the town's small **antiquarium**, including pottery of a unique style. In the vicinity of the town, recent excavations have uncovered part of the **Roman town**. In 1943, Centúripe was one of the strongholds of the German defence of the island against the Anglo-American invasion: following its collapse, after a two-day bombardment, the German retreat was rapid.

Cómiso Town 17 km west of Ragusa (SS115), worth a pause for admirers of 18th c. Baroque.

A colony of Syracuse, this became an important Roman town and then, in the middle ages, a fief of the Chiaramonte and other noble families. In the centre of the town, which steps gracefully up a hillside overlooking a river valley, is the Piazza Municipio. Here a modern fountain is served by the waters of an underground spring, the Fonte Diana, which in Roman times circulated through a bath-house (vestiges of its mosaic pavement lie beneath the Municipio on the west side of the square).

To the north of the square is the **Chiesa Matrice**; to the south, at a higher level, the **SS. Annunziata**. Both churches, which were reconstructed in the 18th c. after the 1693 earthquake, are built on the monumental scale peculiar to this region of Sicily. Their domes dominate the town from afar. From the Piazza Municipio the Via S. Biagio leads to the **Castello Feudale** of the Naselli family who were the feudal lords of Cómiso from the 15th–19th c. From the Piazza S. Biagio the Via Ippari leads to the 13th c. church of **S. Francesco** to which was added, in 1517, the family chapel of the Naselli.

Égadi Islands (Isole Égadi) Group of Islands off the west coast of Sicily, anciently known as the *Aegates*. They are Favignana, Lévanzo and—further west—Maréttimo. In 241 BC, at the end of the first Punic War, the Romans won an important naval victory over the Carthaginians, between Maréttimo and Favignana. The islands are best known for their fishing, both as an industry and as a sport. (For details of boat services see p. 17.)

Favignana (pop. 7000 area 19 sq km) Island 17 km west of Trápani.

This Island, together with the tiny *Formica* to the north-east, is the centre of Sicily's tunny fishing industry. Most popular month for the *pesca del tonno* is May, when the landing of the catch offers a rare spectacle. A fine view of the Égadi and the coastline of western Sicily may be enjoyed from the Monte S. Caterina (302 m). In this mountain are caves with Palaeolithic engravings.

Lévanzo (pop. 300 area 10 sq km) Island 15 km west of Trápani.

This tiny island rises to its highest point at the Pizzo del Mónaco (278 m). It has a number of grottoes of prehistoric interest, the most important the *Grotta del Genovese*. This cave on the west coast has incised and painted drawings of humans and animals from the Upper Palaeolithic period. It may be reached on foot from the village of *Levanzo* ($\frac{1}{2}$hr) or by boat. (For access to this and the caves on Favignana see Museums and Monuments, p. 25.)

Maréttimo (pop. 1100 area 12 sq km) Island 38 km west of Trápani.

The most remote of the Égadi Islands, popular for underwater fishing and the exploration of its marine grottoes (west coast).

Eloro (Helorus) Ancient site, 7 km southeast of Noto. Reached by turning off the Noto-Pachino road after 2 km and then right at next junction. From here, turn left after 4 km (Hotel Eloro) and continue 1 km. From the hotel a track leads south over two headlands. Situated on the second headland, overlooking the sea and the mouth of the River Tellaro, this ancient settlement began life as an outpost of Syracuse in the 7th c. BC. Excavations still in progress have revealed traces of walls and fortifications, which attest to its military significance. The most important discovery to date, the **Sanctuary of Demeter**, has been reconstructed in part in the Noto Museum. Other remains are of a *Doric stoa* and a *theatre* (part of the latter has been carried away by the erosive action of the river).

To the north of Helorus, and best seen from the main road by the junction, is a strange monumental column, known as the **Pizzuta**. This belongs to the 3rd c. BC and is something of a folly, erected as a memorial to a family interred in a burial chamber beneath it.

Enna (948 m) Provincial capital.

Situated in the centre of Sicily, on a mountain commanding the surrounding countryside, this fortress-town has been called, appropriately, the 'Navel' and the 'Belvedere' of Sicily.

History The town stands on the site of *Henna*, a settlement of the Sicels, in the midst of fertile, undulating country which was originally covered by extensive woodland. The ground was fertile enough, in fact, for the growth of the legend of the corn goddesses—the subterranean powers that gave fruitfulness to the earth—which were later absorbed in the Greek legend of Demeter and Persephone. Lake Pergusa, 10 km from Enna, is acknowledged by the Latin poets as the site of Persephone's abduction by the God of the Underworld, Hades.

In 397 BC the town was taken by the tyrant Dionysius I, but later (309 BC) asserted its independence against another tyrant, Agathocles, by joining the cities which opposed him—the Akragantine League. In the Punic Wars, the city came into the possession of both the Carthaginians and the Romans. From 133–132 BC it was the retreat of Eunus in the First Slave Revolt against the Romans.

Enna's defensive position was put to the test by the Saracens (859) who found a way in through the sewers, and by the Normans,

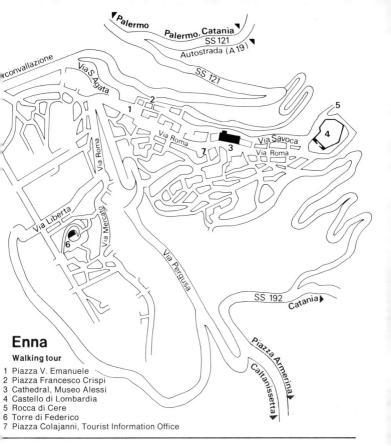

Enna

Walking tour

1 Piazza V. Emanuele
2 Piazza Francesco Crispi
3 Cathedral, Museo Alessi
4 Castello di Lombardia
5 Rocca di Cere
6 Torre di Federico
7 Piazza Colajanni, Tourist Information Office

who were only able to capture the town after a prolonged siege (1087). The town's fortifications were largely the work of the Emperor Frederick II.

Walking tour Starting point: Piazza Vittorio Emanuele. This square is dominated on the north by the 15th c. campanile of the church of **S. Francesco**. From the north-east corner of the square one enters the Piazza Francesco Crispi. This must be one of the most relaxing squares in Sicily, set apart from the traffic with its small garden and fountain (the bronze statue is, appropriately, a copy of Bernini's *Rape of Persephone*). The west side of the square is flanked by the old-fashioned Belvedere Hotel: to the north, a long balustrade makes a gallery for an impressive view of the Madonie mountains and distant Etna, with the old hill-town of Calascibetta in the foreground.

From the south-east corner of the Piazza V. Emanuele the Via Roma leads to the cathedral. On the way it passes three further

squares: the Piazza 6 Dicembre with the neo-classical **Municipio** on the left; the Piazza Coppola with the 15th c. church of *S. Giuseppe* (and, to the south, in Via Candrilli, the *Torre Campanaria di S. Giovanni*, a Gothic survival) and the Piazza Colajanni with the 18th c. church of **S. Chiara**. The cathedral itself stands in another square —the Piazza Mazzini.

Cathedral Founded in 1307, the building was seriously damaged by fire in 1446 and not finally reconstructed until the end of the 16th c. In the transformation from Gothic to Baroque, little of the original may now be seen. The façade is Baroque, as is the tower, a late 17th c. addition. The south side has a 16th c. *door* in the Renaissance style, with a fine relief in the tympanum of *St Martin Giving his Cloak to the Beggar*.

The *interior* of the cathedral is largely of the 16th c. The columns of the *nave* are particularly impressive. Of black basalt, they have elaborate Corinthian capitals and

Piazza F. Crispi, Enna

85

extraordinary bases, carved with grotesque figures. The wooden ceilings of the nave and transepts are very fine, the work of the Neapolitan Scipione di Guido (d. 1604). The same woodworker was probably responsible for the choir stalls. In the *choir* are a series of paintings of scenes from the New Testament by Fil. Paladino (1613). The organ galleries, at the east end of the nave, are elaborately carved, with figures of the *Apostles*. The cathedral **treasury** contains one of Italy's finest collections of church art. To the west of the cathedral is the small *Museo Alessi* (Tues, Thurs and Sat 09.00–12.30). The Via Roma continues east to the citadel rock on which rises the grand mass of the **Castello di Lombardia**. Built by the Emperor Frederick II, the castle was converted into a residence by Frederick III of Aragon. It has an irregular plan and preserves six of its twenty original towers. The entrance is by the ravelin to the south-west, and from here —if and when the gates are open—the interior of the castle may be explored. The first courtyard, with a ruined chapel, is now in use as an open-air theatre. A further courtyard gives access to the *Torre Pisana*, the highest and best preserved of the towers, which offers the pinnacle view of the surrounding country.

If the castle is closed an alternative view— which has the virtue of including the castle— may be enjoyed from the **Rocca di Cerere**, a salient of the citadel rock, where ancient ruins have been proposed as the *Temple of Demeter* (built by Gelon in 480 BC).

Elsewhere in the town, in the *Giardino Pubblico* (follow the Via Roma in the other direction, to the south-west) stands the **Torre di Federico II**, which survives the 13th c. defences of the town. The octagonal tower has three floors; the second with windows added in 1457.

Eraclea Minoa (Heraclea Minoa) Ancient site, 6 km south of junction on SS115, 35 km west of Agrigento.

History Founded by the people of Selinus (6th c. BC) to counter the expanding power of Akragas to the east, Heraclea Minoa played the role of buffer between the rival cities, a role perpetuated in the later struggle between Greeks and Carthaginians. The River Halykos (now the Platani) on which the town was sited, had a special celebrity as the spot where the legendary King Minos landed after his voyage from Crete in pursuit of Daedalus. It was here that he—or his followers—were supposed to have founded a city: certainly he was the inspiration for the name of the later Greek settlement, Minoa. (The 'Heraclea' was added by settlers in the 4th c. BC who worshipped Heracles.)

Towards the end of the 6th c. BC Akragas won control over the city, but a hundred years later Minoa fell victim, together with

Selinus and Akragas, to the massive Carthaginian invasion. It was not until the alliance between the Greek leader Timoleon and the Carthaginians (339 BC) that Minoa was restored to democracy, but in its tightrope position (on the River Halykos, which was the border between Greeks and Carthaginians) its future was precarious. In the Punic War, possession of the city was furiously contested by the Romans and Carthaginians, but even under the iron rule of the Romans the city had little peace. In the two Slave Revolts (*c.* 134 BC and *c.* 104 BC) the city was ransacked, and although— according to an account of Cicero—it recovered, it was finally abandoned at the end of the 1st c. BC.

Tour of the ruins After turning off the main SS115 one reaches a junction. Directly ahead the road descends to the beach and camp site: to the right it leads in 2 km to the Archaeological Zone of Heraclea Minoa.

At the entrance to the site is a small *antiquarium*, with an exhibition of material recovered from the site. Further on are vestiges of the *eastern wall* of the city built during the period of its reconstruction (4th c. BC) and, to the right, a small *theatre* of the same period. The rock from which the *cavea* of the theatre was cut is extremely soft and

has been covered with protective plastic sheets. Note the foundations for the scene building in the orchestra.

To the south lie the newly excavated dwellings of the residential quarter of the city. Most conspicuous is the *Hellenistic-Roman House*, covered by a shelter to protect the mud brick walls. Inside one can see vestiges of wall painting and mosaic pavement. To the north of this area are further remains of walls, broken by the *north gate* and a series of towers.

Érice (756m) Town 14km north-east of Trápani.

If one were to isolate a special corner of Sicily as an example of the achievement of medieval, rather than modern man, it would have to be Érice. The isolation is already there: a mountain top lower than the crag of Enna but more difficult to reach; a sheer climb from the coast at Trápani or from the Palermo road. The achievement is in the tumbled, timeless architecture, a warren of cobbled streets flanked by grey stone houses which conform perfectly not only with the rock on which they are built but with the atmosphere of remoteness which pervades the town.

Érice belonged in turn to the Phoenicians,

Greeks, Romans and Normans, whose motivation towards the site was either religious or military. Evidence of their presence—and their preoccupations—may be found in various parts of the town.

In modern times the port of Trápani has siphoned off the population—and the importance—of Érice. It now belongs to the visitor who seeks a whiff of the past (and of the fresh mountain air) the far-reaching, mystical views and the suspended, uncanny silence that happens in only a few places in the world.

History *Eryx* was a settlement of the Elymians, who inhabited this part of Sicily before the arrival of the Phoenicians. They worshipped here an unknown goddess in a sacred area—probably the site of the present castle—which later became the sanctuary of the Phoenician fertility goddess Astarte, the Greek Aphrodite and the Roman Venus.

During the Carthaginian period Eryx assumed a military significance, evidenced by the remains of walls still visible today. Apart from a brief alliance with Dionysius I of Syracuse during his campaign in western Sicily (397 BC) Eryx remained in Carthaginian hands until its capture by Pyrrhus, King of Epirus, in his similar, short-lived campaign of 278 BC. In the First Punic War a

Érice

Walking tour

1 Chiesa Matrice
2 Museum
3 S. Giovanni Battista
4 Balio
5 Castello Pepoli
6 Norman Castle
(Temple of Venus)
7 Funivia
(cable-car to Trapani)

few years later the possession of Eryx was bitterly contested by the Romans and Carthaginians, the stronghold finally falling to the Romans in 248 BC.

Under the Romans there was a strengthening of the religious identity of the town, with considerable funds expended by the emperors Tiberius and Claudius on the embellishment of the Temple of Venus, which became one of the great shrines of the Roman world. The town, conversely, was allowed to decline, and did not recover its importance until its occupation by the Saracens and subsequent capture by the Normans under Count Roger. The Normans called the town Monte San Giuliano, a name maintained until Mussolini's nostalgia revived Érice (1934).

Walking tour Starting point: **Chiesa Matrice** (Assunta). For visitors travelling by car, this church stands at the southern entrance of the town, inside the Porta Trápani. For visitors using the cable car, the church stands opposite the Stazione Funivia. The *campanile* is the oldest part, built before the church. It was originally a look-out tower, part of the fortifications of Frederick II of Aragon. Both the campanile and church are built of the beautiful grey stone, blotched and gnarled by age, that is typical of the old buildings of Érice. The church, founded in 1314, has a fine Gothic *porch*, added in 1426. The ceiling of the *interior* is also Gothic, but this time from the 19th c.: an extraordinary vault with corded ribs. On the third altar to the right is a fine marble statue of the *Madonna and Child* (1469) attributed to Francesco Laurana but possibly the work of Domenico Gagini.

The *ancient walls* of the town run from here northwards to the Porta Spada. They are in part cyclopean, from the Phoenician period, in part Roman and in part medieval. From this northern walk (Via Rabata) there are some fine views of the coastline.

The direct route to the town centre is by the Via Vittorio Emanuele. In the Piazza Umberto I, in the Municipio, is the **museum**. In the entrance is a splendid *Annunciation*, a marble group by Antonello Gagini: upstairs is a library and the collection of the museum. This includes Phoenician, Greek and Roman antiquities. Some of the material is from the *Temple of Venus*: note especially the 4th c. BC *Head of Aphrodite*.

The Via D. Vultaggio leads from the north side of the square to the Porta Carmine. From here the Viale Nunzio Nasi leads south to the church of **S. Giovanni Battista**, with a 13th c. portal. Inside are statues of *St John the Baptist* and *St John the Evangelist* by (respectively) Antonino and Antonello Gagini. Further south one reaches the **Balio** or **Villa Comunale**, the garden which lies on the plateau of the ancient acropolis. Here, at the south-east corner of the town, stand two castles. The first, the **Castello Pepoli**, is 14th c., with 19th c. modifications. The

Ancient walls, Porta Spada, Érice

ruins of the earlier **Norman castle** lie on the spur of rock beyond. This castle was built on the site of the ancient Temple of Venus. Fragments from the Roman restoration of the temple may be seen in the masonry of the castle, including the *Pozzo di Venere* (bath or well of Venus). From the main tower of the Castello Pepoli one can enjoy incomparable views. To the east, the mountains of Sicily; to the west the port of Trápani and the salt-lakes, with the Égadi Is. on the horizon. On a crystal clear day the island of Ustica may be seen to the north: to the south, the coast of Africa.

The Viale Conte Pepoli leads back to the start of the tour.

Cable-car services to Érice

This is without doubt the best way to visit Érice from Trapani. Motor-cars are extraneous in the cobbled streets of Érice and the town is small enough to be comfortably explored on foot. The cable-car offers a quick service from Trapani, via the Stazione Funivia at the top of the Via Fardella (Bus No 2 or 3 from the town). The service is every hour, on the hour, single or return, from 08.00–14.00 & 17.00–20.00 (summer) and from 08.00–14.00 (winter). The views on the way up, rising over the pine-covered slopes of Eryx, are superb.

For those who prefer to take their car the best approach is the new road from Trápani (14 km) which climbs the north-west side of the mountain.

Etna (3300 m) The highest mountain in Sicily, and the largest active volcano in Europe. Also known as 'Mongibello'.

The cone of Etna, which dominates the eastern coast of Sicily, is 40 km wide and has an irregular conformation, the sides broken by numerous fissures, caused by eruptive pressure from within the cone. Miniature cones have formed along these fissures, providing a kind of 'gas escape' for the hot magma rising in the main cone. The best examples of these smaller cones are the *Monti Rossi*, near Nicolosi, whose name comes from the red ash which formed them.

The whole of the Etna region has been alternately destroyed and created by its volcano. One has only to look at the bed of lava in Catania's Piazza Federico di Svevia or conversely, the lava used in the construction of the 18th c. buildings, to see how this is so. In the same way one has only to admire the green and abundant texture of the coastal region, fertilized by volcanic soil, or gaze in awe at the desolate stretches of ash and lava in the upper region near the cone to become aware of the pervasive power of Etna.

History To the Greek imagination, Etna was variously the forge of the God of Fire, the forge of the Cyclopes who inhabited this coast, or the prison of the Titan Enceladus, who shook the earth in his efforts to break free. The first recorded eruption was in 475 BC (described by Pindar and Aeschylus). Since then there have been more than 130 eruptions, and on some occasions the lava flow has reached the sea. The most serious eruption was in 1669, when a fissure opened to the north of Nicolosi and the lava flowing out, in a swathe 2 km wide, demolished Catania. The most recent eruption, which caused relatively light damage, was in 1979. Unhappily a later explosion in the same year caused the deaths of some climbers.

The history of Etna is not, however, purely of its destructive powers. Its virtues are also recorded. Much has been written about the wine of the region, the product of the fertile lower slopes, and the plentiful citrus. The snow, too, which covers Etna to some extent for at least eight months of the year, has had its commercial uses. Before the age of refrigeration the Bishops of Catania farmed it and sold it abroad, creating a great demand for what was—in the arid regions of the Mediterranean—a great delicacy. A 19th c. traveller wrote: 'This snow is of vast importance to the whole population of Sicily, Malta, and sometimes even Barbary, where ices, during the heat of summer, are among the necessaries of life. The exhaustion of the stock is capable of producing serious disturbances . . .'

Ascent of Etna From ancient times, the climb to the summit of Mt Etna has presented a challenge to travellers. The philosopher Empedocles came up here to discover the secret of immortality and fell into the crater. Later on the Roman Emperor Hadrian was more circumspect, surveying his empire from the rim. Gladstone paid a visit in his journal (1838) and his climb can hardly have been easier than that of his ancient predecessors. In the 19th c. the journey was usually made from Catania, by carriage to Nicolosi; from there the rest of the way was by mule or on foot. Today the approach is still via Nicolosi, ascending to the Rifugio G. Sapienza (1881 m) where one may take the cableway to the summit. With the exception of the last part of the climb, to the actual crater, which must be done on foot

Left: Cable-car, Érice Right: Etna

(381 m), the journey is no longer arduous. It is important, however, that the climber should take the right clothing. Even between June and October, which are the best months to go up Etna, the temperature is cool at the higher altitudes. Extra clothing is recommended, and strong shoes for walking over the lava.

Approaches by car

Route from Catania (south approach) Leaving the city by the Via Etnea, take the Strada dell'Etna for Nicolosi. On the way note the dark brown masses of lava at the roadside, relics of the 1669 eruption. Note also the richness of the terrain. The volcanic soil at the foot of Etna—a product of past eruptions—is extremely fertile. Olives, vines and citrus abound, in competition with the ubiquitous prickly pear. At *Gravina*, 8 km from Catania, one may see the first small craters of Etna, opened in the 14th c. Further on, near *Nicolosi* (16 km) are the craters of the *Monti Rossi*. Now wooded, these were the source of the 1669 lava flow which buried Catania. Elsewhere on this approach the terrain is sparsely wooded: these were the slopes stripped by Dionysius for ship-building in the 4th c. BC.

31 km from Catania (15 km from Nicolosi) a turning to the left leads to the *Grande Albergo Etna*, which is open from Jun–Sep for summer visitors and from Jan–Mar for ski enthusiasts. 2 km further on is the *Cantoniera d'Etna* (rest.) with—need one say—a fine view from the terrace. This is the desert region of Etna: a massive landscape of purple-brown lava and extinct craters. In some places vegetation has regained a foothold, only to be overwhelmed by a later flow of lava.

The climax of the road journey is reached at the nearby *Rifugio G. Sapienza* (1910 m) which is a hotel of the Alpine Club with a bar and restaurant. This is the starting point of the cableway, the *Funivia dell'Etna*. This takes visitors up to the station at *Montagnola* (2500 m, rest.) which lies 700 m below the crater.

The remainder of the trip to the crater is done by jeep. The service operates from 08.30–17.30 with the last descent at 18.00, leaving at least every half-hour. There is an additional night service commencing at 18.00. The charges, subject to alteration, are:

Cable trip and ascent to crater and return (including guide) L12000

Cable trip only (return) 6000

Night service (to crater only) 10% extra

For those not wishing to use the cableway, SITAS minibuses offer a service from the Rif. Sapienza to the crater with a similar tariff. They also operate an extended night service to the crater, which continues until 03.30 and offers a unique opportunity to witness the volcanic phenomena at night. Arrangements for night excursions should be made in advance through SITAS (details from tourist office).

For those with a head for heights and the

smell of sulphur, the climb to the summit of Etna is a memorable experience. The guides know the easiest and quickest route to the crater: 'going it alone' is forbidden. The guides are responsible for visitors' safety, and as explosions from the craters are unforeseeable it is essential to obey their instructions.

The effort, of course, is rewarded, not only with a view that embraces the whole of Sicily, the coast of Calabria, and the Aeolian Islands, but with a close-up experience of the phenomena of a still-active volcano. The crater, filled with its fuming sulphur-crusted lava, is an extraordinary sight: even more so at night when it glows like a devil's furnace. From the rim of the crater one can see clearly the pattern of the previous lava flows from the cone, and the formation of subsidiary cones on the slopes. For those prepared to go up or come down at night, the sunrise—or sunset—make the experience indelible.

Route from Taormina (north approach) From the SS114 11 km south of Taormina (Fiume-freddo) a right turn is made for Lingua-glossa (11 km). The road ascends steeply to *Piedemonte* (348 m) and more gradually to *Linguaglossa* (525 m). This is a resort area, set in a haven of pinewoods and mountain streams. From here one reaches in 15 km the resort village at *Mareneve* (1400 m, rest.). A right turn here leads to the ski-centre of *Piano Provenzana* (1800 m, rest.)—a further 4 km. From Mareneve STAR minibuses are available in good weather to take visitors to the central crater (details from tourist office).

The route continues a further 12 km to *Fornazzo*, passing the turn to *Rifugio Citelli* (1700 m) and crossing the 1979 lava flow north of the village. From Fornazzo one can descend to the A18 or SS114 at Giarre and return to Taormina. Alternatively the mountain route may be continued to the *Rif. Sapienza* via the town of *Zafferana* (600 m).

Bus and train services to the Etna region
From Catania *Trasporti Etna* run a daily bus service to Etna, departing in the morning (07.50, Piazza della Stazione) and returning in the afternoon (16.00). Visitors preferring an excursion around Etna may either make the $4\frac{1}{2}$ hr round trip by train (Ferrovia Circum-etnea, Corso Italia, change at Giarre-Riposto) or combine the services of coach and train in the special 'Giro Turistico dell'Etna'. This tour, available from June to September on Sundays only (price L12500 including excursions) offers a comprehensive and relaxed view of the beautiful Etna region. Further information about these services may be obtained from the Tourist Informa-tion Office in the Corso Umberto.

The route around Etna **by car** is perhaps the most pleasant, as it can be varied according

to taste and offers the most intimate and varied view of the region. There are many attractive and interesting towns and villages en route, including Paternò, Adrano, Bronte, Randazzo and Linguaglossa.

Favignana Island see Égadi Is.

Filicudi Island see Aeolian Is.

Forza d'Agro
Village 4 km from turning off SS114, 10 km north of Taormina.

Despite the regular succession of coach parties that wind up from Taormina to admire it, this old village, perched on its height overlooking the Ionian Sea and the coast of Calabria, retains its 'forgotten' look. Many of the houses were built in the 15th and 16th c., and the higher one climbs towards the ruined medieval castle at the top, the more primitive these dwellings appear, in-habited by donkeys and entwined with the gnarled branches of ancient vines.

In the village are three churches of minor interest. At the entrance, on the left, is the church of **S. Francesco**, with 16th c. sculp-ture, and on the right, following the Via del Municipio, is the church of **SS. Trinita**, with a 16th c. façade and campanile. The Baroque **Chiesa Matrice** in the centre of the village contains various works from the 14th–18th c.

Frazzanò
(550 m) Village 11 km south of turning off SS113 8 km west of Cape Orlando.

During spring and summer the road to Frazzanò offers one of the most delightful drives in the island, along a winding, gently climbing road banked on either side by wild flowers and shrubs. 2 km beyond the village stands the disused Monastery of **S. Filippo di Fragala**, one of the chain of church buildings erected by the Normans along the coastline of Sicily. The monastery, built by Count Roger in the 11th c., stands on a hill overlooking the road and is clearly visible from a distance. To reach it one has to follow the road round to the other side of the hill and then double back up an unmade road to the right.

This old building, doing penance now as a farmhouse, is semi-ruined, but worth a visit for those interested in the early period of Norman architecture in Sicily. The disused church has a T-plan, with three apses, the octagonal drum of the central cupola (the cupola itself has disappeared) and a bell tower. The dome on the latter is 18th c., replacing the original. Visitors who can find someone on the spot to let them in should see the inside of the church which has remains of Byzantine frescoes.

Ganzirri
Fishing village 10 km north of Messina, situated on the edge of a small lagoon filled with mussel-beds. There are some good fish restaurants here.

Mussels and swordfish, Ganzirri

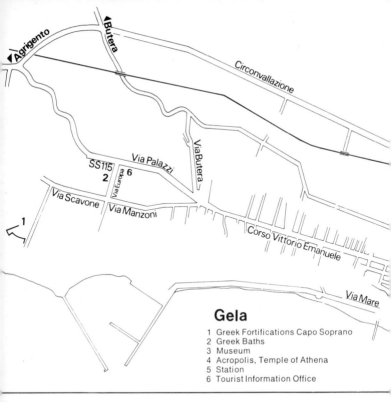

Gela

1 Greek Fortifications Capo Soprano
2 Greek Baths
3 Museum
4 Acropolis, Temple of Athena
5 Station
6 Tourist Information Office

Gela (pop. 55,000) Town on south coast with historic beginnings: now a major centre of Sicily's petro-chemical industry.

History In 689 BC Gela was founded by Greeks from Crete and Rhodes. The site was a ridge originally occupied by the Sicans, near to the river that the earlier inhabitants had called *Gelas*, meaning 'cold'. As the first Greek colony on the south coast and the founder of a satellite colony, Akragas, further to the west, Gela presented a challenge to the great Syracuse. Under the tyrant Hippocrates (492–485 BC) the city reached the height of its power, and came near to conquering Syracuse in a war against that city. Hippocrates' famous successor, Gelon, removed the possibility of further antagonism between the cities by becoming tyrant of both. His alliance with Theron of Akragas later provided a consolidated front against the Carthaginians. Gela was, eventually, taken by the Carthaginians (405 BC) and remained under their influence until Timoleon forged his treaty with them and repopulated the town with Greeks from Chios. In 282 BC Gela was destroyed by the Mamertine mercenaries from Messina, and the tyrant of Akragas, Phintias, transferred its homeless citizens to a new town to the east (the modern Licata). Nothing more was heard of Gela until the Emperor Frederick II refounded the town, with the name Terranova. Gela reverted to its original name in 1927. On 10 July 1943 the Americans landed here during the Allied invasion of Sicily.

The town Modern Gela, dominated by the spectacular oil refineries to the east of the town, has little to commend it to the casual visitor. The ancient town was so thoroughly destroyed that only vestiges remain. The most interesting remains, in fact, are those of the one part of the Greek city to be saved from destruction by a freak of nature. These are the **Greek fortifications** on Capo Soprano at the western end of the city (Via Scavone). No other defensive work of Greek antiquity can match this great wall, more than 200 m long in its best preserved stretch, which was discovered by chance in 1948 after being buried by sand for 2,300 years.

These walls were built by Timoleon as part of his renewal of the city after 338 BC. The wall is of massive construction, the lower

part formed of stone blocks and the upper part of sun-dried bricks. This odd method of building was, in part, an economy, as the stone was not available in the immediate locality and had to be hauled 10km or so from quarries to the west. Also this 'topping-off' was a rearguard action against the rapidly encroaching sand. The height of this part of the wall, built on the dunes, was gradually reduced by the rising sand, and further levels of brick had to be added. The wall that was finally destroyed by Phintias in 282 BC was, in fact, largely buried; a process that had taken, since its construction, little more than 50 years.

The wall as it stands today is in a marvellous state of preservation. The limestone blocks at the bottom, protected by the sand, look as if they are newly cut, and the clay bricks of the upper level have been given a cladding of glass. Additional protection has been afforded by a plastic roof over the whole structure.

Walking along the wall (starting from the spur at right angles to the east end) one can identify the different stages of construction in the clay bricks, where the colour becomes lighter. Other interesting features in the wall are the *postern gate* and *stairway* to the ramparts (viewed from the inside of the wall). Further traces of the fortifications may be seen to the west and north.

In the Via Europa, which joins the Via Scavone to the Via Palazzi, are the remains of **Greek baths** (4th c. BC). The individual basins, which have been restored, make an interesting comparison with the later more communal Roman type of bath-house.

Museum Gela's new Museo Nazionale (for opening hours see p. 25: closed on Tuesdays) is situated on the former acropolis of the Greek city. It contains an impressive collection of finds from local sites.

In the *entrance hall* is displayed material excavated from the acropolis, including Early Bronze Age objects (*Case 1*) which show the site was occupied long before the arrival of the Greeks. Other cases contain relics of the Greek period, demonstrating the formidable talent of the Geloan sculptors. Among them are *antefixes* (roof ornaments) from decorated shrines, in the form of *sileni*, gorgons and harpies (the *silenus heads* in *Case 6* are perfect examples); and the splendid *horse's head* from a temple roof (5th c. BC). The material in *Cases 7–10* should be noted as belonging to the later Greek phase, i.e. the period of Timoleon following the destruction of Gela by the Carthaginians (late 4th c. BC). The elegant *marble bowl* with its fluted base (near the entrance) is from this period. In the middle of the entrance hall are architectural fragments, including two fine *Ionic capitals* (6th c. BC), unusual in Sicily.

In the *gallery* above the entrance hall is material from the minor sanctuaries of Gela. The *north wing* (*Cases 23–31*) contains objects recovered from the city's necropolises, including *sarcophagi* (for interment) and vases for holding the ashes of the dead after cremation. In addition are everyday objects found in the houses built over the burial grounds during Timoleon's reconstruction of the city (4th c. BC).

The *monetarium* (coin room) at the end of the north wing is closed. This is the result of a robbery in 1972 in which most of the museum's priceless collection of archaic (6th–5th c. BC) silver coins were removed. Among the many thefts of art treasures in Sicily in recent years, this was without doubt one of the most shocking. Much of the haul has, happily, since been recovered.

In the *east wing*, amongst many varied finds from local sites, is material recovered from the excavations at Capo Soprano and from the Bronze Age village of Manfria, west of Gela. The *south wing* contains a great variety of exhibits from sites further afield, including Butera, whose necropolis yielded such rich finds in the recent excavations (*Cases 39 and 40*). The central hall houses the impressive *Navarra collection*, on provisional loan to the museum, which includes fine red and black figure Attic vases.

To the east of the museum may be seen remains of houses and shops built during the 4th c. BC reconstruction of the city. Further on, in the gardens, can be seen the sole surviving column of the earlier **Temple of Athena**, thought to have been built to commemorate Gelon's victory over the Carthaginians at Himera (480 BC).

Halaesa Ancient site south of road junction on SS113 24 km east of Cefalù (Castel di Tusa).

This site, a Sicel foundation of the late 15th c. BC, is reached by following the road to Tusa and after 3 km taking a steep track to the right (look out for 'Scavi' sign) which climbs to a disused chapel on the hillside.

From the farmhouse adjacent to the chapel a short walk takes the visitor to the brow of the hill and the remains of the ancient town. Built by the Sicels, the early inhabitants of eastern Sicily, Halaesa reached its greatest prosperity during the Roman period, when it was granted the status of a 'free' city by the Romans in recognition of its loyalty during their wars against the Carthaginians. The security of its site, on a fortified hill, and its proximity to the sea, ensured its success as a merchant city and its decline was only brought about by the punitive taxation of the Roman praetor Verres in the 1st c. BC.

The site is at the moment under excavation and its appeal is confined to the student of archaeology. The *agora* has been partially reconstructed, and there are traces of the *decumanus* (central street), side streets and walls. At the highest point of the hill are the remains of two temples of the 3rd c. BC.

Imera (Himera) Ancient site on west bank of the River Imera (or Fiume Grande) near sea 55 km east of Palermo, 19 km west of Cefalu. The only survival of ancient Himera is its temple, sandwiched between the SS113 and adjacent railway line and the motorway (A19). It can be reached either by descending to the SS113 from the motorway at Buonfornello, or—for those travelling direct on the SS113—by turning off towards the sea just to the west of the river bridge.

History Himera was the first Greek colony to be established on the north coast of Sicily (648 BC). Its founders were Chalcidians from Greece who had earlier colonized Zancle (ancient Messina) on the east coast. It later came under the influence of Theron, the tyrant of Akragas (Agrigento).

As the Greek settlement nearest to the Carthaginian-dominated area of Sicily to the north-west, Himera was at a point of confrontation between two colonizing nations, translated in 480 BC into open warfare. The battle of Himera, between Hamilcar of Carthage and the combined forces of Theron of Akragas and Gelon of Syracuse, was one of the epic conflicts of the ancient world. The Carthaginian forces, coming by land and sea from their colony at Panormus (Palermo) were so massive that they can only have been intent on the conquest of the island, to put a stop to further Greek expansion. Despite their size these forces were however no match for Gelon's strategy and the Greek victory was overwhelming, resulting in the rout of the Carthaginian army and destruction of their fleet.

For 70 years this victory put a stop to the territorial ambitions of Carthage: then, in 410 BC, a second invasion of the island by Hannibal, Hamilcar's grandson, resulted in the total destruction of Himera. Carthaginian expansion stopped here and the resettlement was to the west, at Thermae (Términi Imerese).

The **temple**, built to ccmmemorate the battle of Himera, was destroyed by the Carthaginians in their subsequent retaliation: enough remains, however, to make an interesting study.

The temple was of the Doric order, with 6 columns in the front and 14 at the sides. It has the conventional *pronaos* and *opisthodomos* of the classical temples but an added feature of interest in the stair-wells on either side of the *cella* entrance, from which steps led to the roof of the temple. This feature is also found in temples of the same period at Agrigento (Akragas), which suggests an architectural dialogue between the cities. Supporting evidence is in another architectural ornament common to Akragas and Himera: the striking lion-head water spouts used for channelling water from the temple roofs. No less than 50 of these ornate lion-heads were found at Himera: examples can be seen at the Museo Archeologico in Palermo and the Museo Civico at Términi Imerese.

Isole dei Ciclopi (Islands of the Cyclops)
Group of three rocks off the east coast between Aci Trezza and Aci Castello.

These dramatic rocks (otherwise known as the *Faraglioni* or *Scoglie dei Ciclopi*) are celebrated in legend as those that were hurled by Polyphemus the Cyclops at Ulysses' ship after the hero had blinded the one-eyed giant in his cave.

Itala Village 2·5 km west of road junction on SS114, 20 km south of Messina.
Just beyond the village is the fine Norman church of **S. Pietro**, erected by Count Roger in 1093 to celebrate a victory over the Saracens. To reach the church go through the village and across the bridge, and

ascend the road, which offers beautiful views of the village, for 1·5 km. At the junction, turn left for the church.

The church was built for the Basilian (Greek Orthodox) order, long established in Sicily before the arrival of the Arabs, who banished them. The Normans restored the order in Sicily and the churches built for the Basilians have an identifiable style: three-aisled basilicas with three apses and fine exteriors with blind arcades and interlacing arches. This church is one of the earliest, built 80 years before its more splendid neighbour to the south, the church of SS. Pietro e Paolo. It has been thoroughly restored.

Those with a definite plan to view the interior of the church should contact the priest (*prete*) in the village.

Lampedusa Island see **Pelagic Is.**

Lentini Town 47 km north-west of Syracuse.
History The ancient *Leontinoi* was one of the earliest Greek colonies of Sicily, founded in 729 BC by the Chalcidians of Naxos who, 30 years earlier, had been the first Greeks to settle in Sicily. Its unusual site—this was the first time the Greeks had moved inland—was chosen for commercial and strategic reasons. The town, built on two hills on either side of a valley, commanded the rich arable land to the north and provided a barrier to the expansion of Syracuse to the south. For over 200 years it was an extremely prosperous and successful city: then in the 5th c. BC it was subjected to pressure, first from Gela and then from Syracuse, the latter city finally crushing it in 425 BC.

Thenceforward, and up to the time of the Romans, Leontinoi was dominated by Syracuse, a situation from which alliances with the Athenians and Carthaginians brought only temporary relief. Under the Romans the city declined, recovering a degree of importance only when it was made the seat of a bishopric in the early Christian period. It was taken by the Saracens in 848, and completely destroyed by the earthquake of 1693. The modern town is still an important agricultural centre.

S. Pietro, Itala

Archaeological zone Most of the remains of the ancient city lie in the valley between Lentini and its neighbour Carlentini and on the sides of the opposing hills of S. Mauro and Metapiccola. The approach may be made from either town, though access from Carlentini is slightly easier. The ruins are mainly of the *fortifications*, which follow the line of the two hills: one has however to search very hard—if only for a sense of direction—amongst the thick vegetation. The most interesting details are the pincer-type *south gate* (near it the remains of a Hellenistic necropolis) and the ruins of a 13th c. Swabian *castle* just below Lentini, built over a section of the ancient fortifications.

In the central square of Lentini, the Piazza Duomo, stands the **Chiesa Madre**, restored in the 18th c. after the earthquake. From the north-west of this square the Via 20 Settembre (steps) leads to the Via del Progresso from which one crosses the main road to Via Piave. Here is Lentini's **museum** (Museo Archeologico) which houses finds from the ancient city. Visitors intending to explore the archaeological zone should come here first and study the plans.

Lévanzo Island see **Égadi Is.**

Lilybaeum see **Marsala**

Linosa Island see **Pelagic Is.**

Lípari Island see **Aeolian Is.**

Madonie Range of mountains, north-central Sicily. At their principal peak (*Pizzo Carbonara*, 1979 m) these limestone mountains are second only in height to Etna. The highest peaks are best visited from *Collesano*, where mule trips may be arranged. The most popular centres, both for excursions and for ski-ing, are the *Piano Zucchi* and the *Piano Battaglia*.

Maréttimo Island see **Égadi Is.**

Marsala (pop. 83,000) Town at westernmost point of Sicily, at the centre of wine-producing area and famous for the wine to which it has given its name, 'Marsala'.

History Marsala, the ancient *Lilybaeum*, was founded by Himilco of Carthage in 396 BC, after the earlier Phoenician colony of Motya had been destroyed by Dionysius II of Syracuse. The promontory on which it was built offered a superbly defensive site, and it remained the principal stronghold of the Carthaginians during the consolidation of their power in Sicily. It was never taken by the Greeks (even Pyrrhus stopped at the gates) and succumbed to the Romans only after a 10-year siege (250–241 AD).

Its position on the west coast of Sicily secured for Lilybaeum commercial as well as military advantages. The Saracens, like the Romans and Carthaginians before them, developed their trade with Africa through their port of Mars-al-Allah ('Harbour of God'). Its proximity to Africa, however, made Marsala the target of pirate raids from the Barbary coast and in the end its importance declined in favour of Trápani.

On 11 May 1860 Marsala became the scene of one of the most important events in Italian history when Garibaldi and the Thousand landed here at the beginning of their invasion of Sicily in their campaign for the country's unification. In 1943 the town was severely damaged in bombing raids.

The town In the central Piazza Repubblica stands the **Cathedral** (S. Tomaso di Canterbury). It has a Norman foundation, but the present building is very much of the 18th c. (the upper part of the Baroque façade was completed in 1956). The central dome and east end of the cathedral were shattered by a bomb in the last war, but have since been restored.

Inside, at the foot of the pillar to the left of the choir, note the fine statue of *St Thomas the Apostle* by Antonello Gagini (1516). The Gagini family were responsible for much of the other sculpture in the church, including the altarpiece of the *Passion* to the left of the choir. The chapel to the right of the choir contains the *Tomb of Antonio Liotta* (d. 1512). The cathedral possesses eight magnificent 16th c. *Flemish tapestries* which unfortunately may be viewed only by special permission.

From the Piazza della Repubblica one can walk, by way of Via 11 Maggio, to the 18th c. **Porta Nuova**. 11 May was the date of Garibaldi's arrival, and a plaque on a house near the gate records a subsequent visit by the great general when he was calling on Sicilians to join him on his march to Rome. A bust of Garibaldi commemorating his landing may be seen in the Piazza della Vittoria in front of the gate. Here also one may wander through the pleasant **Villa Cavallotti**, a garden lined with statues of some of Marsala's leading citizens. A belvedere, reached from the gardens, offers a fine panorama of the coast, embracing the Isole dello Stagnone (including ancient Motya) to the north.

Archaeological zone From the Porta Nuovo, take the coast road to the north. At Capo Boeo (on the right, 1 km) are the excavations of the Roman **Lilybaeum**. These excavations are only the beginning of the archaeological exploration of the cape, which promises to yield some fascinating material from the early settlements—including, one hopes, evidence of the Carthaginian colony.

At the moment the principal discovery has been the remains of a **Roman villa** and **baths** of the 3rd c. AD. At the entrance is a 'cave canem' mosaic of a chained dog, leading

The town A pleasant walk may be made along the sea-front, starting from the east at the public gardens (*Giardino Pubblico Jolanda*). Here stand the sad remains of the **castle** built by Count Roger after his capture of the town from the Arabs.

Opposite the gardens is the **Cathedral** (S. Salvatore), with a façade, completed in 1906, which incorporates an interesting 16th c. relief of *Count Roger on Horseback*, trampling on a Saracen. The original cathedral, built by the Normans, was completely restyled in the 17th c., but a little of the early building is retained in the exterior of the apse. Inside the cathedral, in the right transept, is the fine *Tomb of Bishop Monteaperto* (1485) by Domenico Gagini, and in the apse a majestic *Transfiguration* consisting of six marble figures, commenced by Domenico's son Antonello and finished by his grandson Antonino. In the left transept is an unusual work in coloured marble by Marabitti, *Christ Mocked*, in which the veining of the marble simulates the blood and bruises on Christ's body.

The cathedral stands in the fine 18th c. Piazza della Repubblica with, in the centre, a statue of Mazara's patron, *S. Vito*, by Marabitti.

Continuing west along the sea-front one reaches, in about 500m, the Via Marina, which leads to the little Norman church of **S. Nicolò Regale**, built on the site of a Roman house (now covered). The church has been recently thoroughly restored. The interior has been transformed by the removal of the columns, cupola and vault, which have been replaced by a metal and glass structure. The exterior, which appears to retain little of the original fabric, shows the typical triple apse and window arches and crenellation of this period of architecture.

Elsewhere in the town is the 17th c. **Palazzo dei Cavalieri di Malta** (Via del Carmine) which recalls the use of Mazara as a port by the Knights of Malta. The building contains a small library and museum.

into a vestibule. In the centre is the open court, or *atrium* with a fine mosaic of a hunting scene. Note the basin for catching rainwater (*impluvium*) in the centre. Around the *atrium*, on three sides, are baths. On the north side is the furnace which supplied the hot air for the *sudatoria* (sweat rooms).

The pavement to the east has a design in mosaic of the *Seasons*, with the central three-legged symbol of *Trinacria*. To the south, on the other side of the path, are a cistern and traces of grain and wine stores. The Romans, it seemed, knew how to attend to their bodily comforts. That it was usually beyond a reasonable level of self-indulgence will be pointed out by the custodian, who proudly shows visitors the nearby *vomitarium*.

A short excursion may be made from Marsala to the island of Motya, site of Sicily's most important Phoenician settlement. See **Motya**.

Mazara del Vallo
Town on west coast 22km south of Marsala, noted for its busy fishing port (A29).

History A port-of-call of the Phoenicians and later an outpost of Selinus, *Mazara* suffered the same fate as its mother city at the hands of the Carthaginians during their conquest of western Sicily (409 BC). Later on it became a Roman fortress, but did not really flourish as a town until the arrival of the Saracens, who landed here on their mission of conquest in 827. After its later conquest by Count Roger (1075), Mazara became the meeting place of the first Norman parliament.

Megara Hyblaea
Ancient site on east coast, 2km from turning off SS114, 19km north of Syracuse.

History In 750 BC this site, close to the sea by the mouth of the River Cantera, was offered by the Sicel ruler Hyblon to settlers from Megara in Greece. Megara Hyblaea thus became one of the earliest Greek colonies in Sicily—after Naxos but before Syracuse. With the revenue from its maritime trade the town prospered and expanded and 100 years later a party of Megarians set off to found Selinus on the south-east coast.

A rival colony so close to Syracuse could not hope to survive, however, and in 483 BC the tyrant Gelon destroyed Megara Hyblaea. The town was later restored by Timoleon in the late 4th c. BC and most of the ruins are from this period and from the subsequent

S. Nicolò Regale, Mazara del Vallo

period of fortification preceding the Roman invasion. These defences were not strong enough to deter the Romans, who took and destroyed the town in 214 BC.

Tour of the ruins To reach the site, take the turning marked 'Enel Tifeo' to the north of the turning to S. Megara-Giannalena. After 1 km a track on the right leads to the site, passing remains of *archaic walls*. Excavations to the east have uncovered the ancient *necropolis*. In a further 600 m (having crossed the railway bridge) the more intact *western wall* of the pre-Roman (Hellenistic) fortifications will be seen. Following this wall on foot, the visitor will note two projecting square towers, and between them the *western entrance* to the town. At the southwest corner of the wall is the *main entrance* to the town which is of the pincer type, flanked on either side by protective towers. From here the *main street* of the town leads north, passing the remains of *baths* on the right. In 200 m it reaches the *agora* at the centre of the town. To the north of the *agora* are remains of the portico of the *stoa*: to the north again a *sacred area* including a *temple* built in the late 4th c. BC, dismantled to provide building materials for the town's defences before the Roman invasion.

Returning to the road, continue eastwards to the *antiquarium*.

Messina (pop. 275,000) City and provincial capital on Strait of Messina, north-east Sicily.

History Messina was founded by Greeks from Chalcis and Cumae c. 730 BC. The ancient name *Zancle* comes from their word for 'sickle' to which they likened the shape of the harbour. The site was one of the most desirable in the island: a strip of land guarded to the rear by mountains, with a superb natural harbour commanding the strait through which much of the Mediterranean trade was channelled. (In legend, this strait was the lurking-place of Scylla and Charybdis, the first a six-headed monster living on a rock, the second a whirlpool. As Odysseus discovered, it was difficult for sailors to avoid one or other hazard).

Zancle prospered, and within a century of its foundation had started two daughter colonies at Mylae (Milazzo) and Himera. A town of such strategic importance, so close to the mainland of Italy, could not hope however to maintain its sovereignty. In 493 BC it was taken by the Greek tyrant of Rhegium on the opposite coast and renamed *Messana*. It was later contested by Athens and Syracuse, and later still by the Carthaginians, who destroyed the town in 396 BC. Dionysius I rebuilt it, but continued to war for its possession with the Carthaginians, who subsequently reconquered it.

It was finally liberated by Timoleon, but after the death of his successor Agathocles the city again changed hands. This time it fell to a band of Agathocles' mercenaries from Campania, known as the Mamertines ('Sons of Mars'). In the ensuing history of Sicily, the rôle of the Mamertines was critical. Pressed by Hieron II of Syracuse, they formed an alliance with Rome. This gave Rome a foothold in Sicily and was the beginning of the First Punic War.

After their conquest of Sicily, Messana became one of the Romans' most important naval bases in the Mediterranean. It had a similar significance 1000 years later as a port-of-call for the Crusaders on their way to the Holy Land. Richard the Lionheart, whose sister Joan married the Norman King of Sicily, William II, was here to claim her dowry in 1190–91.

The independent spirit which characterized Messina in ancient times prevailed again in her resistance to the cruel Angevins (1282) and in her rebellion against the neglectful Viceroys of Spain in the 17th c. That spirit, however, was not enough to protect Messina from an extraordinary series of catastrophes in the 18th and 19th c. These included epidemics of plague and cholera, major earthquakes and a naval bombardment by the Neapolitans (1848) in which the cannon of 'King Bomba's' fleet were used to quell an insurrection. (The city subsequently became the last in Sicily to be liberated by Garibaldi in 1860.)

The most serious disaster followed in this century (1908) when an earthquake flattened the city and killed 60,000 of the inhabitants. The final trauma was inflicted by the Allied bombers in August 1943, during the German retreat from Sicily.

The city Modern Messina shows little sign today of being the most often, and most thoroughly, destroyed city in Italy. Its low buildings, however, are the result of a height

restriction imposed after the 1908 earthquake. The result is a sprawling modern city, whose only attraction is in its site, on a ledge of land at the foot of the Monti Peloritani, facing, across a narrow strait, the rugged coast of Calabria. The sickle-shaped harbour, with its fortified tip punctuated by the *Colonna Votiva* (a column topped by a statue of the Madonna) is dramatic when viewed from above, and this aspect of Messina is best seen from the *circonvallazione* which runs around the upper town (Viale Italia to Viale Regina Margherita).

Note: the best approach to the city from the A18/A20 is from the *Boccetta* exit.

At the centre of the city is the Piazza del Duomo, totally destroyed in the 1908 earthquake. On the east side is the restored **Fontana di Orione**, a lively fountain by Montorsoli with, at the base, reclining figures representing *rivers* and, at the top, the statue of *Orion*, the mythical founder of the city.

Cathedral This building, originally Norman, has been twice reconstructed in this century: once after the earthquake of 1908 and again after an incendiary bomb fell on it in 1943. These were only the last in the succession of disasters in the long history of this building since its foundation by Roger II in the 12th c., and what exists today is a completely modern construction incorporating fragments from different periods. The church has undergone many architectural changes

in its history and the man responsible for its post-earthquake reconstruction, Valenti, took the opportunity to restore the building to its original Norman form.

Beside it the fantastic Gothic *campanile*, which was also Valenti's inspiration, seems an aberration. Its justification must be that it houses the world's largest astronomical clock, made in 1933. The mechanism is extremely elaborate and may be viewed in action on the west side. The movable tableaux represent, from the bottom: the *Seven Days of the Week*; the *Four Ages of Man* (one every quarter of an hour); the *Sanctuary of Montalto*; *Scenes from the Gospels*; *Delivery of the Letter of the Madonna to the Ambassadors of Messina*. At the next level the two figures of *Dina* and *Clarenza*, heroines of the struggle of the Messinese against the Angevins, are poised to strike the hour. At midday the clock provides, in action, an astonishing spectacle. On the south side of the *campanile*, facing the cathedral, are two dials, one showing the seasons and another the planetary system. Above them a globe shows the phases of the moon.

The three portals of the west front of the cathedral retain much of the original 15th and 16th c. sculptured decoration. The Gothic *central portal* has some unusual carving on either side: pagan in spirit and primitive in execution. A host of *putti* cavort among vines heavy with their fruit: saints and angels look

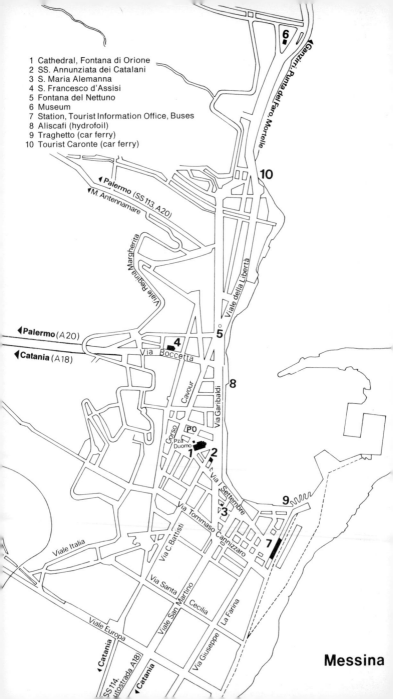

1 Cathedral, Fontana di Orione
2 SS. Annunziata dei Catalani
3 S. Maria Alemanna
4 S. Francesco d'Assisi
5 Fontana del Nettuno
6 Museum
7 Station, Tourist Information Office, Buses
8 Aliscafi (hydrofoil)
9 Traghetto (car ferry)
10 Tourist Caronte (car ferry)

Messina

on benignly. In the tympanum over the door is a *Coronation of the Virgin* by Bonate (1468); in the lunette a *Madonna and Child* by Mazzola (1534). The north and south doors of the cathedral are the work of Polidoro da Caravaggio (16th c.).

The *interior* of the cathedral, with a nave and two aisles, reproduces the Norman original. The nave has monolithic 'antique' columns, pointed arches and a painted wooden ceiling, in the style of the Norman cathedrals of Cefalù and Monreale. Like her sister cathedrals, Messina had fine mosaics: unhappily all these have disappeared and those in the central and side apses of the present building are modern restorations.

The monuments and other works of art in the cathedral are for the most part reconstructions. In the first altar of the right aisle is a restored statue of *John the Baptist* by Antonello Gagini (1525). The next six altars, and those of the opposite aisle, are reconstructions of work by Montorsoli and others. The marble *pulpit* was remade from the original by Calamecca. A door leads from the right aisle to a vestibule from which a further door (left) leads to the *Treasury*. Fortunately the rich contents of this treasury survived both disasters and may be viewed by visitors (mornings only).

Another interesting restoration is the inscribed slab of the *Tomb of Archbishop Palmer*, on the pilaster at the end of the nave to the right. (Archbishop Palmer was the Englishman who married William II to Joan, Richard the Lionheart's sister.) Opposite, by the right hand pilaster of the central apse, is the *Tomb of Archbishop de Tabiatis* by Goro di Gregorio (1333) with fine reliefs.

Other restorations include the elaborate 17th c. *baldacchino*, choir stalls and font.

From the Piazza del Duomo the Via 1 Settembre leads to the Piazza Catalani, in which stands the attractive little church of **SS. Annunziata dei Catalani**. This church, less severely damaged in the earthquake than many of the buildings around it, is one of the most interesting monuments of Norman Sicily, combining elements of Byzantine and

Saracenic architecture. It was built in the second half of the 12th c., but shortened—perhaps after an earthquake—in the 13th c. Its façade, with three portals, dates from the latter period.

The church is best viewed from the east side, where one can see the original *apse*, decorated with two levels of blind arcades, and the *cupola*, on a similarly decorated drum. The *interior* of the church (open mornings only) is Byzantine in style with round arches supported by antique columns (note the typical use of ornamental double columns in the apsidal arch), barrel vaulting and cupola supported by pendentives.

Opposite the church is a monument to *Don John of Austria*, the victor of Lepanto, a bronze statue by Calamecca (1572).

Other places of interest in Messina

S. Maria Alemanna This ruined church of the 13th c. (in the street of the same name off the Via Garibaldi) was shattered by the 1908 earthquake. Unlike the other monuments of the city however, it has been subjected to a barbaric attempt at restoration which must be condemned for the materials used—reinforced concrete—rather than for the fact that the work has never been completed. The interest of the church lies in its totally Gothic character—the only church of its kind in Sicily. It is thought to have been built by an architect from northern Europe.

S. Francesco d'Assisi, in the street of the same name, is a careful reconstruction of the 13th c. original. Worth noting are the single nave, unusually high transept and three deep apses, with ribbed vaults.

Fontana del Nettuno (Fountain of Neptune) On the sea-front, at the meeting of the Via Garibaldi and the Viale della Liberta. This is a reconstruction of the much damaged original fountain by Montorsoli (1557). The figure of *Neptune*, pacifying the sea, stands between the turbulent terrors of the strait, *Scylla* and *Charybdis*. Both he and Scylla are 19th c. replicas of original figures now in the museum.

Museum (Museo Nazionale) At the end of the Via della Liberta, at the northern limit of the town. This museum has Sicily's finest collection of paintings by artists working in the island from the 15th–17th c., many of them enhanced by recent restoration. For opening times see p.25. For opening times see p.25.

In the garden is the debris of the 1908 earthquake: statues, masonry, etc., including, by the entrance, the *Neptune* from Montorsoli's fountain.

Room 1 contains works rescued from churches, including a late 14th c. *polyptych* and a 13th c. *niche mosaic*. *Room 2* has the prize of the collection, a polyptych of the *Madonna and Child Enthroned between S. Benedict and S. Gregorio* and (superior panels) *Annunciation*. This is by Messina's own son,

Antonello da Messina (1473). Also in this room are paintings of the Flemish school, which had considerable influence on Antonello. *Rooms 3 & 4* have other works by Messinese artists including those of Girolamo Alibrandi (16th c.) which show the influence of Leonardo. In *Room 5* are two paintings by Caravaggio, who was in Sicily between 1609–10. These are the *Adoration of the Shepherds* and the *Resurrection of Lazarus.* (The famous Italian artist should not be confused with his namesake Polidoro da Caravaggio whose work is in Room 4.) *Rooms 7–9* are devoted to antiquities from the Hellenistic, Roman and Byzantine periods. *Rooms 10–12* contain works of art recovered from churches destroyed by the earthquake, including a graceful marble *Madonna col Bambino* (15th c., school of Laurana) and a marble *ciborium* (16th c., school of Gagini), both in *Room 11*. *Room 13* has church treasures.

Excursions from Messina

A pleasant drive may be made from Messina to the north-eastern tip of the island at *Punta del Faro.* The route passes through several fishing villages, including *Ganzirri* with its lake and mussel beds. Fine views of the Strait and the coastline of Calabria may be enjoyed, particularly from the cape itself, which is marked by a massive pylon carrying electricity from the mainland. To the west is Messina's bathing resort, *Lido di Mortelle.*

Mountain explorers will enjoy the trip to *M. Antennamare* (1124m). This is reached by the SS113 from Messina, turning left at S. Rizzo. The journey along the wooded spine of the Peloritani mountains, with views of the coast to the north and east, is exhilarating. Distance: 22km.

Boat services

For boat services to **Reggio Calabria**, **Aeolian Is.** and **Naples**, see p. 17.

Milazzo Town and seaport 45km west of Messina (A20).

Built on the neck of the Capo di Milazzo, the spearhead peninsula that points towards the Aeolian Islands, Milazzo is well placed as a stepping-off point for the exploration of Sicily's northern group of islands.

History The ancient name of the town was *Mylae*, a small settlement established here by the Greeks of Zancle (Messina) in 716 BC. Its strategic position ensured an eventful history for Milazzo, which has been, up to modern times, the victim of innumerable invasions, sieges and bombardments.

The Athenians conquered it in 427 BC: the Greek tyrants of Syracuse, after the rout of the Athenians, later embraced it. A critical naval battle was fought here between the Romans and the Carthaginians in the First Punic War (260 BC). The result, a Roman victory, contributed to their eventual naval supremacy in the Mediterranean.

Warring Roman generals, Saracens and Christians, Spanish and British have all contested Milazzo, which must have welcomed the final arrival of Garibaldi in 1860, driving the Neapolitans before him, in his pursuit of a united Italy.

The town For foreign visitors, Milazzo is mainly identified as the port of embarkation for the **Aeolian Islands**. Steamship and hydrofoil services operate daily between Milazzo and the main islands (for details see p. 17).

Boats leave from the Molo Luigi Rizzo, where tickets may be bought at the agents' offices. There are several hotels and restaurants conveniently situated in the area of the port. Further on towards the peninsula, one may see evidence of Milazzo's other important activity: fishing. At night, along the Marina Garibaldi, the tunny fishermen land their catch: under the light of small fires the knives go to work, cleaning the huge fish for market.

Castle On a high point of the peninsula overlooking the town stands the great castle reconstructed by Charles V in the 16th c., and restored in the 17th c. From ancient times this site has been fortified and defended by successive rulers of Sicily: the last to surrender it were the Neapolitans, driven here by Garibaldi's Thousand in 1860. The castle is reached by turning inland from the Marina Garibaldi (the quickest access is from the Via Cristoforo Colombo). Unfortunately the castle is now used as a prison and can only be viewed from the outside. The *keep* and *north wall* are particularly impressive, as is the site itself, overlooking the sea on either side of the peninsula. Beyond the castle a road runs along the head of the peninsula to the lighthouse on the tip of the Capo di Milazzo. The return journey to Milazzo can be made by the road on the western side, completing a circular tour of the peninsula (total distance 12 km).

Mili S. Pietro Village 3 km from junction on SS114, 9 km south of Messina.
Just before the village, tucked into the hillside below the road, is an old Basilian monastery founded by Count Roger in 1082. Its centrepiece, the tiny church of **S. Maria**, may be recognized by its little central dome and semi-circular apse. This precious relic of the Norman conquest of Sicily is now unhappily derelict. The monastery, which was confiscated by the new Italian state after the unification of 1860 and subsequently abandoned, has become a farmhouse. The church is locked, but with a bit of luck someone may be on hand to open it. The *portal* is 16th c., at some time restored, but the *interior* is in an advanced state of decay. One can distinguish in the murk the typical Basilian form: a small dome at the east end; a central apse and two side apses. A stone in the nave marks the burial place of Count Roger's son, Jordan.

Módica Town in south-east Sicily 12 km east of Ragusa, built on two levels at the foot (*Módica Bassa*) and on the flank (*Módica Alta*) of a mountain spur. The town has some fine churches of different periods.
Most notable for the beauty of its façade and the elegance of its siting is the church of **S. Giorgio** (Chiesa Madre). This church is in Módica Alta and is reached on foot from the Corso Umberto, on the western side of the town, going up a little side street (Corso Garibaldi) to the left of the large 18th c. church of S. Pietro. Continuing the ascent one eventually sees the *façade* of S. Giorgio above, on the right, at the top of a flight of steps. The church was erected between 1702 and 1738 and the graceful façade was the model for many other churches in the region. Other churches of interest are the 15th c. **S. Maria di Gesù**, at the northernmost point of Módica Alta, which retains a Catalan-Gothic *doorway*; the church of the **Carmine** (Piazza Giacomo Matteoti, off the Corso Umberto) which also retains a fine 15th c. *doorway* and *rose window*; and the church of **S. Maria in Betlem**, in the Via Marchesa Tedeschi, off the Corso Umberto. The last-named church was originally built in 1400, but reconstructed in the 18th and 19th c. after the 1693 earthquake. Inside, to the right of the altar, is the remarkable *Cappella del Sacramento*, which combines the styles of almost all the periods of Sicilian architecture.

S. Giorgio, Módica

Mondello Village 13 km north-west of Palermo which has given its name to the capital's main bathing resort, *Mondello Lido*. The village itself, which has a small fishing harbour, sits on a headland closing in a beautiful sandy bay—now the most popular beach in Sicily.

Monreale Town 8 km south-west of Palermo, whose singular attraction, apart from a marvellous view of the Conca d'Oro, is the **Cathedral** which is acknowledged as the finest example of Norman church architecture in Sicily. Visitors without personal transport may take a bus (No. 9) from the Piazza 13 Vittime.

The cathedral is on the east side of the town and is quickly reached in a short (20 minute) journey by car from Palermo. It stands between the Piazza Vittorio Emanuele and the Piazza Guglielmo, and there is reasonable space for parking.

The story behind the foundation of the cathedral is interesting, and rather bizarre. It was the inspiration of William II, the third Norman King of Sicily (1166–1189). William had inherited the throne from his father, William I, while still a child, and during his minority was very much under the thumb of the powerful Archbishop of Palermo, Gualtiero Offamilio (Walter of the Mill). Archbishop Walter had his own plans for the building of a cathedral —the present Santa Maria dell' Assunta, in the city of Palermo—and the only way that William could challenge his power was by building his own cathedral. The site chosen was Mons Regalis (the Latin name for Royal Mountain, later to become the Italian Monreale) which was part of the royal estates created by King Roger to the west of the city. William was anxious to keep the building of his cathedral a secret, and as a subterfuge a Benedictine abbey was founded on the site, its church becoming, later on, the new cathedral and the abbot its bishop. To secure the foundation, the abbey was endowed with vast possessions of land and the titles to various castles and villages, all of which became the property of the new bishopric.

The *exterior* of the cathedral shows the same mixture of architectural styles found in the other great Norman cathedrals in Palermo and Cefalù. The west front is flanked by two square towers. The one on the left, which has lost its upper tier, has battlements and arrow-slits. Conflicting in style with the rest of the façade is the 18th c. *porch*, which would look happier on a monument of Renaissance Rome. This portico replaced the original narthex, but the upper part of the Norman façade with its interesting arches has survived.

The porch is closed by railings which barricade the fine *west doors* of Bonanno da Pisa (1186). These magnificent doors are cast in bronze, with reliefs of scenes from the Old Testament. They may be viewed more closely on application to the sacristan, who will open them for visitors.

On the right of the cathedral is the building which has largely replaced the old Benedictine monastery founded by William II. It is now the *Istituto Statale d'Arte per il Mosaico*, but parts of the old monastery may be viewed in the mornings. It contains a notable painting above the grand staircase of *St Benedict Distributing the Bread* by the 17th c. master Pietro Novelli, who was born in Monreale.

An arched entrance to the right of the building leads through a courtyard to a fine *belvedere* overlooking the valley of the Oreto.

On the left of the cathedral (north side) is a 16th c. *arcade*, the work of two of the sons of the great sculptor Antonello Gagini. Here is the main entrance to the cathedral, with bronze *doors* by another imported artist, Barisano da Trani (1179). His work is more formal than Bonanno's and includes, with much complicated decorative work, seated figures of saints.

Walking around to the *east end* of the cathedral, one can admire the intricate patterns on the stonework of the exterior of the three *apses*. The intersecting arches and medallions, of different types of stone, are similar to those at the east end of Palermo cathedral and show the Arab influence that was so strong in Siculo-Norman architecture.

Interior The cathedral is entered by the north door, already described. The interior is its greatest glory. It is improbable that any church of the period had more exhaustive care or skill lavished on its internal decoration. The Cappella Palatina, for all its richness, is overshadowed by the scale of Monreale. The space seems entrapped here in a huge casket, lined with gold, and once again, as at Cefalù, one's attention is drawn to the commanding presence of the *Christ Pantocrator*, supreme in the semi-dome of the apse.

The columns of the nave—nine on each side —are Roman. The wooden ceiling of the nave is a replacement, the original having been destroyed by fire in 1811. The ceiling of the choir, however, survived the flames, although it has subsequently been much restored. The marble pavement of the cathedral is 16th c.

The **mosaics** cover the walls of both aisles, the west wall, the arches of the nave, and the central and side apses. The area covered by mosaic is calculated to be greater than that in any other Christian church. The mosaics were commenced at the time of the construction of the cathedral (c. 1170) and finished in 1182, i.e. about 40 years later than the similar series of mosaics in the Cathedral of Cefalù. They are, accordingly, further away from the Byzantine tradition, and have lost much of the stylized formality that typifies the earlier

period. What they gain in naturalism, however, the Monreale mosaics seem to lose in impact. The best comparison lies in the two Pantocrators: the one at Cefalù with elongated yet human and compassionate features, the one here, at Monreale, more realistic but remote and untouching.

In such a splendid gallery (the cathedral is 100m long by 40m wide) the mosaics offer a comprehensive exposition of the Christian story. The series begins on the right-hand side of the nave, over the arch nearest to the choir, with the *Creation*. The Old Testament story continues, as in the Cappella Palatina in Palermo, on two levels: around the clerestory and over the arches. It embraces the west wall of the cathedral and completes the cycle at the end of the nave, before the choir, on the north side.

The mosaics of the aisles are devoted to the *Teaching of Christ*, and include scenes of His miracles. On the wall of the aisle to the

Façade, east end and apse

right of the choir are further scenes from the New Testament, including the *Temptation of Christ*, the *Entry into Jerusalem* and the *Betrayal of Christ*. On the wall of the aisle to the left of the choir the story continues with scenes of the *Passion*.

The mosaics of the small apses on either side of the central apse are devoted to *St Peter* (right) and *St Paul* (left), with the scene of each saint's martyrdom over the arch in front of each apse.

In the central apse we return to the focal point of this great firmament of mosaic, the *Christ Pantocrator*. Here Christ is shown in benediction and in this gesture, emphasized by the enfolding drapery over His shoulders and extended arm, He seems to embrace the world. In the vault above are the strange six-winged *cherubim*, also seen at Cefalù, and below them, *archangels*. On the face of the arch of this vault is the *Annunciation*. Below Christ, in the curve of the apse, is a *Madonna and Child Enthroned, with Archangels and Apostles*. Below them, and elsewhere in the sanctuary and choir, are numerous *saints*. Among them (centre of lower row on right of east window) is *St Thomas*, the famous Thomas a'Becket who was Archbishop of Canterbury under Henry II and who was murdered in 1170, hardly more than a decade before this commemorative mosaic. It is interesting to note here that William II, the patron of Monreale, was married to one of Henry II's daughters (Joan). The championing of Becket was probably done to spite the English king, who was little loved by his offspring.

On the walls above the choir are scenes from the *Birth and Early Life of Jesus*, starting on the south wall (upper level) with the *Annunciation* and ending on the north wall (lower level) with the *Baptism of Christ*.

Above the royal throne, on the left-hand pillar of the choir, is the mosaic of *Christ Crowning William II*. This is greatly inferior to the work from which it was derived (*Christ Crowning Roger II* in the Martorana) and students of the mosaic work of the Byzantine period who compare the treatment of the figures will see how much inspiration was lost in the 40 years between the two works. The mosaic over the bishop's throne, on the right, shows *William II Offering the Cathedral to the Virgin*.

On the right of the choir are the *Royal Tombs* of William I (d. 1166) and of William II (d. 1189). A door leads off to the 16th c. Baroque *Cappella di San Benedetto* which has a relief of St Benedict by Marabitti (1760) over the altar. On the left of the choir, to the north, are further tombs of the family of William I. More Baroque decoration, this time in the more effusive style of the 17th c., is in the adjoining *Cappella del Crocifisso*. Leading off this chapel is the *Treasury* (admission charge). At the west end of the south aisle a door leads to a steep flight of steps ascending to the roof. There is an admission charge and 180 steps, but the view is more than a consolation.

Cloister (entrance fee, access from south side of Piazza Guglielmo, to the right of cathedral) Hours: 09.00–15.00 (last entrance 14.30) Sun & hol 09.00–13.00 (last entrance 12.30). Closed Tues.

When churches with cloisters are such a rarity in Sicily the discovery here of one of the finest medieval cloisters in Italy is a special pleasure. Visitors to Rome will find in these elegant arcades all the subtleties of carving and decoration familiar to them from the Romanesque cloisters of the same period, in such grand churches as S. Paolo fuori le Mura and S. Giovanni in

Laterano. Most reminiscent are the twin columns, some of them elaborately carved, others inlaid with beautiful mosaic patterns in the Cosmatesque style.

But while making this comparison one cannot overlook the differences that give the Monreale cloister its own special character. First, the arches are not rounded as in the Romanesque churches but given a slight point: an Arabic touch that finds an echo in the patterning of the arches. The second unique detail is the variety of the capitals which top the columns. In all there are 216 capitals, paired together on the double columns and elaborately carved. They are the work of artists from southern Italy, whose skills were given free reign by their Sicilian masters. The result is a fascinating miscellany of motifs, taken from nature, mythology and the Bible, and scenes narrated, almost in the round, on the joined capitals. Such scenes are either taken from everyday life (the vintage is a popular subject) or from the Bible. As elsewhere in the cathedral, the King's seal is on this cloister. One of the carvings represents *William II Presenting the Cathedral to the Virgin Mary.*

In the south-west corner of the cloister, in its own colonnaded enclosure, is a delightful *fountain*, formed of a single decorated column topped by a little cluster of lion-head spouts.

Monte Pellegrino (606 m)   Mountain dominating Palermo and the Conca d'Oro from the north (see **Palermo**, Excursions)

Monte San Calogero see Sciacca

Morgantina Ancient site, near village of Aidone, 15 km north-east of Piazza Armerina. Approaching from Catania, the best route (65 km) is the SS192, linking with the SS288. Approaching the site from Piazza Armerina (SS288) turn left after 8 km before entering Aidone (sign-post Catania). After 2 km, rejoin the 288 and turn right. In a further 3 km, look out for the sign 'Scavi Morgantina'. A left turn takes us in 2 km to the site.

History Sited on a ridge (Serra Orlando) the ancient city was founded by Greeks from Katane in the 6th c. BC. There is evidence of earlier settlement going back as far as the 12th c. BC, and it is apparent that the ancient inhabitants, the Sicels, lived here as a subordinate population of the Greeks. The city reached the peak of its development under the later Greek tyrants, from Timoleon to Hieron II, and most of the visible ruins date from this period (4th–3rd c. BC).

The ruins The site is entered from the south-west. On the left is a *gymnasium* of the Roman period, and on the slope to the right *public buildings.* Before us, in a valley between two low hills, lies the large *agora* with a *portico* on the left. In the centre

Cloister and fountain, Monreale

of the agora is a flight of steps in the shape of a trapezoid which connected the upper to the lower agora. This was also used as a stand for assemblies. To the west of this are the rectangular excavations of the *macellum* or provisions market.

On the hill to the north are the recently excavated houses of the *residential quarter*, with—at the top and to the right—the *House of Ganymede*. Preserved here are two mosaics, one representing *Ganymede* (damaged), the other geometric.

On the hill to the south is a small *theatre* and in front of it a *sanctuary* dedicated to Demeter and Persephone.

To the east of the agora lie the *granaries* and *pottery*.

Motya

Motya (Mozia) Ancient site on island of San Pantaleo, 1 km off west coast, 9 km north of Marsala.

This site is of special interest to the historian and archaeologist, as it is the only comprehensive Phoenician site in Sicily. Much of the preliminary excavation was done by Mr J. Whitaker, head of the wine-exporting family who own the island. Since his death excavations have continued sporadically and it is hoped that future discoveries will give us greater knowledge of these early settlers of western Sicily.

To reach Motya, a turning should be made off the secondary road between Trápani and Marsala at Spagnuola (19 km south of Trápani, 9 km north of Marsala: watch out for signpost 'Mozia'). A track (keep bearing left) leads to a jetty, where a signal—white handkerchief, waved vigorously—should bring a response from the boatman on the far shore. The best time to come here, to ensure getting across, is early in the morning.

History Motya began as a Phoenician trading post in the 8th c. BC. The small island, just off the west coast of Sicily, was perfectly situated to command their main trading route—the strip of the Mediterranean between Sicily and their colonies in North Africa. Later on, during the Carthaginian period, the island was fortified and became their major base in Sicily, a supply depot for the war materials shipped in from Carthage for the campaigns against the Greeks.

In 397 BC, the peak year of the power of Dionysius I, the Greeks were laying siege to Motya. The historian Diodorus has described the fantastic effort of the Greeks to reduce the Carthaginian stronghold. Catapults and siege-towers were used, the latter built to a height of six stories to match the height of the buildings on the island. The defenders finally succumbed and the city was totally destroyed. It was, however, an unsatisfactory conquest, for Dionysius had to return to Syracuse and leave a garrison at Motya. The inevitable sequel was the reconquest of the island by the Carthaginians, the following

year, under the leadership of Himilco. But there could be no future for such a devastated city, and the population was moved to the new stronghold of Lilybaeum.

The ruins The landing-place is near the museum, which houses an interesting collection of finds from Motya, from the burial ground of Birgi on the mainland, and from Lilybaeum.

The island is best explored by following the coastline, on which remains of the ancient fortifications, including towers and gates, may be seen. Working in a clockwise direction one discovers first—100m south of the *museum*—the *House of Mosaics*. This was built in the 3rd c. BC on the site of an earlier Phoenician house, and has a courtyard with a fine black-and-white pebble mosaic (before the finer tesserae were introduced by the Romans, pebbles were used for this type of pavement). Further on (120m) are the remains of a *barracks* and beyond (300m) the *south gate*. Beside this is the *cothon*, a small artificial dock. This Phoenician harbour, the only one in Sicily, was lined with stone. Its narrow entrance could be closed to an enemy.

Continuing around the west coast to the north side of the island, one reaches the excavations of the *Phoenician burial grounds*. Here were found small amphorae containing human and animal bones, evidence of the Phoenician custom of sacrificing children and small animals to appease their gods.

110

Further on is the *north gate*, which had a double entrance. From here a *causeway*, below the level of the water, connects Motya to the mainland at Birgi, the site of another burial ground. In their attempt to obstruct Dionysius and the Greeks, the Carthaginians destroyed part of this causeway: but the Greek tyrant was able to rebuild it and resume his attack.

Inland from the north gate are the remains of a 6th c. BC *Phoenician sanctuary*. The tour is completed by returning along the east coast to the museum.

Naro Town 11 km south-east of junction on SS122, 21 km north-east of Agrigento.

The interest of this attractive hill town lies in the architecture surviving from the 13th c.: the battlemented walls and the **Castello dei Chiaramonte** at the highest part of the town. There are also a number of 17th c. Baroque churches. Externally, the most exuberant of them is the church of **S. Francesco**, in the Piazza Garibaldi. Internally, one must admire the **Chiesa Matrice** in the Via Lucchesi (off the Piazza Garibaldi) with its rich stucco work and sculpture by the Gagini.

Naxos Ancient site on Capo Schiso, 4.5 km south of Taormina. The site is best reached through Giardino: Capo Schiso and the ruins of Naxos lie to the south.

History This was the first colony founded by the Greeks in Sicily, c. 757 BC. The settlers were Chalcidians from Euboea and Ionians from Naxos in the Cyclades. Although the site was well chosen the colony did not develop as rapidly as those that followed it. The reason was almost certainly that as the first colony it acted as the springboard for the others. Naxiots founded Katane (Catania) and Leontinoi (Lentini): both cities which grew and prospered to a much greater extent than Naxos.

In 490 BC Naxos fell to Hippocrates of Gela, and later on was dominated by Hieron I of Syracuse. During the war between Syracuse and Athens it sided with the latter, an alliance which brought the inevitable reprisal of Syracuse. In 403 BC Dionysius I completely destroyed the town.

The ruins Originally, the walls of Naxos enclosed Capo Schiso. Now their visible remains are largely concentrated on the south-western extremity of the city, on the bank of the Santa Venera River. The wall here consists of one long stretch (280 m) of large blocks of lava, the *muro megalitico*. This meets, at the south-west corner of the town, the *muro poligonale*—another wall of smaller polygonal blocks which fit precisely together, like the walls of similar construction in Delphi and other sites in ancient Greece.

In the angle formed by the two walls lies the sacred area of Naxos, probably dedicated to Aphrodite, with the foundations of a 5th c. BC *temple*. Nearby, under protective roofs, are the interesting remains of two ancient *brick kilns* (6th c. BC).

Extensive excavations are now in progress at Naxos (a complete citrus grove has been taken over by the Soprintendente Antichita) and one can only guess at the revelations to come in this largely unexplored site of Greece's first Sicilian colony.

At the point of Capo Schiso (reached by the sea promenade) is a newly-opened **museum** with further remains, in its garden, of the ancient walls.

Nebrodi Mountain chain in northern Sicily, between the Madonie in the west and the Peloritani in the east. Highest point: Monte Soro (1847 m).

Nicolosi see **Etna**

Nicosia Town in eastern Sicily, 48 km from the north coast.

Its position to the south of the coastal mountain range of the Nebrodi put Nicosia on the map in medieval times as a stopping-place on the road from Messina to Palermo, the route used by travellers before the construction of the coast road. The old buildings of the town, stacked against the steeply-pitched hillside, make an impressive and irregular composition, completed by the ruined Norman castle at the highest point. The town is full of churches, too numerous to detail, that bear in their fabric the texture of old Sicily. Most impressive is the 14th c. **Cathedral** (S. Nicola) in the Piazza Garibaldi. The façade preserves a *doorway* with a finely-carved arch of the period: the figures of *Virtues* and the four *lions* being late 16th c. additions. The fine Gothic *campanile* is also 14th c., the *portico* on the left side 15th c. Inside the cathedral note the beautiful engraved *choir stalls* (1622) and work by the Gagini (*pulpit*, *font*) and Marabitti (*Monument to Alessandro Testa*, right of entrance).

Higher up is the church of **S. Maria Maggiore**, founded in the 13th c., but destroyed in the 18th c. by a landslide. The reconstruction has incorporated a fine Baroque *portal*. Inside the church is the so-called *Throne of Charles V*, supposed to have accommodated the great Emperor during his progress through Sicily in 1535. There is also a monumental marble *polyptych* by Antonello Gagini in the presbytery, completed in 1512, with *Scenes from the Life of the Virgin*.

Noto Town in south-eastern Sicily 32 km south of Syracuse. Outstanding for the symmetry of its street plan and the quality of its architecture.

After the earlier town, Noto Antica, had been destroyed by the 1693 earthquake, the present town was constructed on a new site, 16 km from the old. It accordingly presents, to the eye wearied by the concrete development of the coast, a refreshing picture of Spanish Sicily, characterized by the exuberant Baroque typical of the region.

Walking tour The focal point of Noto is the Piazza Municipio, with the cathedral to the north, at the head of a flight of steps, and the Municipio to the south. (Cars may be parked in the square.)

The splendid *façade* of the **Cathedral**, mounted on its broad, gently-stepped plinth, is one of the sights of Noto. In the morning the stone is near-white in the clear light: later on, as the sun sets, the full richness of the stone's natural golden colour emerges. The cathedral was finished in 1776: much of the decoration inside is modern.

Opposite the cathedral is another fine façade: that of the Municipio, the 18th c. **Palazzo Ducezio**. The convex centre of this arcaded front is a pleasing variation. To explore Noto the visitor is recommended to go on foot, as follows:

East of the cathedral To the right of the cathedral is the *Bishop's Palace*: to the right side of the square in front of it is the church of **SS. Salvatore**, backed by its convent (now a seminary). On the opposite side of the Corso Vittorio Emanuele is the church of **S. Chiara**. This has an unusual elliptical form, as will be best seen inside. Also inside (2nd altar on the left) is a *Madonna and Child* by

Antonello Gagini. Continuing to the east one may have a view, up the Via G. Zanardelli, of the extraordinary undulating Baroque of the exterior of the convent of SS. Salvatore, already mentioned. This elaborate treatment makes an interesting comparison with the more formal church of **S. Francesco d'Assisi**, opposite, also built in the early 18th c.

In the convent building (No 134 Corso Vittorio Emanuele) is Noto's small **museum**. Half of the museum—the most interesting part—is devoted to finds made at Eloro (Helorus), the Greek site which lies on the coast south of Noto. Especially fascinating is the reconstruction of the *Sanctuary of Demeter and Kore*. The eastern wall of the sanctuary is here reassembled, showing the votive statuettes fixed in position. Also shown are three *bothroi* (the votive holes in which the sacrifices were made).

West of the cathedral To the left of the cathedral is the *Palazzo Sant'Alfano*. Facing it, across the Via Corrado Nicolaci, is the **Palazzo Villadorata** (1737). The extraordinary perspective of this building is best appreciated by walking up the Via Nicolaci. The way in which such a versatile—almost eccentric—edifice was designed to conform with the steep rise of the street is a tribute to the skill of the architect, P. Labisi. His achievement lies also in the skilful merging of the glorious Baroque balconies in the strictly classical façade: balconies supported by monsters, maidens, cherubs, winged horses and lions. At the top of the street, closing off the perspective, is the concave façade of the church of *Monte Vergine*, in the Via Cavour.

Cathedral, Noto

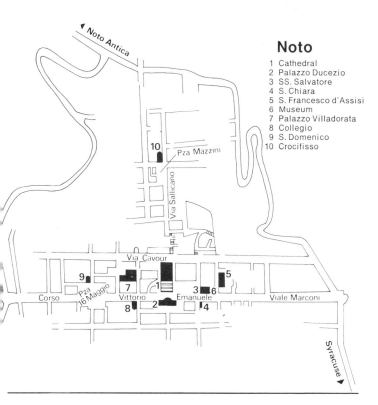

Noto

1 Cathedral
2 Palazzo Ducezio
3 SS. Salvatore
4 S. Chiara
5 S. Francesco d'Assisi
6 Museum
7 Palazzo Villadorata
8 Collegio
9 S. Domenico
10 Crocifisso

Balcony, Noto

Returning to the Corso, continue west past another fine 18th c. church, the **Collegio**, to the Piazza 16 Maggio. This is Noto's central square, where the Netini—as the people of this charming town are known—gather for the evening gossip. On the north side of the square is a small garden with a fountain topped by a 16th c. figure of *Hercules*, recovered from Noto Antica. Behind is the church of **S. Domenico**, whose graceful convex façade turns a rich golden colour at sunset.

North of the cathedral Steps lead up from behind the cathedral, and to the right of the *Palazzo Astuto* in the Via Cavour, to the Via Sallicano. From here one soon reaches the Piazza Mazzini, with the church of the **Crocifisso** on the north side. The façade of this church is incomplete. On either side of the entrance portal is a Romanesque *lion*, recovered from Noto Antica. Inside the church is a unique work: the only signed sculpture by Francesco Laurana in Sicily. This is his *Madonna della Neve* (1417).

Noto Antica Medieval site, 16 km northwest of Noto. Reached by turning off SS287 10 km north of Noto, 21 km south of Palazzolo Acréide.

This is the old Noto, destroyed by the earthquake of 1693. The ruins are very sparse, but the excursion, through a varied countryside, is very pleasant. 2 km after passing the convent of *S. Maria della Scala*, the ruins of the east wall of the old city will be seen across a valley. The road leads round to the entrance, an arch set between crumbling ramparts. To the right are the remains of a castle, much overgrown by foliage. The rest of the ruins which lie on either side of a track running on from the entrance, are similarly obscured, and it is necessary to leave the track to explore them.

After 1 km the track reaches a shrine, where it forks. The left hand track peters out amidst more ruins: the right hand track continues for 1 km to the **Eremo della Madonna della Providenza**. This old convent, founded in the 18th c. in remembrance of the earthquake, houses fragments of some of the destroyed buildings in its corridors. The adjacent church, its plaster riddled with wasps' nests, looks ready to join the ruins it commemorates.

Ortygia see **Syracuse**

Palazzolo Acréide Town 43 km west of Syracuse, associated with the ancient city of Akrai just outside it to the west.

The central square of the modern town, the Piazza del Popolo, is dominated by the huge 17th c. church of **S. Sebastiano**. From here the Via Maestranza and the Via Garibaldi lead the visitor to the heart of the 18th c. town, which was created, like so many towns in this region, after the disastrous 1693 earthquake. In the Piazza Umberto I stands the impressive church of **S. Paolo**, with an exuberant porticoed façade.

The route to Akrai (signed 'Teatro Greco') is via the Corso Vittorio Emanuele. This leads from the Piazza del Popolo already mentioned, and one should note, at the beginning of the Corso, the fine 18th c. buildings of the **Palazzo Iudica** (No 10) and the **Palazzo Pizzo-Guglielmino** (No 38). At the end of the Corso, in the higher part of the town, stands the church of the **Immacolata**, where admirers of Francesco Laurana should pause to do homage. In the nave is another of his beautiful *Madonna and Child* statues (1470). From here the road leads (500 m) to the entrance of the ancient **Akrai**, founded by the Greeks of Syracuse as a military outpost in 664 BC. (The archaeological zone is closed to visitors between 13.00 and 15.30.)

The outpost, which later became a thriving town, was strategically sited on a hill (771 m) between the Anapo and Tellaro Rivers. The town reached its greatest prosperity in the 3rd c. BC, during the stable rule of Hieron II of Syracuse. After a period of decline under the Romans it came to the fore again as a centre of Christian worship: evidence of this is in the multitude of rock-cut tombs on the site.

Tour of the ruins A short walk from the entrance is the small **Greek theatre** (Teatro Greco) built in the 3rd c. BC. Well preserved are the 12 rows of seats and the pavement of the orchestra, also the base of the scene building. In front of the latter is a Roman addition: the foundations of a stage. Just to the north of the theatre are the openings of two Roman-Byzantine grain silos.

To the west of the theatre is the *Bouleuterion*, or Senate council chamber, which consisted of a rectangular room with semicircular seating. The area to the west of this has been identified as the *agora*. Behind the theatre, to the south, are two quarries, the **Intagliata** and the **Intagliatella**, which contain rock-cut catacombs and dwellings of the Byzantine period. A third quarry, known as the **Templi Ferali**, lies to the south-east. These quarries were originally reserved

Theatre, Palazzolo Acréide

for the worship of ancestors who were venerated as heroes—a cult which will already be familiar to those who have visited Syracuse. In the walls of the Intagliatella are recesses for commemorative tablets; also an interesting relief of the 2nd c. BC which combines a Greek scene (*Heroes Banqueting*) with a Roman scene (*Heroes Offering Sacrifice*).

Although the memorials to the Greek dead were inside the town, it should be noted that they were buried outside the walls, as revealed by the discovery of a large necropolis to the east. The Christians, on the other hand, were entombed within the walls, in the catacombs to the south.

If a custodian is available, it is best to tour the site in his company. There are many nooks and crannies to explore in these quarries and he will know the most interesting. There is also the outside chance of an unaccompanied explorer missing his footing and either disappearing down an ancient *pozzo* (well) or falling into a rock-cut tomb!

A guide will also be necessary for a visit to the **Santoni**. These are twelve representations of the eastern goddess Cybele, with lions and attendant figures, cut out of the rock in the nearby valley of the Santicello. They were carved in the 3rd c. BC, close together in a row. The origins of the cult of Cybele in Sicily are not clear, although it is known that the goddess was worshipped in Corinth, the mother city of Syracuse. Originally the figures would have been covered in stucco and painted: now they are badly worn and protected by locked cupboards, which the custodian will open for visitors.

Palermo

Palermo (pop. 663,000) Capital of Sicily and one of Italy's principal ports (A19, A29). Undoubtedly this is also one of the most magnificently situated cities in Italy. The plain in which it stands, enclosed by mountains, is called the *Conca d'Oro*, or 'Golden Shell'—a name attributed to its shape and its fertility. The first is defined most obviously by the curve on the map of the SS121, Palermo's *circonvallazione*: the second by the endless groves of citrus and other rich vegetation that holds the city in a green embrace, best seen from one of its mountain approaches (either from Montelepre, Monreale, or Altofonte). It is these mountains which are the key to the whole effect: headed to the north by the hunched mass of Monte Pellegrino and to the south by the higher but more distant Monte Grifone.

History Such a site could not fail to capture the imagination of the seafaring Phoenicians, who founded a colony here in the 8th c. BC. There is no definite record of a Phoenician name for the settlement (the name 'Ziz' appearing on Phoenician coins of the period has been suggested) and the ancient port is generally known by the name given it by the

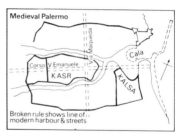

Medieval Palermo

Broken rule shows line of modern harbour & streets

Greeks, *Panormos* (meaning 'all-haven'). Apart from brief incursions by Hermocrates and Pyrrhus, the Greeks themselves were never in possession of the city. It remained —with Solus to the east and Motya to the south—one of the three strongholds of Punic settlement in Sicily until its conquest by the Romans in 254 BC.

The Roman Panormus was one of the five cities of the province accorded a special status by Rome, exempting it from tribute. It was later one of the first bishoprics of the early Christian Church. In the 5th c. AD the barbarians swept across Sicily and Panormus became a stronghold of the Goths. Delivered by Belisarius in 535 AD, it remained for three centuries—with the rest of Sicily— a part of the Byzantine Empire.

Panormus became 'Balerm' under the Arabs and 'Palermo' under the Normans. These conquerors were the most significant in the history of Palermo, both bringing to the city their very different, but equally stimulating, cultures.

Under the Saracens, who conquered the city in 831 AD (after a year's siege, and at the cost of nearly its entire population of 70,000) Palermo became the capital of an emirate and one of the great centres of Arab civilization. By the end of the 10th c. the city was beginning to take the shape which is still at the heart of modern Palermo. To the east was the harbour whose name—*Cala*—is retained today in the old port. To the south of the harbour was the *Kalsa* (again the name prevails), which was a walled quarter reserved for the Sultan and his court. To the west, on high land between two rivers was the *Kasr* (now *Cassaro*) or citadel—where the Palace of the Normans stands today. On either side—to the north and south of the two rivers—the first suburbs were created. Like the other parts of the city these were walled and became quarters with their own distinct character.

In 1072 the Saracen capital fell to the Normans under Roger de Hauteville (Count Roger). There was not, however, the butchery that accompanied the Saracenic conquest. The Normans' primary instincts were commercial and they maintained the same administrative system that had operated

PALERMO

*'Description of the capital of Sicilia—
may Allah give it back to the Muslims!*

*Ancient and elegant, splendid and
passing fair, she rises before you like
an enchantress, enthroned among
her open spaces and her plains that
are like unto one garden. With
spacious alleys and main thoroughfares she dazzles the eye with the
rare loveliness of her aspect. A
stupendous city, like Cordova in her
architecture, her buildings all of cut
stone . . .*

*The king found in her every pleasure
of the earth and made her the capital
of his Frankish realm . . .*

*What delights he has there—may
Allah prevent him from enjoying
them!'*

Ibn Jubair, an Arab travelling in Sicily
1184–5

under the Saracens. They also allowed the
Moslem inhabitants full civic freedom and
the right to practice their religion. Most sig-
nificantly, they employed Arab craftsmen to
construct and decorate their buildings, and
it is to this Norman fostering of the skills of
the conquered race that we owe the survival
of so much of their art.

The man who did most to create the splendours of the Arabo-Norman city was Roger
II (1130–54), son of the conquering Count. In
addition to great architectural achievements
(the Palace of the Normans and Cappella
Palatina, and the churches of the Martorana
and St John of the Hermits were built during
his rule), Roger was responsible for the lay-
out of the great parks, used for hunting and
other pursuits, in the surrounding countryside. His work was continued by his successors and by the end of Norman rule (1194)
the city of Palermo—with a port commanding
trade routes from Africa, Europe and Asia—
had become one of the most prosperous and
splendid cities of the Mediterranean.

Under the Emperor Frederick II (Frederick I
of Sicily), who had his court here (1198–
1250), the city continued to flourish, and to

its other attributes were added the intellectual activity he stimulated. The birth and growth of Sicily's vernacular poetry and the pursuit of the sciences—particularly mathematics, medicine and natural history—were the accomplishments of this period. After so much sweetness and light it was inevitable that the Palermitans should react violently to the vicious rule of Charles of Anjou (1268–82) and it was in Palermo—at the church of S. Spirito—that the rebellion against the French Angevins (the Sicilian Vespers) broke out.

The long period of Spanish rule—starting with the Aragonese kings and ending with the Viceroys—had an increasingly oppressive effect on the city. The main impact was architectural. In the 16th c. the two rivers which ran through the city were drained and filled in and the walls of the old suburbs destroyed. A new port was created to the north of the city, and the large thoroughfares, which still control Palermo's traffic flow, were constructed. The 17th c. saw the building of much of the fine Baroque architecture which gives the old part of Palermo its present character.

Under Bourbon rule (1734–1860) Palermo was a poor relation to Naples, capital of the Kingdom of the Two Sicilies. Twice, however, as a result of the French occupation of Naples (1799 and 1806) Ferdinand IV brought his court here, and some of the rooms he used, decorated in the Bourbon style, may be seen in the Palace of the Normans.

In 1820 and 1848 the people of Palermo rebelled against the Bourbons. With a population largely sympathetic to the cause of liberation and the unification of Italy, Sicily made a good starting point for the campaign of Garibaldi and the Thousand. On 27 May 1860, after fierce street fighting in which the citizens played a heroic part, the Bourbon troops were routed and the triumphant Redshirts—who had landed in the island only two weeks previously—occupied the city.

After unification Palermo found a new status as one of the principal cities of the Kingdom of Italy and developed rapidly as a commercial and cultural centre through which the awakening South could effect a greater participation in the affairs of Europe. In 1946 it became the capital of the autonomous Region of Sicily, with its own Parliament.

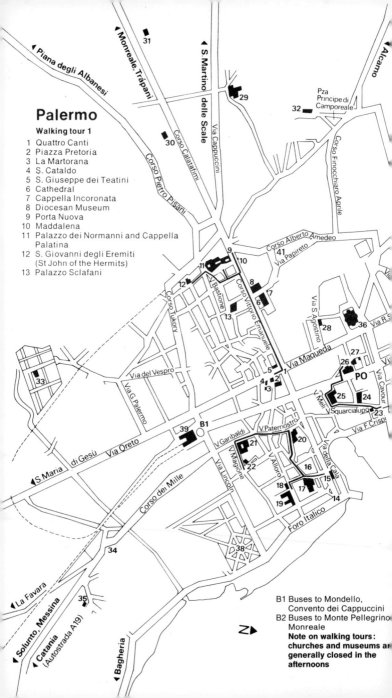

Palermo

Walking tour 1

1 Quattro Canti
2 Piazza Pretoria
3 La Martorana
4 S. Cataldo
5 S. Giuseppe dei Teatini
6 Cathedral
7 Cappella Incoronata
8 Diocesan Museum
9 Porta Nuova
10 Maddalena
11 Palazzo dei Normanni and Cappella Palatina
12 S. Giovanni degli Eremiti (St John of the Hermits)
13 Palazzo Sclafani

B1 Buses to Mondello, Convento dei Cappuccini
B2 Buses to Monte Pellegrino, Monreale
Note on walking tours: churches and museums are generally closed in the afternoons

Walking tour 2

14 Porta Felice
15 S. Maria della Catena
16 Giardino Garibaldi
17 Palazzo Chiaramonte
18 La Gancia
19 Palazzo Abbatellis (National Gallery)
20 S. Francesco d'Assisi, Oratorio di
   S. Lorenzo
21 Palazzo Aiutamicristo
22 La Magione

Walking tour 3

23 Piazza S. Giorgio
24 S. Zita, Oratorio di S. Zita
25 S. Domenico, Oratorio del Rosario di
   S. Domenico
26 Olivella
27 Archaeological Museum

28 S. Agostino
29 Convento dei Cappuccini
30 Cuba
31 Cubula
32 Zisa
33 S. Spirito
34 Ponte dell'Ammiraglio
35 S. Giovanni dei Lebbrosi
36 Teatro Massimo
37 Politeama Garibaldi
38 Orto Botanico
39 Station
40 Tourist Information Office
41 Papireto Market

The modern city The extensive development to the north of the city, seen by visitors arriving from the airport, is a mask over the face of the real Palermo. Likewise, the seaward approach, though dramatic in terms of landscape, offers in close-up only the unattractive view of the seafront—so thoroughly bombed during the last war and still only partially renewed. Only when one is on foot, and exploring at one's leisure, can one discover the true fascination of the inner city with its labyrinthine streets, Spanish and Norman palaces and churches, and the essentially Palermitan atmosphere which can only be described as a perplexing—and often provoking—mixture of calm and vitality. The vitality has many guises. At one extreme is the Via Roma in the rush-hour: a corridor of noise with every driver jostling for position and resting his elbow on his horn. The Quattro Canti too, at the heart of the old city, which at least has a policeman to adjudicate. In the evenings the Palermitan on foot creates another kind of bustle. The activity is concentrated here on Palermo's 'West End' which lies very approximately between the two great opera-houses, the Teatro Massimo and the Politeama Garibaldi. The latter overlooks the double square of the Piazza Ruggero Settimo and the Piazza Castelnuovo with its garden—a favourite spot for open-air concerts and folk-lore festivals. The link with the Teatro Massimo is the Via Ruggero Settimo, and in this area is the greatest concentration of cinemas, restaurants, bars and *pasticerrie*, which provide a focus for the night life of the city.

Vitality is found on a smaller scale in the Papireto market, not far from the cathedral, where one can buy any variety of 'folk' souvenir, from a piece of the tail-board of a Sicilian *carretta* to a marionette in a full suit of armour. This is the art of the *artigiani*, the Sicilian craftsmen whose work is inseparable from the traditions of the island. This combination of art and tradition will best be enjoyed by a visit to the *opera dei pupi*, one of the tiny marionette theatres tucked away in the back streets of the city. Here one can behold, on a diminutive stage, the re-enactment of the legendary battles of Orlando and Rinaldo, the crusading knights, against the Moorish infidels: an entertainment that happily still enthrals the Palermitans as much as the tourists.

For calm, one does not have to search too far. In the old part of the city one can pause for a while in the gardens of the Villa Bonanno, by the Palace of the Normans, and find that one is in the company of a large number of like-minded Palermitans. A more rarified calm may be found nearby in the exquisite cloistered garden of the little church of St John of the Hermits, surely one of the most treasured corners of old Palermo. For those who enjoy tranquillity on a larger scale there

are the gardens of the Villa Giulia and the Orto Botanico (Botanical Gardens) on the Via Lincoln, or—on the north side of the city —the Park of the Favorita. Gardens apart, one cannot equal the experience of that embalmed silence, a thousand miles from the din of traffic, that exists in the gem-like Arabo-Norman interiors of the Cappella Palatina and the church of the Martorana. These places of worship, created by the servants of Allah and of God alike, have a universality that crosses the barriers of creed: few can fail to find peace within their walls.

Walking tour 1 (see map) *Quattro Canti— Piazza Pretoria—La Martorana—S. Cataldo —S. Giuseppe dei Teatini—Cathedral— Museo Diocesano—Porta Nuova—La Maddalena—Palazzo dei Normanni—Cappella Palatina—S. Giovanni degli Eremiti—Palazzo Sclafani*
At the intersection of the Via Maqueda and the Corso Vittorio Emanuele, the **Quattro Canti** or 'Four Corners' is still the hub of old Palermo. Heavy motor traffic, however, has made an irrelevance of this 17th c. curiosity, with its extravagant Baroque decoration. The four corners, once a tribute to the glories of Imperial Spain, are now scorned by the heedless activity of the modern city, and it is difficult for the visitor to get a good view of the façades without getting caught up in the maelstrom. Each façade, angled across the corner, has three cornices. The top is dominated by the imperial eagle, the centre one by a patron saint of the city and the lower one by a Spanish king of Sicily. At ground level there is a fountain at each corner, supporting a figure of one of the *Seasons*. The Viceroys of Spain are also commemorated, their names inscribed on plaques above each fountain.
Immediately to the south of the Quattro Canti, off the Via Maqueda, is the Piazza Pretoria. Dominating this square is the large **Fontana Pretoria**, a rather elaborate fountain on which the nymphs and river-gods seem to have created their own population problem. This fountain is 16th c. Florentine work and was originally intended for a villa: in 1573 it was acquired by the city of Palermo.
On the south side of the square is the **Palazzo del Municipio**, formerly the Pretorio (magistrate's office) a 16th c. building with 19th c. restorations. On the east, from the same period, is the church of **S. Caterina**. This is a convent church and is almost invariably closed, but it is worth checking the south door (overlooking the adjoining Piazza Bellini) in case it chances to be open. The *interior* of the church is worth seeing for its fine Baroque decoration, and there is a statue of *St Catherine* by Antonello Gagini in the right transept.
Opposite S. Caterina, on the south side of the Piazza Bellini, are two churches which be-

tween them bridge 500 years of Palermo's history. The high podium on which they stand —a section of the old city walls—sets them apart, appropriately, from the whirl of modern Palermo.

La Martorana One of the most beautiful and interesting of Sicily's smaller churches: not to be hurried by those who have elsewhere enjoyed the extraordinary synthesis of Norman, Byzantine and Arab skills that characterizes Palermo's contribution to Christian art.

The church, originally named S. Maria dell'Ammiraglio, was founded in 1143 by Roger II's admiral, George of Antioch. Its name was changed when in 1433 it became the church of an adjacent Benedictine convent, founded by Eloisa Martorana in 1194. The present bizarre mixture of Norman and Baroque architecture dates from the alterations to the church carried out in the 16th and 17th c. The old narthex and entrance portico were demolished to make way for the present enlarged narthex, with its Baroque façade on the north; later on the old Greek-style apse was enlarged into the present choir. Fortunately the original body of the Norman church, capped by its central dome, survives. So too does the beautiful 12th c. **campanile**. This structure, though now deprived of its cupola, retains four tiers with double windows in the Arabo-Norman style. As they ascend they become lighter and more graceful, the top two levels with rounded and recessed corners set with classical columns similar to those used in the windows.

The conflicting styles of the church's exterior are repeated inside. The builders of the 17th c. *narthex* were able to utilize the columns and capitals of the Norman portico, which happily were not overwhelmed by the subsequent Baroque decoration (Borremans). Also preserved from the old portico are two *mosaic panels* (on the original west wall) which have lost a little of their charm in some heavy-handed restoration. In *George of Antioch Kneeling at the Feet of Mary* (left) the figure of the church's founder has been particularly badly handled. More impressive is the panel showing *Roger II Crowned by*

Above: Piazza Pretoria   *Martorana, S. Cataldo*

Christ (right) the only portrait we have of the Norman king. At the south side of the narthex is a 12th c. wooden door with Arabic carving, a rare discovery in Sicily.

The nave of the church continues the contrast, with Norman columns topped by Corinthian capitals supporting arches and vaults decorated in the Baroque style. At the third arch, however, one has entered the Greek cross and returned to the full glory of the Norman-Byzantine church with its festival of brilliantly coloured **mosaics**. The founder of the church, himself a Byzantine, employed Greek artists to carry out the work, and one sees here the perfect expression of a golden age, echoed at Monreale, Cefalù and the Cappella Palatina. The mosaic of the cupola, *Christ with Archangels*, shows the seated figure of Christ surrounded by archangels. The Greek inscription in the roundel reads 'I am the Light of the World. . . .' In the octagonal drum below the cupola are portraits of eight *Prophets*, and in the corner niches, the four *Evangelists*.

Below the drum, in the east and west arches of the crossing respectively, are the *Annunciation* (note the unusual representation of the Virgin with the distaff on her lap) and *Presentation in the Temple*. In the vault of the arch leading into the choir are the figures of the archangels *Michael* and *Gabriel*. The choir itself is decorated in the Rococo style and seems sadly at odds with its Byzantine setting. The apses on either side of the choir contain mosaics of saints: on the left, *St Joachim*, on the right, *St Anne*. Further saints are in the vaults on either side of the crossing, in the medallions of the archivolts, and in the upper part of the south wall. Elsewhere the treatment is decorative, and one can find particular delight in the rich blue star-spangled vaults of the side aisles.

In the eastern vault of the nave are two mosaics worth careful study. On the north is a delicate *Nativity* showing the Infant Jesus in swaddling clothes, touched by a ray from the Bethlehem star. Included in the scene is a smaller group, showing the midwives preparing to bathe the Holy Infant (is the one on the left testing the water?). On the south curve of the vault is the *Death of the Virgin*, showing the Virgin's swaddled spirit being accepted by Christ, with angels poised to convey it to Heaven.

The walls were originally panelled in marble, in a similar style to the beautifully inlaid floor.

S. Cataldo (opposite the Martorana) With the nearby San Giovanni degli Eremiti, this church is the best example of the fusion of the Norman and Arabic styles in Palermo. The church was built by the Normans c. 1160, and served as the private chapel for an Italian nobleman. This was less than a century after the Norman conquest of Sicily and the Arab architects that were employed have

left their influence in the three little domes, the denticulated roof and the Arabic inscription running along the top of the building.

The church is usually shut, but the custodian of the Martorana will open it on request. The *interior*, which was used for secular purposes until its restoration in 1885, is quite bare. The plan is basilican, without a central dome, and the three domes rest on arches supported by columns. Apart from the marble pavement in *opus Alexandrinum* and the Byzantine altar, the capitals of the columns are the only decorative part of the old church to survive. One of these capitals, on the north side of the church, has an unusual basket-work design, Byzantine in origin.

On the opposite side of the Via Maqueda is the *University of Palermo*, and next to it, at the corner of the Quattro Canti, the church of **S. Giuseppe dei Teatini**, an early 17th c. building with a splendid interior decorated by the leading artists of the Baroque epoch. The central *dome*, supported by four pairs of gigantic columns of grey marble, was painted by the Flemish artist Borremans, who also worked on the Martorana and other churches in Palermo. Sicilian artists are also represented: Marabitti by the two sculptured figures of *angels with stoups* on either side of the west entrance and Siragusa by a bas-relief of the *Madonna with Angels* (altar of south transept, 1800). In the north transept is a Pietro Novelli painting, *S. Gaetano*. An unusual and pleasing feature of this church is the series of small cupolas with lanterns in the side aisles, one over each of the five bays.

Roger II Crowned by Christ, Martorana

From the Quattro Canti, the Via Vittorio Emanuele leads west to the Piazza della Cattedrale.

Cathedral (Santa Maria dell'Assunta) A complicated, but strangely impressive building of many different styles. It is approached from the south, through the cathedral garden, and to assist one's orientation it is important to realize that this south side is now to all intents and purposes the front of the cathedral with the entrance portico on the left. The real front is of course on the west of the building, overlooking the Via Bonello, but the entrance here is now closed.

The cathedral, founded in 1185 by William II's English archbishop Walter of the Mill (Gualtiero Offamilio), stands on the site of an earlier Latin basilica, converted into a mosque by the Arabs. Before the present building was erected the Normans had already added chapels to the old basilica, and a vestige of one of these, the Cappella dell' Incoronata, still survives (see below). Alterations and restorations have continued to the present day, and the cathedral is a compendium of contrasting architectural styles, harmonized by the restful ochre colour of its stone. Before going into the cathedral the visitor should make a tour of the exterior, which having suffered fewer Baroque accretions is more pleasing than the interior. (The exception to this is of course the great dome, added to the cathedral by Ferdinando Fuga in the late 18th c. Internally quite harmonious, it makes a totally incongruous appendage to the Arabo-Norman exterior.)

The tour begins at the west end of the cathedral. This is dominated by the massive *campanile*, restored in the 19th c., which is joined by two supporting arches to the main building. The *west front*, opposite, is topped by two towers of the 14th c., similar in style to the much earlier campanile of the Martorana. Over the elaborate Gothic *doorway* is a small tabernacle containing a *Madonna and Child*. The decoration here is all of the 14th and 15th c. and assiduously reproduces the zigzags, arabesques and other decorative details of the earlier Arabo-Norman architecture.

Facing the north-west corner of the cathedral, on the other side of the street, are the sad remains of the **Cappella dell'Incoronata**. This chapel was built by Roger II and was part of the old basilica that was pulled down to make way for the present cathedral. The removal of this earlier building isolated the chapel, which explains why the width of a street now lies between it and the cathedral. The chapel was used for the coronation of the Norman kings (hence the name) and the *loggia* to the west was where the new monarch showed himself to the people. This loggia is still reasonably intact, but the chapel itself was largely destroyed by fire in 1860. Following the street along the north

side of the cathedral, the visitor reaches the *east end*, which though thoroughly restored retains much of the 12th c. fabric. The blind arcades with their intersecting arches on the exterior of the three apses, the medallions and other decorative elements, are Arabic and show that craftsmen of the conquered race were employed on this building as on other smaller churches of the period. Two flanking towers match those at the western end of the cathedral.

Returning to the *south side* of the cathedral one can see the patterns continued, and merging together in the warm yellow texture of the stonework. A Gothic touch is added by the 15th c. **porch**, through which the cathedral is entered. Though a later addition to the cathedral, this porch shows an Arabic influence and includes an interesting detail: one of the columns supporting the entrance portico bears an inscription from the Koran and may well be a survival from the conversion of the earlier church into a mosque. The fine *doorway* is by Gambara (1426) and the carved *wooden doors* by Miranda (1432).

Interior The form of the interior is a Latin cross, with a nave and two aisles. The decoration, in the Baroque style, is part of the transformation of the church by Fuga in the late 18th c.

Turning to the left on entering by the south door, the visitor will immediately see a magnificent memorial to the years of Sicily's greatness: the six **Royal Tombs** in the double chapel at the top of the south aisle. Four of these tombs are canopied, the other two set in the walls on either side. The four canopied tombs contain the remains of some of Sicily's most noted monarchs. The chronological sequence of these tombs is best understood if one starts at the back with the tomb on the left. This is the tomb of the great Norman king, Roger II (d. 1154). Beside it is the tomb of his daughter Constance (d. 1198). Constance married the Holy Roman Emperor Henry VI (who crowned himself King of Sicily) and it is his tomb which stands in front on the right. In front on the left is the tomb of their son Frederick II, who after his father's death (1197) became Holy Roman Emperor and King Frederick I of Sicily. His tomb also contains the remains of the little-known Aragonese King Peter II—an odd bedfellow for 'Stupor Mundi'.

The canopies on these tombs are particularly fine. Those at the back are of white marble inlaid with mosaic, those in front of porphyry. Two other tombs are set in the wall on either side of the central group. The left wall holds the sarcophagus of Peter II's brother Duke William (d. 1338) and the right wall the sarcophagus of Emperor Frederick II's wife, Constance of Aragon.

Passing along the south aisle, note the elegant canopied *stoup* (1553) by the 4th pillar. This was matched to the earlier and finer

stoup on the opposite side of the nave, by the 4th pillar of the north aisle. In the 4th chapel of the south aisle, next to the entrance, is a painting by the 17th c. artist Pietro Novelli, *Madonna and St Ignatius*. Continuing to the south transept, note the *statues* in the niches by Antonello Gagini (1535). These belong to a high altar which the great sculptor designed for the cathedral, now dismantled. Other sculptures from this former high altar are the *Apostles* in the choir and the relief of *Christ* on the present altar. To the right of the choir is the *Cappella di S. Rosalia*. Here are kept the relics of Palermo's patron saint, in a silver urn usually hidden from view. On the walls marble reliefs show right: *S. Rosalia Quelling the Plague* and left: *Procession of the Relics of the Saint*.

From the south transept a doorway leads to the *Treasury* (apply to the sacristan, L100). This contains the precious crown of Constance of Aragon, wife of the Holy Roman Emperor Frederick II. The crown, which is shaped like a cap and studded with jewels, was recovered from the tomb of the Empress when it was opened in the 18th c. To the east of the Treasury is the *Sacristy*, with ornately carved doors by the Gagini.

On special request, the sacristan will conduct visitors to the *Crypt*, where there is a further sculpture by Antonello. This is on the *Tomb of Giovanni Paterno*, the Archbishop who commissioned so much of the master's work. Also in the crypt is the *Tomb of Archbishop Gualtiero Offamilio* (d. 1190), the cathedral's founder.

The north transept of the cathedral contains a 14th c. *crucifix* mounted above a bas-relief of the *Passion* (Gagini school). The north aisle contains three pieces of interest. In the end chapel, next to the transept, is a *Madonna and Child* by Francesco Laurana (1469), the master of Antonello Gagini and one of southern Italy's most influential sculptors. Halfway along, by the 4th pillar, is the *stoup* already mentioned, thought to be the work of Antonello's father, Domenico (late 15th c.). In the 2nd chapel, further along, is another group from the former high altar of the cathedral.

From the west side of the cathedral a short diversion (not part of this tour) may be made to the Papireto market, by way of the Via Bonello and the Via Papireto. This market will interest those who prefer genuine folk craft to the souvenir variety.

From the cathedral the tour continues westwards to the Porta Nuova. This elaborate Renaissance-style gateway was built as a triumphal arch to the Emperor Charles V after his capture of Tunis (1535). It was rebuilt in 1667 after destruction by lightning. By the Porta Nuova, on the north side of the Corso, stands a frail memorial to the 12th c., the church of **La Maddalena**. This church, now a chapel of the Carabinieri, stands within the courtyard of their barracks. (Permission to view it must be obtained from the Carabinieri.) One of the few surviving churches of the Arabo-Norman period (built by Walter of the Mill), the Maddalena was

Left: Cathedral, east end
Above: Palace of the Normans

Palazzo dei Normanni (Palace of the Normans) Otherwise known as the Palazzo Reale (Royal Palace), this is for many the highlight of a visit to historic Palermo. It stands at the highest point of the old city, on the site of the fortress built by the Arabs. The Norman building was begun by Roger II and continued by the successive Norman kings who used it as their principal palace. Externally most of the building is now 17th c., but a Norman tower survives. This is the *Torre di Santa Ninfa*, also known as the *Torre Pisano*, which sits squarely in the centre of the building topped by the incongruous dome and masts of the observatory. The arcading over the windows is Norman, but the windows themselves are modern.

The Palace now consists of a number of buildings joined together, used as Government offices. Here too is the Chamber of the Regional Parliament of Sicily, a splendid role for the building which has for so long been the seat of power in the island. The Palace is approached from the east, from the terrace overlooking the attractive gardens of the Villa Bonanno. An archway gives access to a 16th c. Renaissance *courtyard*, surrounded by a porticoed gallery at three levels. A staircase leads up to the first floor.

Cappella Palatina Open daily 09.00–13.00. Afternoons 15.00–18.00 (winter 15.00–16.30). Closed in the afternoon on Thursday, Sunday and holidays.

The art of Arab and Norman have nowhere reached such a perfect fusion as in this beautiful chapel of the Norman kings, the creation of Roger II. Built between 1132–40, it possesses a mosaic interior of outstanding beauty, one of the finest creations of Byzantine art.

little more than a ruin before its restoration as a chapel. In plan it is like the church of S. Cataldo, a basilica with three bays. The roof of the nave, however, is flat; as are those of the aisles—although a little of the original barrel vaulting of the latter may be seen at the east end. The dome has disappeared, and the walls have undergone some reconstruction, but the original antique columns with their 12th c. capitals survive.

Christ Pantocrator, Cappella Palatina

The exterior is barely relevant: a porticoed façade decorated with a modern mosaic. The chapel is entered through a small narthex, which provides a necessary pause before the stunning spectacle of the interior. Like the other churches of the period in Palermo the plan is of a simple basilica, with a nave and two aisles. Unlike them, however, the choir is raised, five steps up, with a small aisle on either side. The altar is also raised, and the effect is to take the eye upwards, first to the semi-dome of the apse with its *Christ in Benediction* and then beyond it, irresistibly, to the honeycomb of gold which has as its centrepiece one of the most beautiful of all cupolas. This is a delight which cannot be deferred, and none would wish to, for this is the starting point of all the treasures of the Cappella Palatina, which seem to radiate from it.

Mosaics The *Christ Pantocrator* in the cupola is gentle but omnipotent: in the roundel we read in Greek 'The sky is my throne; the ground my footstool'. Around the Pantocrator is the most delightful band of *angels* that one could hope to see here on earth, the four Archangels distinguished by their orbs and wands. In the four niches of the pendentives are the *Evangelists*. The first words of each of the relevant gospels are inscribed

on the twin arches of these niches, in Latin and Greek. Between the niches, on the faces of the octagon, are the figures of the four major Prophets: *John the Baptist, Solomon, Zachariah* and *David*. The latter figure, positioned above the apse, is 19th c. work and occupies the space of a former window. Note also the eight portraits of *Minor Prophets*, immediately below the cupola.

Further inscriptions run around the square base of the octagon: the upper one, in Greek, contains a record of King Roger's dedication of the chapel to St Peter and St Paul in 1143. On the arch over the apse is the *Annunciation*: on the opposite arch, the *Presentation in the Temple*. In the vault over the apse, in a central roundel, note the symbols of *etoimasia*, the throne of the Last Judgement. These are the cross, crown of thorns, lance and sponge, and, on a small throne, the dove, closed book, and cushion with the four nails. On either side, on the curve of the vault, are the *Archangels Michael and Gabriel* in adoration of the *Christ in Benediction* in the semi-dome of the apse. Below this Christ, the central mosaic of the apse strikes a jarring note. It is a sentimental work of the 18th c., depicting a seated *Madonna* between *saints* (these figures are slightly earlier).

On the north wall of the chapel to the left of the choir and between two windows, is a compelling mosaic of the *Three Fathers of the Church*: St Gregory, St Basil and St John Chrysostomon. The dual inscription in Greek and Latin suggests that this work was a collaboration between Greek and Sicilian artists.

The mosaics of the small apses on either side of the central apse will be described together. The figures in the centre of the apses are 18th c., that in the left apse showing *St Joseph with the Holy Child*, that in the right showing *St Anne with the Infant Mary*. The semi-domes of these apses contain, on the left, a portrait of *St Andrew* (replacing an earlier St Peter) and on the right, *St Paul*. Above the left apse is one of the earliest mosaics in the chapel, a *Madonna and Child* of the 12th c. This is the work of a Greek artist, traditionally Byzantine in its formal treatment of the drapery and in the elongated features of the Madonna. Of the same period is the *Nativity* over the right apse, very similar to that in the Martorana. It contains superb details. In a narrative composition the three Magi are shown first approaching on horses and then offering their gifts to the new-born King. Similarly, the Child is shown again, below the Nativity scene, taking His bath. Seated in the lower left-hand corner, Joseph seems as much 'out of it' here as in the Martorana.

The mosaic, which is taken adroitly round the corner on the south wall, is the beginning of the New Testament cycle which continues on three levels with the *Dream of Joseph, Flight into Egypt, Baptism, Transfiguration, Resurrection of Lazarus,* and *Entry into Jerusalem*. This is a particularly fine series. On the vault is the *Pentecost*, with various saints and apostles receiving the Holy Spirit in the form of a dove.

On the wall of the south aisle are mosaics (many greatly restored) depicting scenes from the lives of St Peter and St Paul. These belong to the end of the 12th c., which makes them slightly later than those of the east end of the chapel already described. They are probably the work of Sicilian craftsmen, following the style of the Greek mosaicists who did the earlier work. It is interesting to note that the inscriptions are now in Latin rather than Greek. From the east the scenes are: *Paul receiving the order to persecute the Christians; Paul struck by the voice from Heaven; Paul baptised by Ananias; Paul's dispute with the Jews and flight from Damascus in a basket; Peter in prison; Peter escaping from prison guided by an angel.* On the opposite wall (north aisle) the series continues, from the west, with *Peter healing the cripple; Bringing Tabitha back to life; Peter meeting Paul; Peter and Paul before Nero; Fall of Simon the Sorcerer.*

The mosaics of the nave are the work of

Sicilian artists (from 1158 onwards) and are inferior to the other mosaics of the period in this chapel. The scenes are from the Old Testament and relate the first 32 chapters of Genesis, from the *Creation* to *Jacob's Flight with the Angel*. The story is on two levels, starting with the upper row on the right side of the nave.

A much later mosaic, dating from the 14th–15th c., is to be seen at the west end of the chapel, over the dais of the King's throne (itself richly decorated in geometric mosaic). This shows *Christ enthroned between St Peter and St Paul*, with above them, the *Archangels Michael and Gabriel*.

Other features The columns of the nave are antique, of granite and cipollino. The lower part of the walls and the floor are inlaid with marble, as are the front of the choir and the pulpit. To the side of the pulpit is a superb **Paschal candlestick**—a Norman–Romanesque work which shows extraordinary imagination, and a little eccentricity. Plants and animals intermingle on the shaft in a naturalistic fantasy; half-way up Christ sits in a mandorla surrounded by angels. The most astonishing feature of the interior is, however, the **ceiling** of the nave, an outstanding example of the art and craftsmanship of the Arabs employed by the Normans

Paschal candlestick, Cappella Palatina

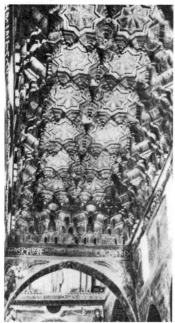

It is this sort of contrast which makes the art of medieval Sicily, springing from the gifts of so many different cultures, such a fascinating study. The intriguing inclusion of a crowned Swabian eagle in the centre of the ceiling is explained by a 13th c. restoration. Other rooms of the palace are decorated in the 18th c. Bourbon style, a reminder of the occasions when Ferdinand IV of Naples (Ferdinand I of the Two Sicilies) had his court here. It is also possible to view the assembly chamber of the Sicilian Parliament when this is not in session.

Leaving the palace, turn right and descend the steps from the Piazza del Parlamento to the Via di Bastione, which is followed to the right. The Via dei Benedettini, on the left, leads to the church of **S. Giovanni degli Eremiti**. Hours: 09.00–13.00 & 15.00–18.00 (May-Sep); 09.00–15.00 Oct–Apr. Sun & hol 09.00–13.00 only. Closed Tues.

The name of this unusual and attractive Byzantine church ('St John of the Hermits') is a derivation of the name of an earlier Byzantine church, St John Hermetis, an attribution which itself came from a Greek temple on the site (Temple of Hermes). The old church belonged to a Benedictine monastery, founded in the 6th c. This was destroyed by the Arabs, who built a mosque on the site. Later on the Norman King Roger refounded the monastery and incorporated the mosque in a new church (1142). The estates granted to the monastery by the king made it the richest in Sicily, and the abbot was given the rank of bishop and made chaplain to the king. The church, which was restored in the 19th c., has now been deconsecrated.

With its plain exterior, capped by a square tower and pink domes, this church, like S. Cataldo, is very Moorish in character. The *interior* is of special interest. The nave has two bays, each surmounted by a large dome. Between the bays, the arch is broken by a decorative window—an unusual feature. (This window is a copy: the original is in the Museo Nazionale.) At the east end are three apses. Over the left apse is the tower, with a small dome: there are similar domes over the central and right-hand apse. From the latter apse there is access to a small rectangular chamber, the old Arab mosque. A delightful feature of the church is its 13th c. cloister, enclosing a beautiful little garden with a well in the centre. The twin columns and arches of this cloister are reminiscent of the larger cloisters of the same period at Monreale and Cefalù.

in the construction of the chapel. The ceiling is carved with star patterns and stalactites, and is beautifully painted with Kufic inscriptions, flower and animal motifs, and scenes of courtly life. In their use of figurative themes the Fatimid artists were working, in a non-Islamic building, outside the conventions of Islamic religious art which forbade the representation of the human form. Christian symbols were added in the 15th c. restoration. **Royal apartments** (Hours: 09.00–12.30 Mon, Fri & Sat only)

On the second floor of the palace (main staircase) are some of the surviving rooms of the former royal apartments of the Norman kings. Visitors are conducted by a custodian to the most important of these, the **Sala di Re Ruggero** (Room of King Roger). This room makes an interesting entry in the record of the art of the Byzantine era. The **mosaics** which richly decorate walls and ceiling (12th c.) are totally pagan in content and there is no other work of the period to compare with them. The artists were Muslim, and the subjects confined to scenes of hunting and wild animals. The border patterns, decorative treatment of foliage and stylization of the animals show a strong Persian influence; but there is an odd contradiction in the introduction of a pair of centaurs, with bows and arrows, over one of the doorways.

Those wishing to return to the Quattro Canti may like to stroll through the pleasant garden of the *Villa Bonanno*, which occupies most of the Piazza Vittoria. In the south-east corner of the square is the **Palazzo Sclafani**, built in 1330. The imposing Gothic-Renaissance façade of this building overlooks the adjacent Piazza San Giovanni.

Above: Ceiling, Cappella Palatina
S. Giovanni degli Eremiti

Walking tour 2 (see map) *Porta Felice—S. Maria della Catena—Palazzo Chiaramonte —La Gancia—Palazzo Abbatellis (National Gallery)—S. Francesco—Oratorio di S. Lorenzo—Palazzo Aiutamicristo—Magione*

If a visit to the National Gallery of Sicily in the Palazzo Abbatellis is planned, this tour must be made in the morning, as the gallery shuts at 2 pm (1 pm on Sundays and holidays, closed on Fridays). Another reason for avoiding the early afternoon is that churches are often shut at this time.

At the east end of the Corso Vittorio Emanuele is the **Porta Felice** (1582–1614) built as a counterpoint to the Porta Nuova and as a gateway to the city from the sea. One of the massive and elaborate piers was damaged in the aerial bombardment of the last war, but has been faithfully restored. The same cannot be said for the general area of the old port (*Cala*) to the north, or the old quarter of the city known as the *Kalsa* to the south. These streets of shattered buildings have become the burrows of Palermo's poor. Knowing what will replace them one cannot spontaneously wish them away: there is, however, little hope of restoration.

Westwards along the Corso is the church of **S. Maria della Catena**, built in the 15th c., which miraculously escaped the bombing. 'Catena' refers to the chain which was drawn across the old harbour at this point to seal it from attack. The church—the only one of its style in Palermo—is Catalan-Gothic with a strong dash of Renaissance: the attributed work of the architect Matteo Carnelivari whose clever fusion of the architectural influences of the period may also be seen on this tour in the Palazzo Abbatellis and the Palazzo Aiutamicristo. The low arches of the *portico* are typical of the style: combining gracefully with the square corner pillars and decorative parapet. The three *doorways* have reliefs by Vincenzo Gagini. Although the church seems invariably shut it is worth a second try (afternoons and evenings are best) to see the *interior*, with its ribbed Gothic vault contrasting—but not conflicting —with the classical columns of the nave, supporting the same elegant low arches seen in the portico.

Crossing the Corso, one enters the large Piazza Marina, with the **Giardino Garibaldi**. Horticulturists will enjoy themselves in this

splendidly overgrown garden in which statues of Garibaldi and his followers are as prolific as the plant life. Particularly impressive are the two giant banyan trees (Indian fig) whose branches are supported by their long pillar-like shoots.

During the Spanish period this square was used for jousting and feasts: a romantic picture that is easy to recreate under the looming medieval façade of the **Palazzo Chiaramonte**, on the east side of the square. This building, otherwise known as 'Lo Steri' (from the Latin *Hosterium* or fortified palace) was begun in 1307 by the Chiaramonte, at that time the most powerful family in Sicily. It was later used as a palace by the Spanish Viceroys and as the headquarters of the Inquisition, whose victims were kept in the dungeons. For defensive reasons the palace has no windows at the street level, but those of the upper floors (restored) are very fine, the arches decorated with lava inlay work. The *interior* of the palace, closed since 1966 for restoration, has in its great hall a painted wooden ceiling of the 14th c., a remarkable Sicilian work with strong Saracenic influence. Another treat in store when the palace is re-opened is the fine inner *courtyard*, surrounded by a loggia with pointed arches. In the open courtyard to the right of the palace is the little church of **S. Antonio Abate**, also built by the Chiaramonte.

The Via 4 Aprile leads to the Via Alloro. Facing the end of the street is the 15th c. monastery church of **La Gancia** which—if it is open—is usually entered through a courtyard on the other side. The church contains sculpture by Serpotta (chapels on either side of the choir) and Antonello Gagini (choir piers and 6th chapel on north side) and paintings by Vincenza da Pavia (*Marriage of the Virgin*, chapel to left of choir; *Nativity*, 2nd chapel on north) and Antonello da Palermo (*Madonna del Monserrato*, 2nd chapel on south). The *organ* at the west end is late 17th c.

Next to the church is the **Palazzo Abbatellis** (National Gallery). (For opening times, see p. 25, and note at introduction to tour.)

The building housing Sicily's national art collection is a fine example of an architectural style little seen in Sicily. Built in the late 15th c. by Matteo Carnelivari for the Patella family, its Catalan-Gothic style is modified by Renaissance elements.

The *doorway* is very unusual, its naturalistic treatment a prophecy of *art nouveau*. Inside there is a courtyard with a two-storied *loggia* on one side, recently restored. The Renaissance influence is seen here in the relationship of the two arcades, the lower larger than the upper. How much of this—or any other part of the palace—is original is not clear, as the building was considerably altered during the period in which it was used

Above: Palazzo Chiaramonte
Left: Cala

as a Dominican convent (1526–1943) and much damaged by bombs in World War II. It was restored in 1954.

Ground floor From the courtyard, a door leads into *Room 1* which contains fragments of the medieval city. Most interesting is the elaborate *door-frame* recovered from the Benedictine convent—now demolished—next to the Martorana church. The carving here is Arabic, of the 12th c. *Room 2* contains relics of churches of the 14th and 15th c., including the *Sarcophagus of Cecilia Aprile* (1495), the work of the school of Francesco Laurana. In an ante-room is the huge **fresco** from the Palazzo Sclafani, *The Triumph of Death* (15th c.). Here the figure of Death rides with macabre glee over his victims, felled by his arrows. The small *Room 3* has three particularly beautiful objects: a huge Saracenic majolica *vase* (14th c.) a section of a *ceiling* (12th c.) covered with Arabic motifs, and three fine 16th c. *plates*. In *Room 4* is one of the gallery's treasures, the superb **Bust of**

Vigilia and a *crucifix* by Pietro Ruzzolone, both Sicilian artists. In the small *Room 10* is the gem of the collection, the **Annunciation** of Antonello da Messina. The Madonna is here captured at the moment of receiving the annunciation, looking up from the book she is reading. Her attitude and features are perfectly composed, and only her uplifted right hand expresses her wonder. This subtle but intensely moving portrait is without doubt the masterpiece of Sicily's greatest painter. Also in this room, but overshadowed by the major work, are three panels of a triptych by the same artist, representing the saints *Girolamo, Gregory* and *Augustine*.

Rooms 11 and *12* contain works of other 15th and 16th c. Sicilian artists, notably Riccardo Quartararo whose *Sts. Peter and Paul* and *Coronation of the Virgin* are impressive. The remaining rooms of the gallery contain work of non-Sicilian artists. In *Room 13* the Flemish school includes a magnificent triptych by Mabuse (*Malvagna Triptych*) which

Eleonora of Aragon by Francesco Laurana. In this and the two adjacent rooms (*Nos 5 & 6*) are further sculptures of the 15th and 16th c., some by the Gagini. Note particularly in Room 5 the charming *Portrait Bust of a Young Man* by Antonello Gagini.

First floor Sicily's finest paintings are concentrated in the ten rooms on this floor. From the staircase, follow the loggia to *Room 7*, which contains early work from Sicily and southern Italy (13th–14th c.). *Room 8* contains fine work by the 'Maestro del Polittico di Trápani' (Master of the Polyptych of Trápani) and the 'Maestro delle Incoronazioni' (Master of the Coronation of the Virgin), two unknown but superb artists of the early Renaissance. *Room 9*, the largest in the gallery, has work of the 14th and 15th c., including paintings by Tommaso de

portrays the Virgin and Child surrounded by a joyfully musical group of angels and flanked by St Catherine and St Dorothy. On the reverse side is Adam and Eve.

Room 14 contains works by 16th c. Italian and Flemish artists. *Room 15* is devoted to works by Vincenzo da Pavia (1518–57) and *Room 16* has 16th–18th c. Italian and Flemish work including a fine Pietro Novelli (*Communion of St Mary the Egyptian*). *Room 17* has 18th c. tapestries.

Returning to the Piazza Marina, the visitor will notice on the south side the *Palazzo S. Cataldo*, a 19th c. Gothic building imitating the style of an earlier 15th c. palace that stood here. Further on, past the 15th c. church of *S. Maria dei Miracoli*, the Via Merlo leads directly to the church of **S. Francesco d'Assisi**.

Above: Annunciation (left)
S. Francesco (right)

This church, fronted by a small square, belongs to the 13th c. with subsequent alterations in the 16th, 18th and 19th c. A radical restoration, following severe bomb damage in the last war, revived the original 13th c. form. The façade has a beautiful Gothic *portal* (note zig-zag carving of the period) and an intricate *rose window*, similar to that of the church of S. Agostino.

Interior Here the church shows the work of different periods and different masters. The spacious nave was restored to its original form by the removal of the Baroque decoration. Four *statues* by Serpotta (1723) are by the central pillars: another four by the west door. The first three chapels in the south aisle have 15th c. Renaissance arches: the fourth, with a 14th c. Gothic arch, contains the *Tomb of Elisabetta Omodei* (1498). The first chapel of the north aisle has two *Madonnas* by Domenico Gagini: the fourth chapel a superb *arch* by Francesco Laurana and Pietro de Bontade (1468). The arch is one of the earliest and most important pieces of sculpture in Sicily's late-flowering Renaissance.

Next to the church (No 5, Via Immacolatella) is the **Oratorio di S. Lorenzo**, a small separate chapel decorated by the elegant stuccoed reliefs and statues of Serpotta (1687-96).

Over the arch before the altar is the figure of *St Francis*: opposite, above the entrance, a relief depicting the *Martyrdom of St Lawrence* (the saint, having offered the poor and the sick as the 'treasures' of his church to the Roman prefect, is being roasted on a gridiron). Other reliefs around the walls show scenes from the lives of the two saints. To those who have seen the other oratories decorated by Serpotta there will be a familiarity in the tumbling *putti* and other figures on the walls, and the ten statues of the *Virtues*. To be noted also are the beautiful carved *stalls* inlaid with mother-of-pearl. It was from this chapel that the *Nativity* of Caravaggio—the artist's finest work in Sicily—was stolen in 1969.

The Via A. Paternostro leads to the Piazza della Rivoluzione, scene of the Palermitan revolt against the Bourbons in 1848. The inscriptions on the *fountain* in the centre commemorate the event.

To the south is the Via Garibaldi, the street by which Garibaldi and the Redshirts entered the city in 1860. Its continuation, further south, is in the Corso dei Mille or 'Street of the Thousand'. Dominating the Via Garibaldi is the **Palazzo Aiutamicristo**, the work of Matteo Carnelivari (1490-95). This has the same Catalan-Gothic form of the other buildings by this architect already seen on this tour (Palazzo Abbatellis, church of S. Maria della Catena), but the façade has less architectural detail and at ground level has been defaced by modern shopfronts.

The finest surviving part of the palace is the *courtyard* (entrance through gateway at No. 23, and left through the first court). This preserves on one side a portico, with the elegant low arches of the period, and a superior *loggia* with more pointed arches.

The next street on the left, Via della Magione, leads to the pleasant Norman church (founded 1150) of **La Magione**, painstakingly rebuilt after its near destruction by bombs in the last war. The church, set back from the bustle of this quarter in its pleasant garden, breaks away from the Norman model with its unusually high nave. Otherwise the traditions are observed: the marble columns, slightly pointed arches, and triple apse. The wooden ceiling (1947) is a fine replica.

From the left aisle of the church a door leads to the restored remains of one side of the original *cloister*. Study of the surviving capitals of the colonnade has suggested that this was the work of the masons responsible for the cloister of Monreale Cathedral.

Oratorio di S. Lorenzo
Stucco by Serpotta

Walking tour 3 (see map) *Piazza S. Giorgio— S. Zita—Oratorio di S. Zita—Oratorio di S. Domenico—Olivella—Museo Nazionale Archeologico*

In the Piazza S. Giorgio stands the church of **S. Giorgio dei Genovesi**, built for the Genoese seamen of Palermo at the end of the 16th c. On the south side of the square, integrated in a new *palazzo* is the campanile of the 14th c. church of the Annunziata, destroyed in 1943. Also surviving on the west side is its beautiful Gothic *portal*, now the entrance to the Conservatory of Music. From the square, the Via Squarcialupo leads past the church of **S. Zita** (also known as the parish church of S. Mamiliano). Founded in the 14th c., this church was rebuilt in the 16th c. and again after the war. Students of Antonello Gagini will find his work in the 2nd chapel to the left of the choir (*Tomb of Ant. Scirotta*), the 2nd chapel to the right of the choir (*arch*) and in the central apse (*altarpiece*).

The Via Valverde, beside the church, leads to the entrance, at No 3, to the **Oratorio di S. Zita** (if there is no reply here, try the door to the left of the west entrance of the church: the oratory is closed between midday and 4pm). The decorative reliefs in this chapel must rank as the greatest achievement of Giacomo Serpotta, master-modeller in stucco, who took 32 years to complete the commission (1686–1718). The versatility of the medium and its master is expressed to the full in the riot of figures, garlands and scrolls that adorn the walls, framing with a rhythmic agitation the more sedate and smaller scale reliefs depicting scenes from the *New Testament*. The most elaborate work is on the west wall. The panels here are gamely supported by *putti*, who are also hanging onto the backdrop, a vast celestial shroud. The centrepiece is a beautifully contrived scene of the *Battle of Lepanto* with (below) the superbly modelled figures of two boys, on either side of the trophies of war.

Returning to the Via Squarcialupo and continuing to the Via Bambinai, we reach the small Piazza Valverde whose buildings of the 16th and 17th c. are sadly ruinous. The church of *S. Maria di Valverde*, which retains its campanile, has an impressive Baroque *interior* with walls and decorations in marbles of many colours (note illusionistic architectural frame of 1st chapel to right). This is much ruined and the ceiling has largely collapsed.

Further on we may again admire the work of Serpotta in the **Oratorio del Rosario di S. Domenico** (open daily 09.00–18.00: ring bell at No. 16). Here the figures are seen in juxtaposition to a number of paintings by artists working in 17th c. Palermo, including Giordano, Stomer and Novelli. The ceiling (*Coronation of the Virgin*) is by Novelli. Van Dyck

also visited the city (1624) and his altarpiece (*Madonna of the Rosary with St. Dominic and the Patronesses of Palermo*) was a commission of that visit. Against these fine paintings Serpotta's figures are incidental: but here they seem to be more readily fulfilling their role of Baroque decoration than in the oratories in which they provide the main theme. The *putti* are certainly more relaxed, playing any number of mischievous games: and the *Virtues* are a pleasant confection. The Via G. Meli leads up the flank of the church of **S. Domenico** to the Piazza of the same name, a rallying point for Palermo's *carrozze* (in the middle, the *Colonna dell'Immacolata*). The square is overshadowed by the great 17th c. façade of the church, Palermo's 'Westminster Abbey'. Among the great men entombed or commemorated here are the heroes of the Sicilian *Risorgimento* (Ruggero Settimo, Emerico Amari, Francesco Crispi), the artist Pietro Novelli and the vernacular poet Giovanni Meli.

Following the Via Roma northwards from the Piazza S. Domenico turn left before the huge *Post Office* (1933) and then bear right into the Piazza dell'Olivella where stands the 16th c. church of the **Olivella**. This is another church that suffered severe bomb damage, as will be seen by the restoration at the east end. The church has some notable paintings and statues, including two works by the Tuscan painter Filippo Paladino (*Martyrdom of St Ignatius*, left transept; *Madonna and Saints*, right transept) and two statues by the Palermitan sculptor Marabitti (*Sts. Peter and Paul*, high altar). Much of the elaborate marble inlay work of the Baroque decoration survived the bombs: note particularly the elaborate work in the 3rd chapel on the left, with a ceiling fresco by Pietro Novelli.

Museum (Museo Nazionale Archeologico) This impressive collection is housed in a building constructed around the cloisters of a 17th c. monastery. (For hours, see p.25.) **Ground floor** The *entrance court (1)* was originally the smaller of the two cloisters. In the centre is a 16th c. *fountain* with the figure of a triton. The *long gallery (2)* contains *amphorae* and anchors recovered from the sea off the north-west coast of Sicily. Two small rooms (*3 & 4*) leading off the courtyard contain *Egyptian and Punic sculpture* (7th–4th c. BC) from Carthaginian settlements (Solus, Motya, etc.). The *main courtyard (5)*, originally the large cloister, contains fragments of the Roman period. On the far side, *Rooms 6–10* are devoted to the museum's most prized archaeological exhibits, the discoveries made at Selinunte and Himera. *Room 6* contains Greek inscriptions, *Room 7* some of the two-headed stone *stelae* from the Sanctuary of Demeter Malophoros at Selinunte. From Room 7 steps lead down to *Room 9*, in which part of the terracotta entablature of Temple C at Selinunte has been

National Archaeological Museum, Palermo

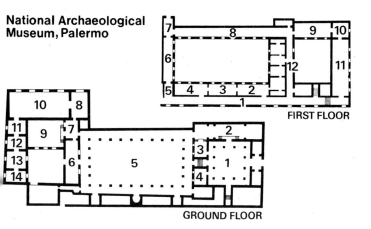

FIRST FLOOR

GROUND FLOOR

reassembled from fragments. *Room 8*, reached from Room 7, has a collection of magnificent *lion's-head water spouts* from the temple at Himera (5th c. BC) destroyed by the Carthaginians.

The next room (*10*) contains an exhibition of the finest Greek sculpture in Sicily, the **Metopes of Selinus**. Along the wall to the left of the entrance are metopes from Temple C; along the wall to the right are metopes from an unidentified temple. Both these temples belong to the early 6th c. BC, and it is interesting to compare the archaic sculpture of these metopes with the more life-like treatment of the metopes of Temple E, which belongs to the later, classical period (c. 480 BC). Also in this room are two half-metopes from Temple F, of the same period, showing battles between gods and giants (*Gigantomachia*).

Rooms 11–14 contain the Museum's *Etruscan collection*, with material from Chiusi in central Italy. This includes an *oinochoe* (wine-cup) of the 6th c. BC, decorated with the figures of Perseus and Medusa. The material ranges from the 7th–1st c. BC, the later work showing Roman influence.

First floor This is reached by a staircase leading from the entrance court. The *North Gallery* (*1*) contains the *Topographical Collection of Greek and Roman Sicily*. The objects are not only artistic (bronzes, vases, etc.) but functional (note particularly the water-pipes from the Roman aqueduct at Términi Imerese). Of special interest are the Hellenistic-Roman funerary *stelae* from Marsala with painted portraits of the deceased. The three rooms *2–4* (*antiquarium*) parallel with the gallery are reserved for finds from Selinunte. At the end of the gallery, turn

right. *Rooms 5 & 6* have Greek pottery and terracotta votive figures of the 6th–5th c. BC from various sites. *Room 7* has an interesting collection of lamps from the Phoenician period to the Middle Ages. The *South Gallery* (*8*) is lined with a large collection of votive figures, found at the Sanctuary of Demeter at Selinunte. At the end of the gallery, to the right, *Room 12* is devoted to a collection of finds from the area of Palermo, including vases from a cemetery of the Carthaginians. Up the steps, *Room 9* contains bronzes, including a 3rd c. BC *ram*, which once flanked the gateway of the Castello Maniace in Syracuse. Note also the group showing *Hercules Killing the Arcadian Stag*, a Roman copy of a Greek original, found in Pompeii. *Room 10* contains Greek sculpture, including part of the frieze of the Parthenon, and Roman copies. *Room 11* has Roman sculpture and mosaics.

Second floor This is closed indefinitely for restoration, and the arrangements are likely to be changed. In the *North Gallery* (*1*) are finds from the Palaeolithic and Mesolithic periods, including casts of incised drawings found at Addaura on the north flank of Monte Pellegrino. Parallel to the gallery, *Rooms 2–9* have material from the Neolithic period to the Bronze Age. *Rooms 10–12* progress to the Iron Age, and in the adjacent *West Gallery* (*13*) are early Greek ceramics (Corinthian and proto-Corinthian ware). Greek ceramics of later periods are in the *South Gallery* (*14*) which features black-on-red ware (6th c. BC) and *Room 15* which features red-on-black ware (5th–4th c. BC). *Room 16* has frescoes from Solunto (1st c. BC) and mosaic pavements from Palermo (3rd and 4th c. AD).

Other places of interest in Palermo
Centre

S. Agostino This church lies three streets to the south of the Teatro Massimo. In the Via S. Agostino, which leads to the church from the Via Maqueda, is one of Palermo's liveliest street markets.

The church was built in the 13th c. by two of Sicily's great feudal families, the Chiaramonte and the Sclafani. Its fine *doorway* (note lava inlay) and the *rose window* are Gothic elements to be recognized in other churches of the period in Sicily (in Palermo, the Church of S. Francesco). A 15th c. addition, introducing a touch of the Renaissance, is the fine *doorway* on the right side of the church by Domenico Gagini (the lunette is by another sculptor).

The *interior* of the church is 17th c., with stuccoes by Serpotta (1711–1729). The statues are of *Saints* and the *Virtues*, and one should note how cleverly the artist has built up the figures of *St Monica* and *St Augustine*, on either side of the altar, from volumes of cloud. A door leads from the north side of the church to the *cloister* where recent restoration work has revived a doorway flanked by double windows of the Chiaramonte style (14th c.).

West

Catacombe di Convento dei Cappuccini (Catacombs of the Convent of the Capucins) In the Piazza Cappuccini off the Via Cappuccini (Bus No 5 from Stazione Centrale, Bus No 23 or 27 from Corso V. Emanuele.) Open daily 09.00–12.00, 15.30–17.00.

The attraction of this chamber of horrors, one of the 'sights' of tourist Palermo, can only be put down to its appeal to the curiously morbid—or morbidly curious—among us. Once curiosity is satisfied, however, there can be few who care to return to this grisly glimpse of Palermo's past.

The catacombs were originally reserved for the deceased Capucins of the Convent, many of whom died in the service of the sick during a 16th c. plague. Their order was subsequently greatly venerated by the Palermitans, to the extent that their catacombs became a sought-after preserve for the dead of the richer families. Throughout the 17th, 18th and 19th centuries the members of these families were laid to rest here. Their 'rest', however, must seem a slight parody to the modern visitor, viewing the stark remains of 8000 of Palermo's most notable citizens arranged along the corridors.

Some are in niches, others in glass cases. The majority are propped against the walls, and one is here reminded of the rows of marionettes hanging behind the scenes in the *teatro dei pupi*. The bloom on the cheeks of the paladins is not to be seen, however, on these skeletal grotesques. The staring skulls are, one senses, making their mute

protests against the maladroit work of the dessicator. This was the earthern drier in which the bodies were placed to drain off their fluids: after eight months or so they were put out in the sun to complete the process. The bodies were then wrapped in straw to return them to reasonably lifelike proportions, dressed in their own clothes and put on display for the relatives, who presumably had waited in some suspense to renew the acquaintance of their dear departed.

This was the most common method of 'preserving' the bodies. Another, more effective, method was to treat the bodies in an arsenical bath, which petrified them. Two of these corpses may be seen in the first corridor leading on from the foot of the stairs. This is the 'Corridor of Men': other corridors are reserved for women, priests and philosophers.

Best preserved of all is little Rosalia Lombardo, admitted to the catacombs in 1920 by special permission (no other bodies have been admitted since 1881). The secret of her perfect preservation, the result of a series of injections, died with the doctor who achieved it.

Cuba This small Norman palace, once a feature of King William II's royal park, is now hidden from view in the barracks at No 100 Corso Calatafimi (Bus No 8 or 9 from Piazza 13 Vittime, No 32 from Corso V. Emanuele). Visitors may enter the barracks to view the palace, but may not take photographs.

Built in 1180 the Cuba was originally in the middle of an artificial lake and there are still traces of a watergate on the exterior. It is very similar in plan to the Zisa, on which it is modelled, and has the same blind arcading on the walls, a feature of Arabo-Norman architecture. There is also an Arabic inscription on the outer wall. The interior had a central hall which rose to the full height of the building. It is thought that this hall was covered by a dome, which would suggest the origin of the building's name (the Arabic *Kubbeh* or 'dome'). Traces of decorative plaster work, including stalactites, have been found.

Cubula This means, literally, 'little Cuba', and is a small domed Norman pavilion which like the Cuba once stood in William II's park. It is now tucked away in the middle of a citrus grove in the old garden of the Villa Napoli (access through modern block at No. 575 Corso Calatafimi: then through gate to right which will be unlocked by custodian). The Cubula is on the same bus routes as the Cuba.

Zisa This is the finest Norman palace in Sicily. It has, without doubt, seen better times, and one can only deplore the neglect of the authorities which has allowed it to become a near-ruin. (Bus Nos 17 and 20 from Stazione Centrale, alight at the Piazza Principe di Camporeale.)

Situated in the quarter on the west side of the city which has taken its name, it was built by the two Williams (I & II) in the second half of the 12th c. as a pleasure palace in their park outside the city. The name 'Zisa' comes from the Arab *aziz*, meaning 'magnificent': a name which brings a touch of irony to a building which—after surviving eight centuries—has reached its present state. The protective wall that now encloses the palace is significant: built not so much to save a historic monument from the actions of vandals as to prevent visitors from being injured by falling masonry. Access (ring bell at side door) is limited to a peek inside the wall: visitors who show a genuine interest and concern may, however, be escorted round the exterior by the custodian.

The building is quadrilateral with three stories and turrets on two sides. An Arabic frieze running along the top was adapted into battlements in the 16th c. The original double windows have disappeared, the inevitable consequence of the building's use as a dwelling place in the years of its decline. The doorways of the main front, however, have retained their form with their slightly pointed Saracenic arches.

The main entrance, with double columns on either side, leads through a Baroque arch (replacing an earlier ogival one) into the most beautiful part of the palace—the *vestibule*. This has recesses on three sides with stalactite vaults and marble and mosaic decoration on the walls. In the central recess the mosaic frieze (which may be covered during restoration work) has a pattern of three roundels, the outer two featuring peacocks on either side of a palm and the centre two hunters with bows. Immediately below this mosaic is a niche decorated with an imperial eagle from which water issued, running down a carved slab flanked by inlaid steps into a channel in the floor. The water then ran out to a fish pond in front of the palace.

This fountain, an oriental delight found nowhere else in Sicily, is part of a concept

that must engage our concern as well as our curiosity. The Norman pleasure palace, with its echo of luxury—the just reward of the achievements of those amazing, adventurous knights—is a unique inheritance of our Mediterranean civilization that must at all costs be preserved.

Near the palace in the Via dei Normanni is the old *Chapel of the Zisa*, now incorporated in a Baroque church. (Note the curved exterior of the apse and the internal dome over the choir.) Both church and chapel are now being restored.

The palace and fountain of the Zisa

South

S. Spirito (dei Vespri) This attractive and unusual Norman church (in the cemetery of S. Orsola, open 09.00–12.00) may be reached by bus (No 2, Corso Tukory). By car, take either the Via Oreto to the south of the city, turning right at the Via Mendola, or the Corso Tukory turning off to the south at the Via Filicuzza. Both these roads join the Via del Vespro (the traditional route until its northern end became one-way). This leads to the *Cemetery of S. Orsola*, created in the grounds of the church in 1782.

The church of S. Spirito was founded by William II's archbishop, Walter of the Mill, in 1178. Its other name, the 'Church of the Vespers', recalls the incident here in 1282 when a Sicilian bride was insulted, at the hour of Vespers, by a French officer serving the detested Charles of Anjou. The resulting revolution, the Sicilian Vespers, swept the French from Sicily.

The church contrasts in style with many of the other Norman churches of the period. The main difference is the gabled roof over the crossing, in place of the dome. The exterior decoration is also distinctive, the windows with an arcading of black and white stonework (lava and tufa) and the apsidal east end combining a pattern of interlacing arches with the corduroy stonework of the windows.

Interior The church has a central nave divided from the side aisles by round columns of lava, supporting slightly pointed Saracenic arches. The wooden ceiling of the nave, and of the raised roof of the crossing, show traces of the original decoration. Note also the little round windows in the side aisles, clerestory and east end with their restored Saracenic lights.

The church is invariably in use for burial services: if it should be closed, apply to the custodian of the cemetery for admission.

Ponte dell'Ammiraglio (Bus No 21/31, Corso dei Mille) This old Norman bridge, which stands in the square of the same name on the Corso dei Mille to the south of the city, was built by the admiral George of Antioch in 1113. It originally spanned the Oreto, which has now been diverted. On 27 May 1860 the Garibaldini, entering the city from the south, had their first clash with the Bourbons here.

S. Giovanni dei Lebbrosi (St John of the Lepers) Not far from the Ponte dell'Ammiraglio, off the Corso dei Mille, is this charming, partially reconstructed Norman church (open approx. 08.30–10.00, 17.00–20.00).

Built in 1072 on the remains of an Arab castle it is one of the oldest churches in Sicily, a prototype of the Arabo-Norman churches of the period. Typical features are the three apses and dome (the Greek-style east end), the wooden ceiling and Saracenic windows (both restorations), and the small engaged columns flanking the central and side apses. The less familiar *campanile* (1934) and the pillars of the nave are also reconstructions. The name of the church comes from a leprosarium that used to adjoin it, now demol-

S. Spirito

ished. Fifty years ago the church was derelict and might have suffered the same fate. Happily it was restored and we see it now in a garden, its serene grey stone a perfect blend of old and new—a testimony to an enlightened recognition of the value of the Norman heritage.

Favara Situated in Brancaccio, on the south side of the city, this old Norman palace is best reached by car, and can be included in an excursion to S. Maria di Gesù (see *Excursions*) via the Corso dei Mille. The route is: right at fork, after Ponte dell'Ammiraglio (Via Brancaccio) then after 1 km, crossing railway twice, turn left at junction (statue). In 500 m, at junction of Via Conte Federico and Via Emiro Giafar, is the palace.

Otherwise known as the *Castello di Mare Dolce* ('castle of the sweet water'), this palace was built by the Normans on the site of an earlier palace of the Emir Giafar (early 11th c.). The artificial lake created by the Arabs on three sides of the building became a natural adjunct to the pleasure palace of the Normans. The lake is no longer there: in its place is a green sea of citrus trees.

The exterior of the palace is extremely simple, relieved only by the decorative arched recesses of the windows. In the centre of the north-west wing (the front from the approach described) is a small *chapel*, topped by a little tower which is in fact the elongated drum of the cupola. On either side of the chapel the rooms are inaccessible: the palace is, in fact, occupied by a large number of people who have converted it into dwellings or built on to it.

The layout of the palace will be best appreciated by going through the arch to the left. One can see that unlike the other Norman palaces of Palermo it was built as a series of rooms around a courtyard. Remains of the vaults of the arcade of this courtyard are still visible in the fabric of the modern dwellings.

Like its sister palace the Zisa, the Favara is in urgent need of restoration, even at the cost of rehousing its present occupants. This would surely bring some life and grandeur back to a building that is now little more than a neglected curiosity.

Through the gate to the right of the palace one can wander around the outer walls. Note the traces of cement used to keep the walls of the palace watertight.

S. Giovanni dei Lebbrosi   Above: Favara

North

Parco della Favorita (Park of the Favourite)
This large public park lies to the north-west
of Palermo, on the west flank of Monte Pellegrino. The main points of interest to the
visitor are the Chinese Pavilion and the
Ethnographic Museum at the northern end
of the park, just inside the main entrance.
Bus Nos 14, 15, 33 and 37 (Stazione Centrale)
pass this entrance. The route by car from
the centre of the city is Via della Liberta—
Piazza Vittorio Veneto—Piazza dei Leoni—
Viale del Fante.

The park was laid out by the Bourbon King
Ferdinand in the early 19th c. The architect
Marvuglia built for the pleasure of the king
and his queen the **Palazzina Cinese**, ex-
ploiting the current craze for 'chinoiserie'.
This exotic pavilion also served as refuge
for the royal couple during the French occupation of Naples. Nelson, at that time an ally
of the Neapolitans against the French, was
entertained here with Lady Hamilton. The
pavilion, to the left of the entrance, is currently closed to the public.

Museo Etnografico Pitre (Pitre Ethnographical Museum) Next to the Palazzina Cinese.
Founded in 1909 by G. Pitre, this is Sicily's

finest folk art collection, and well worth a
visit for those interested in the island's folk-
lore and artefacts of the more recent past.
The ethnographic library specialises in
Sicilian folklore. (Museum hours: 08.30–
15.00, Sun & hol 09.00–13.00; closed Fri.)
The collection is housed in the former servants' quarters and stables of the Bourbon
King. The exhibits include:
Workaday objects Fishing nets and tridents,
agricultural tools, rustic furniture and domestic implements. Note particularly the
wooden cow and goat collars, engraved by
the shepherds.
Costumes and embroidery Note particularly
the traditional costume of the Albanian im-
migrants of Piana degli Albanesi and the fine
carpetwork (Erice).
Ceramics These include decorative jars and
figures (a delightful assortment, from grand
admirals to rustics) mostly from the pottery
centres of Caltagirone, Collesano and S.
Stefano di Camastra.
Carriages and harness In the former stables
are carriages of the Palermitan Senate; also
traditional Sicilian carts and trappings. Here
too is the *Puppet Theatre* and *Exhibition of
Childrens' Games*.

Palermo: Panorama of the city

Excursions from Palermo

Monte Pellegrino This excursion may be made by bus (No 12 from Piazza 13 Vittime) but is preferable by car. Driving up Goethe's 'most beautiful headland' the motorist may elect to pause—at a convenient lay-by—for the best views. There are also steps, for those who scorn the easy life, at the foot of the Via Pietro Bonanno. (These steps are used by the pilgrims to the Sanctuary of S. Rosalia, at the top of the mountain. In their yearly pilgrimage, on September 4th, they climb barefoot.)

Half-way up is the *Castello Utveggio*, a former hotel now closed to the public. Before the closure the terrace of this hotel offered one of the finest views of the Conca d'Oro. Further on is the **Sanctuary of S. Rosalia**, of which Goethe said: 'In all Christendom . . . there may well be no other sacred spot as naively decorated and touchingly venerated as this.' Here, in fact, at the side of a 17th c. convent, is the *grotto* in which the bones of Palermo's patron saint were found. These relics, now in the cathedral, miraculously alleviated the plague of 1624, since when Rosalia has been the most venerated saint in the island. Her mantled effigy, the gift of the Bourbon King Charles III, lies in the grotto, which has been converted into a chapel. The water flowing down the rock walls of the grotto is supposed to be miraculous.

A turning to the right leads to the colossal bronze *Statue of S. Rosalia*, commanding marvellous views of the Gulf of Palermo, the Aeolian Isles to the north and Etna to the south. From here one can continue down the west side of the mountain to join the main Palermo–Mondello road.

S. Maria di Gesù This 15th c. church lies to the extreme south of the city, on the north of Monte Grifone, and offers a pleasant excursion to those who have seen all the main sights of the city and have a little extra time. The direct route is by the Via Oreto to Guadagna and thence by the Via S. Maria di Gesù (Bus No 10 from Via Maqueda). Those travelling by car, however, may prefer to take a different route, taking in places of interest to the south of the city. The Corso dei Mille leads to the *Ponte dell'Ammiraglio* and the church of *S. Giovanni dei Lebbrosi*: from here the Via Brancaccio leads to the *Palazzo Favara* (see above). From the Favara one quickly reaches the *Circonvallazione* to the south: shortly on the left is the old road (Via. S. Maria di Gesù) which leads to the church.

The attraction of S. Maria di Gesù is its site, above an old cemetery on the flank of Monte Grifone, and the fine view it offers of Palermo, either from the terrace in front of the church or from the belvedere above. In the middle of the terrace stands a lovely

S. Maria di Gesu

17th c. *fountain* ornamented with lions and *putti*. The most interesting details of the church itself are the *doors*, which show a varied range of architectural styles. At the west end is a fine Renaissance portal (late 15th c.) with figures of the *Apostles with the Creed* on either side of the door. On the left side of the church the arched doorway is crowned by a tabernacle with a relief of the *Madonna* (16th c.), and to the left of this doorway is the entrance of the *Cappella la Grua* in the Catalan-Gothic style. Inside are remains of 15th c. frescoes. Inside the church, to the right of the choir, is a fine *tomb* (Antonio Alliata) by Antonello Gagini.

S. Martino delle Scale A short run (13 km) to the west of the city (leave by Via Giuseppe Pitre) offers a glimpse of the quiet life in this village-cum-hill resort, with its fine Benedictine abbey.

The popularity of the mountains as a monastic retreat is also shown at *Baida* (turn right after 5 km, at Boccadifalco) which has its own convent, founded in the 14th c. for the Cistercians. The *church* of this convent preserves its original façade, with a later Renaissance *portal* (1507) by Vanelli. Inside (1st altar on left) is a statue of *St John the Baptist* by Antonello Gagini. The drive along the ridge to Baida offers splendid views of Palermo (Bus No 23 from Piazza Marina).

8 km from Boccadifalco, in a beautiful setting of pine forest, is the Abbey of **S. Martino delle Scale**. This abbey has a long history. Founded by St Gregory the Great in the 6th c., it was destroyed by the Arabs in 820 and rebuilt in the 14th c. The buildings of the convent are now largely 18th c., by the architect Marvuglia.

The **church** (1561–95) contains many paintings of the period, including Ribera's *St Dominic* (2nd altar on left); Paladino's *St Martin* (left transept) and Novelli's *Madonna and Sts Benedict and Scholastica* (right transept) and *St Benedict* (choir). Note also, in the choir, the finely engraved *stalls* (16th c.).

The large **convent** to the rear of the church contains, in the vestibule, a marble group by Marabitti, *St Martin and the Beggar*. The refectory has a ceiling by Novelli: *Daniel in the Lions' Den*.

Boat services

For boat services to **Ustica**, **Trápani**, **Cagliari**, **Genoa**, **Naples** and **Tunis**, see p. 17.

Panarea Island see **Aeolian Is.**

Pantálica Ancient site west of Syracuse, reached by SS124 and then side road to Ferla (53 km). 9 km from Ferla the road reaches the general area of the site, a limestone plateau between two deep river gorges. (Look out for the signs to the right of the road marking the footpath to the south necropolis.) *Important note:* There is as yet no access by car to the site from the nearby village of Sortino.

History Pantálica has a double significance in Sicilian prehistory, both as the proposed site of the ancient *Hybla* and as the greatest area of rock-cut tombs in the island. The date of these tombs (13th–8th c. BC) relates to the earliest recorded settlement of the plateau, by indigenous peoples driven inland by the immigration of the Sicels and other tribes from Italy. The defensive advantages of this plateau, with the deep gorges of the Anapo and its tributary on either side, will be appreciated by the visitor. The Sicel occupation of the site has been related to the legendary king Hyblon who ruled a large part of eastern Sicily in the 8th c. BC, i.e. at the time of the Greek colonization. The ancient city succumbed, in fact, to Greek expansion, and it is interesting that its demise coincided with the foundation of the Syracusan colony of Akrai to the south.

Tour The most remarkable feature of Pantálica is the series of **rock-cut tombs** (there are around 5000) in the limestone walls of the two river gorges. At the first stopping point, a footpath leads along the southern edge of the plateau, overlooking the valley of the Anapo. The rock-cut tombs here, part of the *south necropolis* of the ancient settlement, were reserved for members of individual families. During the 4th–6th c. AD they were used as cave-dwellings by refugees from the barbarian invasions: two of them were converted into *chapels*.

The footpath leads eventually to the other necropolises of Pantálica (north-west and north) but the visitor may prefer to return to the starting point after a short walk and continue the exploration by car. 500 m further along the road a sign marks the *north-west necropolis*: at this point it is quite fun to try out the echoes. In another 500 m a sign marks the rough road up to the *anaktoron*, or prince's palace—the only survival, apart from vestiges of walling, of the ancient city. 1 km further on, a sign marks the approach to the *north necropolis*, also cave dwellings of the Byzantine period (*la Cavetta*).

Pantelleria (pop. 9,000, area 83 sq km) Island 100 km off south-west coast of Sicily, 70 km east of Tunisia. (For air and boat services, see p. 17.)

This is the largest of Sicily's minor islands. Volcanic in origin, Pantelleria had its last eruption in 1891, 5 km off the north-west coast. There is still considerable volcanic activity in the island, including thermal spas. At the centre of the island are the craters of two large volcanoes, the *Montagna Grande* (836 m) and the *Montagna Gibele* (700 m). Although the island is treeless it has prolific vines, producing a celebrated muscatel.

History The island has a long history. On the west coast are traces of prehistoric settlement. Its proximity to Africa brought colonization of the island (ancient name *Cossyra*) by the Phoenicians, and it was later an important staging post for the Carthaginians during their campaigns in Sicily. The Romans took the island in 217 BC, after which it followed the fortunes of the rest of Sicily. Its location was such, however, that Pantelleria could never play a conspicuous role in the Mediterranean. In the 16th c. the island was pillaged by Corsairs and Turks: in the last war, as a fortress of the Axis powers, it was the target of a naval and air bombardment lasting 33 days (the Allies finally took the island on 11th June 1943).

Pantelleria, the island's main port, has a number of hotels and an airport 4 km from the town. The island offers a number of attractions for long-term visitors: all quickly reached from the town. 3 km to the south are the Neolithic sites of *Mursia* and *Sesi*. To the east (5 km) is the *Bagno dell'Acqua*, a crater-lake whose waters are supplemented by hot springs—delicious for bathing. On the coast, a little further on, is the *Cala dei 5 Denti*, a fantastic rock formation which is better viewed from the sea. (There is a boat trip around the island from Pantelleria port.) For the energetic, tours may be made by mule and foot via S. Vito to the crater of the *Montagna Grande*, where one can observe the phenomenon known as the *favare* (jets of hot water vapour) and enjoy a view of the whole island.

Castle, Paternò

Paternò Town 20 km west of Catania, on circum-Etna route.

On a high rock of black lava overlooking the town is the Norman **castle**. (If the custodian is not on the spot, the key may be obtained from the Municipio in the town.) This castle was built by Count Roger in 1073, restored in the 14th c. and again in 1900 and 1958 (following war damage, when it was used as an observation post by the Germans). On the ground floor is a *chapel* with traces of frescoes. By stairs, built into the thickness of the walls, one reaches the first floor, with four double windows, and the second floor with its central room, dramatically illuminated by two vast *double windows*. From the terrace at the top of the building one can enjoy a fine panorama, embracing Etna and the plain of Catania. Preparations have been made for the use of the castle as a civic museum; but final arrangements await the disposal of material from the museum at Syracuse.

Pelagic Islands (Isole Pelágie) This small and remote group of islands lies to the south-west of Sicily. For details of boat services, see p. 17.

Lampedusa (pop. 4500 area 18 sq km) 250 km from Sicily, this is the most distant of the minor islands.

The island, which is non-volcanic, has little natural vegetation and depends for its existence on sponge-fishing and what can be cultivated from the rocky soil. Traces of Phoenician, Greek, Roman and Arab occupation have been found, but the first significant population of the island was by the Neapolitans in 1847.

17 km to the north-west of Lampedusa is the uninhabited island of *Lampione*.

Linosa (pop. 500 area 5·4 sq km) 42 km north of Lampedusa, this island is volcanic in origin and has some extinct craters. Agriculture and fishing sustain the meagre population.

Penisola Magnisi see **Thapsos**.

Pergusa (667 m) Lake 10 km from Enna (2·25 km × 1·1 km).

This, according to the legend, is where Persephone, daughter of Demeter, was abducted by Hades. The lake, which has no apparent outlet, was thought to be the entrance to the Underworld.

Petralia Soprana (1147 m) Town 39 km west of Nicosia (SS120).

Standing on a high spur of the Madonie mountains, this town, with its sister Petralia Sottana, is among the most dramatically situated in Sicily. At the heart of the town the church of **SS. Pietro e Paolo** combines architectural features of different periods: a squat *tower* with a double-arched window (15th c.), a 17th c. *portico* with double columns and a Catalan-Gothic *portal*.

Petralia Sottana (1000m) Town 46km west of Nicosia (SS120).

Its commanding situation on the southern slopes of the Madonie, with the blessings of cool climate and beautiful wooded landscape have made this a popular summer resort. An added attraction is the *ballo della cordella*, a traditional dance festival which takes place every year in September. In the town is the church of the **Assunta** (Chiesa Matrice) rebuilt in the 17th c. but preserving a Catalan-Gothic *portal* of the 16th c.

Piana degli Albanesi (700m) Town 24km south of Palermo.

Originally known as *Piana dei Greci*, this was a settlement of the Albanians who came to Sicily in the 15th c. The people of the town still use their native tongue and worship in the Greek rite. During religious festivals and ceremonies traditional Albanian costumes are often worn. In the long sloping main street stands the Greek Orthodox church of *S. Demetrio*. On a hill to the south of the town is an *obelisk* in the place where Garibaldi camped during his advance from the west coast (24 May 1860) and planned his strategy for the march on Palermo.

Piazza Armerina (721m) Town 36km south of Enna

The name of this town, the second largest in the province of Enna, is inseparable from the Roman mosaics at nearby Casale (p. 65). Built on three hills, it is topped on the highest point by the dome of its cathedral, which is best reached from the lower town by the Via Garibaldi. At the foot of this street, near the large Piazza Umberto I, stands the plain 13th c. church of *S. Giovanni di Rodi*. As its name suggests, this was a chapel of the Knights of St John.

The Via Garibaldi ascends to the Piazza Garibaldi. From here the Via Cavour climbs steeply to the Piazza Duomo. In the centre of the square is the *Statue of Marco Trigona*, the nobleman who founded the cathedral in 1604. On the south side is the fine 18th c. *Palazzo Trigona*. (It is interesting to note the prominence of the Spanish eagle on this building and the cathedral; a reminder of the period of the Viceroys.)

Cathedral This 17th c. building incorporates a 15th c. *tower*, on the right side, which belonged to an earlier church. Note the two levels of Catalan-Gothic windows that survive (blocked in) in the lower part of the tower. The fine Baroque *entrance* of the cathedral was added in 1719.

Interior To the right of the nave, the elaborate *arch* of the baptistery (school of Gagini)

1 S. Giovanni di Rodi
2 Cathedral
3 Castle
4 Tourist Information Office

Piazza Armerina

belonged to the earlier church. The cathedral has two important treasures. One, which we cannot see, is a Byzantine *Icon of the Madonna*, kept in a silver case on the high altar. This precious work was the gift of Pope Nicholas II to Count Roger before his conquest of Sicily and has been given the name *Madonna delle Vittorie*. The other treasure, in the chapel to the left of the choir, is a beautiful painted *crucifix* (1485). The reverse side of the crucifix is also painted, with a figure of *Christ Risen*. The *Treasury* contains some fine objects.

The street to the right of the cathedral (Via Floresta) leads to a 14th c. *castle* (not open to the public). From here the Via V. Emanuele II leads back down to the Piazza Garibaldi. The churches of Piazza Armerina, mostly late Renaissance or Baroque in style, are too numerous to mention in detail, and many of them are now derelict. The town reached its greatest splendour in the Middle Ages under the Normans and Aragonese, but little survives from this period. The best example is the church of **S. Andrea** (1096) which lies to the north of the town (Via Guccio, 10 min. drive). Frescoes from this church, discovered during recent restoration, have been removed to the Palazzo Abbatellis in Palermo.

On 15th August every year the people of Piazza Armerina celebrate the 'Palio dei Normanni' in honour of their patron saint, S. Maria delle Vittorie, whose icon is in the cathedral. The arrival of Count Roger with the icon is re-enacted in an historical cavalcade on the first day, and on the second day are games and competitions on horseback, reminiscent of the 'Palio' of Siena.

The Roman mosaics at **Casale** are reached from the south of the town (5 km). The ancient site of **Morgantina** lies to the north (15 km).

Punta del Faro
North-eastern point of Sicily (see Messina, Excursions).

Ragusa
(502 m, pop. 59,000) Provincial capital, south-eastern Sicily.

The site of this beautiful old town in the Val di Noto is spectacular: a ridge of rock between two river gorges with a depression dividing it into two prominences. On the western, higher prominence is the main, and newer part of the town: to the east, slightly lower, is the old town, *Ragusa Ibla*.

History The old part, Ibla, derives its name from a settlement of the Sicels, *Hybla Heraia*. As a fortress town of the Byzantines it was overwhelmed by the Arabs in 848, and subsequently taken by the Normans, who

created the county of Ragusa. In 1296 the county of Ragusa was united with that of Módica by the Chiaramonte family. The destruction of the 1693 earthquake caused a new town to be built on the higher ground to the west. This had a separate identity until it was united with Ibla as the provincial capital. Ragusa's prosperity is ensured by its location in one of Italy's richest oil-producing areas: the modern industries of the town have not, however, impinged too much on its cultured, Baroque character.

Walking tour Starting point: **Ponte Nuovo**. This graceful bridge spans the gorge of the Torrente S. Domenica on the south side of Ragusa, on the way into the town from the railway station. Beneath it is a garden and sports stadium, and the entrance to the museum (the latter is most easily reached by steps leading down at the side of the Hotel Mediterraneo).

Museum (Museo Archeologico Ibleo) This new museum, founded in 1960, houses an interesting collection of material from local sites, from the prehistoric to the Byzantine periods. The nucleus of the exhibition is the collection from the Greek site of *Camarina* (6th c. BC) which includes a reconstruction of part of the necropolis with the amphorae and sarcophagi in the position in which they were found in the tombs.

From the Ponte Nuovo the broad Via Roma, with its shops and pavement cafés, leads north. A right turn at the Corso Vittorio Veneto leads into the Piazza S. Giovanni, dominated by the huge and imposing façade of the **Cathedral** (S. Giovanni Battista) built 1706-60. This façade has all the ingredients of the 18th c. Baroque of Sicily's deep south: Corinthian columns, statues, cornices and volutes. The whole effect is dramatised by the siting of the cathedral, on a balustraded terrace above the level of the square.

From the north-east corner of the square the Corso Italia runs eastwards, past the modern *Post Office*, to the Via 24 Maggio, where one commences the descent by steps to the old town. Near the top of the steps is the church of **S. Maria delle Scale**. Originally 15th c., this attractive little church was reconstructed after the earthquake. Part of the portal of the original building was restored, and some of the internal architecture. Of the latter, one can admire the four *arches*, of different styles, that grace the chapels to the right of the nave. Particularly fine is the arch of the second chapel, Catalan-Gothic in style, and

Cathedral, Ragusa

S. Giorgio

ture of its many churches, which rose up after the earthquake of 1693: the Baroque expression is given full range in many interpretations. To the left of the church of the *Anime del Purgatorio*, at the foot of the old town, the Via del Mercato climbs to the summit. After 500 m, a right turn (Largo Camerina and Via Conte Cabrera) leads to the Piazza Duomo.

This square offers the best approach to the majestic golden *façade* of the church of **S. Giorgio**. Completed in 1775 (architect Rosario Gagliardi) this church is the ultimate achievement of the Baroque in southern Sicily, the rhythms of the slightly curved, subtly receding façade and the exuberant, but not too elaborate ornaments fusing to create a superbly graceful effect. Inside, the church is illuminated by the lantern of the large cupola, an addition of 1820. Note the inscription over the inside of the west door to St George, the patron saint of Ragusa.

In the Via 25 Aprile, running from the foot of the Piazza Duomo, is the *Palazzo Donna-fugata*, which houses a fine private collection of Italian and Flemish masters. In the Piazza Pola the façade of the church of *S. Giuseppe* echoes the spirit of S. Giorgio: further on, the Via 25 Aprile terminates at the entrance to the Giardino Ibleo. Before visiting the garden, a moment should be spared for the ruined church of **S. Giorgio Vecchio** to the right. Preserved in the west

that of the third chapel, which is Renaissance. Over the altar of this chapel is an unusual bas-relief in terracotta, the work of the Gagini, depicting the *Transition of the Virgin*.

From the terrace of the church one can enjoy a superb view of **Ragusa Ibla** on its winding spur, the closely-packed and irregular buildings making their own dramatic landscape. Descending to the foot of the new town, one then makes the climb to the old. Ibla's essential charm lies in the architec-

Above: S. Giorgio Vecchio
Left: Giardino Ibleo

wall, which survived the 1693 earthquake, is a beautiful Catalan-Gothic *portal* of the late 15th c. In the lunette is a relief of *St George and the Dragon*.

The **Giardino Ibleo** is one of the most pleasant of Sicily's urban gardens, with an abundance of flowers, trees and fountains and the added feature of an uninterrupted view from the very edge of Ragusa's spur. The garden has in its grounds no less than three churches: *S. Domenico*, *S. Giacomo* and the *Cappuccini Vecchi*, the last named with paintings by Novelli.

The return to the upper town may be made by a bus (No 3) which departs on the hour from the Piazza Pola.

Randazzo (754m) Town 70 km north-west of Catania on circum-Etna route.

There is something unexpected about Randazzo: not merely its sudden appearance in the empty landscape of Etna's hinterland but in the character of the town itself. The medieval aspect of the buildings, with their walls of dark lava, stirs up a feeling of the past.

Least expected is that this town, the nearest to Mt Etna (the crater is only 15km from here) should have managed to survive the multitude of earthquakes and volcanic eruptions that have devastated this area through the centuries. A thriving town during the Swabian and Aragonese periods, it is calamitous that Randazzo should have suffered its first destruction in the last war, when the Germans dug in here before their final retreat across the Strait of Messina. The subsequent Allied bombing damaged many of the old buildings before the town was finally wrested from the Germans (13 August 1943).

Randazzo's principal monuments are the three churches of S. Maria, S. Nicolò and S. Martino. Each is in a different quarter of the town and up to the 16th c. served as the mother church of separate communities. It was finally resolved, in 1916, that S. Maria should be the 'Matrice'.

Built in the early 13th c., the church of **S. Maria**, at the east end of the Corso Umberto I, is one of the few examples of Swabian church architecture in Sicily. The surviving parts of the original building are the *south wall*, with its irregular doors and windows (the *portal* is 16th c. Catalan-Gothic) and the three towering *apses*. The façade of the church is broken by a campanile, both restored in the 19th c. The use of white limestone in the decorative elements provides a striking contrast to the dark lava of the building. The *interior* of the church is vast, with tall columns of lava flanking the nave. The transept and dome, which have detracted considerably from the harmony of the old church, are additions by Marvuglia (1804).

Further west the Corso Umberto I reaches the Via degli Archi, which has remains of medieval arches. This street leads to the church of **S. Nicolò** in the square of the same name. This large church is a patchwork of successive periods of architecture. It was founded in the 14th c. and Frederick II of Aragon, who spent his summers in Randazzo, made it the meeting place of the civic assembly. Some of the original structure may be seen in the east end (apse and transept) and it is interesting to note that part of the buildings around the square are of the same period. The façade is 17th c., the campanile 1789: more recent fabric belongs to the restoration following bomb damage in the last war. The church contains works by Antonello and Giacomo Gagini, and one should note particularly Antonello's statue of *St Nicholas*, on a plinth sculpted with scenes from the saint's life, in the left transept.

In the north-west corner of the square (Via Duca degli Abruzzi) is the *Palazzo Finocchiaro* of 1509—an interesting mixture of Gothic and Renaissance. Returning to the Via Umberto I, the visitor will notice the

S. Maria, Randazzo

vestiges of the old buildings which survived the 1943 bombings. Most interesting is the *Palazzo Scala* (No. 219-221) which was used as a summer residence by Joan, the English wife of the Norman king William II, by members of the Swabian and Aragonese royal families, and by the Emperor Charles V.

In a square at the end of the Corso Umberto I is the church of **S. Martino**. This church—originally 13th-14th c.—is still recovering from serious war damage. In contrast to the sober and uninspiring façade (17th c.) the 14th c. *campanile* has a touch of fantasy. The coupled windows, with their multiple frames banded alternately with white limestone and black lava, the beautiful white triple window at the top, the battlements and crowning octagonal cusp, are features of a totally individual expression of medieval architecture. The church contains a number of works of the 14th and 15th c.—most notably the marble *font* by Ang. Riccioda Messina (1447) to the right of the main entrance.

Near the church are the remains of a medieval *castle*.

Salemi Town in western Sicily in Val di Mazara (38 km east of Marsala), situated amidst beautiful vine-covered hills.

The area was badly hit by the 1968 earthquake and thousands were made homeless: evidence of the impact of the earth movements on the buildings may best be seen at the highest point of the town.

Here stands the **castle** built by the Emperor Frederick II (13th c.) with its prominent cylindrical *tower*, badly shaken by the earthquake, now girt with iron bands. It was on this tower that Garibaldi planted—with his own hands—the tricolor of the new Kingdom of Italy when he arrived here with the Thousand after their historic landing at Marsala. A plaque in the wall near the castle records that at Salemi, on the 14 May 1860, Garibaldi declared himself Dictator of Sicily in the name of King Victor Emmanuel. This made Salemi, in a brief moment of glory, 'the first true capital of United Italy'.

Salina Island see **Aeolian Is.**

S. Angelo Muxaro Village 15 km north of junction with SS118 (Raffadali) 16 km north of Agrigento. (5 km from Raffadali take sharp left at S. Elisabetta.)

Sican **tombs** were found in 1932 on the south and west sides of the hill on which this village stands. The route to the village, through the Valley of the Platani, is very beautiful—but the rewards are limited. A guide will be necessary both for the location and exploration of the tombs, which are reached from a point on the road half-way down the hill. Ask in the square—and hopefully a willing youth will present himself.

The tombs are cut out of the rock, and some of those higher up and later in date (8th-5th c. BC) are 'beehive' in form. The largest of these, known as the *Tomba del Principe*, was converted by the Byzantines into a chapel, known as the *Grotta di S. Angelo*.

S. Biagio Village on north coast on SS113 west of Milazzo.

A brief pause should be made in this traffic-ridden village for a look at a newly-discovered **Roman villa** of the 1st c. AD, just to the south of the main road. The custodian will be found at No 615 (butcher's).

Approximately half the villa has been excavated and before looking at the site it is a good idea to refer to the plan in the small *museum*. So far the visible ruins are of part of the *entrance court* and *peristyle*, the adjoining *tablinum*, with a fine geometric mosaic floor, and—to the east—the *baths*.

S. Maria di Maniace (Abbazia di Maniace) Convent 1.5 km from turning off SS120 13 km west of Randazzo in Etna region.

This old convent, also known locally as the 'Castello', was founded by the Normans on the site of a famous battle (1040) in which the Greek General George Maniakes defeated the Saracens during his abortive attempt to reconquer Sicily for the Byzantine Empire. In 1799 the Bourbon King Ferdinand IV presented the abbey, together with the title of Duke of Bronte, to Admiral Nelson—at that time his ally in the war with France. After Nelson's death it passed on to his heirs who transformed the convent and grounds into a beautiful house and garden. The 6th Duke of Bronte (3rd Viscount Bridport) who died in 1969, devoted his life to the care of this estate and restored the little **church** of the convent. Built at the end of the 12th c. this church has a fine *portal* with a pointed arch and capitals carved with figures. Unhappily the apses were destroyed in the 1693 earthquake, but apart from this the interior retains its Norman form, including much of the original wooden *ceiling*.

SS. Pietro e Paolo Church 5 km from road junction on SS114 (A18) south of S. Teresa di Riva. This road, signposted Limina/Antillo leads first to the small village of Scifi. Before Scifi, and after crossing the river bridge, turn right onto an unmade track leading to the church. From here, the river bed, which is dry for most of the year, may be crossed on foot and the ascent made to the church.

This well-restored church, beautifully sited on a terraced hill on a bend of the River Agro, is the best surviving example of the monasteries of the Basilian (Greek) order endowed by the Normans in the 12th c. A Greek inscription over the west door records that the church was built for the Greek Abbot, Teosterictos, in 1170–72. The exterior walls have an interesting Saracenic pattern of interlacing arches on two levels, the upper level crowned by battlements. The combination of red brick, white limestone and black lava, and the use of chequerboard and other patterns, lends an interesting variety of colour and design to the building. The plan of the *interior* is a nave with three bays and, at the east end, three apses. Over the central bay, and over the crossing, are domes, the first supported by pendentives, the second by a Moorish 'honeycomb'.

SS. Trinità di Delia see Castelvetrano

Sciacca Town on south coast, noted as a centre for thermal cures.

Although the precise date of its foundation is uncertain the Roman name for the town, *Thermae Selinuntinae* ('Baths of Selinus') links Sciacca with the Greek colony of Selinus to the west. The medicinal properties of the thermal springs which are a feature of the town were as much appreciated by the Romans as by contemporary visitors.

The town Sciacca's old buildings show a great variety of styles. Entering from the west through the **Porta S. Salvatore**—an elaborate survival of the 16th c. fortifications of the town—one might anticipate a wealth of Baroque. Instead there are two palaces and two churches, just inside the gate, which incorporate features of different inspirations. To the right is the church of **S. Margherita**, (1342) with a Gothic west door and—on the north side—a later *portal* (16th c.). This beautiful door, facing the Via F. Incisa is by the great Renaissance sculptor Francesco Laurana (in the lunette, *St Margaret and Angels*).

Opposite is the odd-looking church of the **Carmine**, its incomplete 18th c. façade retaining the rose window of an earlier Gothic church. Further on, at No 48, is the **Casa Arone** which retains 15th c. double windows. A finer medieval palace, in the Corso Vittorio Emanuele to the north, is the **Palazzo Steripinto**. This building, with its unusual and attractive *punta di diamante* stonework and swallow-tail battlements is 15th c.

The Corso Vittorio Emanuele leads east to the large Piazza Scandaliato, open on the south side to the sea. From here the street continues to the Piazza Don Minzoni, dominated by the ungainly façade of the **Cathedral** (S. Maria Maddalena). This is an incomplete 18th c. restoration of a 13th c. building, of which only the exterior of the three apses remain. The front and sides of the cathedral are decorated with statues by the Gagini, salvaged from the earlier church.

Cupola, doorway and exterior SS. Pietro e Paolo

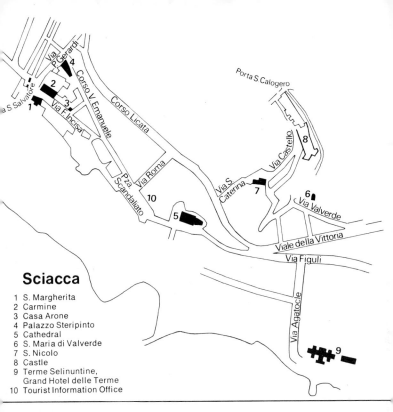

Sciacca

1 S. Margherita
2 Carmine
3 Casa Arone
4 Palazzo Steripinto
5 Cathedral
6 S. Maria di Valverde
7 S. Nicolo
8 Castle
9 Terme Selinuntine,
  Grand Hotel delle Terme
10 Tourist Information Office

The Corso Vittorio Emanuele ends at the Piazza Friscia. From the Viale della Vittoria the second turning on the left leads to the church of **S. Maria di Valverde** or **delle Giummare**, originally Norman but entirely restored in the 16th c. in the Catalan-Gothic style. The rather severe battlements contrast oddly with the Baroque portal (18th c.). A church that has survived more or less intact from the Norman period is the inconspicuous **S. Nicolò** (to reach it, follow the Via Valverde to the west).

From S. Nicolò the Via Castello leads up to a ruined 14th c. *castle*: to the north, near the *Porta S. Calogero*, is a stretch of the town's 16th c. *walls*.

Terme Selinuntine Sciacca's thermal establishment, the largest in Sicily, is situated on the seafront to the south-east of the town. Next to it is the *Grand Hotel delle Terme*, where one can also obtain thermal treatments. The sulphur water which rises naturally here is used for mud-cures, baths and inhalations, the conditions treated varying from arthritis to skin diseases and respiratory complaints. Treatment is available throughout the year.

In a small river valley just outside Sciacca to the east are the *Antiche Terme*. This thermal bathing place is now disused—but the stream is still full of sulphur.

Monte S. Calogero 8 km north-east of Sciacca is this isolated mountain (ancient name *Kronios*) where the mysteries of natural phenomena are additionally imbued by legend. Emanations of hot vapour have made the grottoes in this mountain into steam baths, a purpose for which they have been used since prehistoric times. The carving of benches and the cutting of passages as part of the adaptation of the grottoes to this function was attributed by the ancient Greeks to Daedalus, the legendary master-craftsman who, after building the labyrinth at Knossos must have felt very much at home in these tortuous caverns. Adding to the dark mystery of the *stufe* was the recent discovery (by explorers wearing special breathing equipment) of Copper Age pots in the inner recesses of the caves. Human remains, too, showed that it required more than ritual objects to satisfy the gods of the underworld.

The temperature in these sweating-grottoes, known as the *Stufe Vaporose di S. Calogero* is between 38/40°C (100/104°F). The grottoes are accessible through a modern thermal establishment incorporated in a hotel, the *Hotel delle Stufe* situated below the *Sanctuary of S. Calogero*. Those wishing to visit the grottoes other than for medical reasons must obtain special permission (enquire at the Tourist Office in the Piazza Scandaliato).

Scicli Town in south-eastern Sicily, 10 km south-west of Modica and situated on the same river.

A small town, but with some of the most stunning architecture of 'Spanish' Sicily. Destroyed by the 1693 earthquake it was built anew like Ragusa, Noto and other towns in this region, and has a similar aspect of 18th c. Baroque. This is best seen in the beautiful central square, backed by the sheer hill which was the site of the medieval city up to the 14th c.

Despite the obvious advantages of its setting beneath high cliffs and by the channel of the *Torrente della Cava S. Bartolomeo*, the most eye-catching façade must be that of the church of **S. Bartolomeo** (turn right at top of square).

Segesta Ancient site in north-western Sicily, reached from A29 autostrada 8 km west of Mazara del Vallo junction or by turning off the SS113 Partinico-Trápani road, at a point 13 km west of Alcamo.

History Segesta was founded in the 12th c. BC by the Elymians, the tribe who predominated in the north-western part of Sicily before the arrival of the Phoenicians and Greeks. The history of the city was very

154   *S. Bartolomeo, Scicli*

much affected by its geography. An alliance with the Phoenicians in the west was inevitable: so, too, was the resulting conflict with the Greeks. This had its focus in an interminable war with the Greek colony of Selinus to the south, which the Segestans tried to resolve by an alliance with Athens. This alliance came to an abrupt end with the disastrous defeat of the Athenians at Syracuse in 413 BC.

A more successful alliance was with the Carthaginians, who destroyed Selinus and repelled the attacks of the Syracusan tyrant Dionysius, who laid siege to Segesta in 397 BC. The Greeks finally had their retribution, however, when Agathocles sacked the city in 307 BC. The inhabitants were either slaughtered or sold into slavery, and a new population drafted in by the tyrant. But later on these new Segestans, who had taken on the identity of their hapless predecessors, submitted readily to the Carthaginians when they regained control of the city. Segesta's last alliance, which involved a treacherous betrayal of the Carthaginians, was with the Romans. Its reward was the status of a free city, exempt from tribute to Rome.

The city, which has now almost disappeared completely, was destroyed by the Saracens in the 10th c. All that survives is the temple already mentioned, the theatre on the hill of Monte Barbaro, and the less accessible remains of a sanctuary.

Temple This is without doubt one of the finest surviving examples of classical temple architecture. Although unfinished, it is the consummation of the Doric style, in a setting that few of the other monuments of the Golden Age can match: a low hill straddling a wide fertile valley with gently rising hills on all sides, and no more sign of human habitation than when it was described by Goethe, two centuries ago.

This temple shows that despite their opposi-

tion to the Greeks of Selinus and Syracuse, the Elymians were a totally Hellenized people. A popular theory is that the temple was built to impress the Athenians as part of a public relations act to secure the alliance. The subsequent abandoning of the temple at the time of the Athenians' defeat by Syracuse would make sense if, as the evidence suggests, an Athenian architect had been employed.

The temple is peripteral and hexastyle with 14 × 6 columns. Although the columns, entablature and pediments are complete, the temple has no cella or roof, and it is clear that these were never constructed. The unfinished condition of the temple is also shown by the lack of fluting on the columns and the rough, unsquared corners of the abaci. The blocks of the steps retain the bosses used to assist in the lifting of the stone, and the top of the stylobate is missing the blocks between the columns, which would have been the top step.

A short drive (but a long and arduous walk) up the adjacent hill of Monte Barbaro brings the visitor to the site of the ancient town, flanked to the west by traces of fortifications. At the highest point is a fine theatre (3rd–2nd c. BC) with a diameter of 63 m and 20 rows of seats cut out of the rock. The scena has disappeared, but this can hardly be a loss when one is offered such an eye-watering view of the valley below and a distant glimpse of the sea at the Gulf of Castellammare.

At the foot of Monte Barbaro, to the south-east, recent excavations have uncovered a 6th c. BC sanctuary.

Selinunte (Selinus) Ancient site on west coast of Sicily 5 km south of junction of SS115 and SS115D 37 km west of Sciacca.

History The ancient Selinus took its name from the river running to the west of the site (now the R. Modione) named after the wild celery (selinon) growing on its banks. Founded (c. 650 BC) by the Greeks who had settled Megara Hyblaea on the east coast, Selinus became the westernmost Greek colony in Sicily.

The virtue of the site was more in easy access than impregnability: a river on either side of the acropolis provided the city with two harbours, serving as outlets for the produce of the fertile hinterland. Its position on the western coast of Sicily, commanding a shoreline stretching 100 km from the River Mazarus to the River Platani, ensured a close commercial contact with Africa. It was this proximity that shaped Selinus' relations with the Carthaginians, who, sailing from Africa, had entrenched themselves in the north-west of Sicily. The Selinuntines, though Greek, had no desire to confront the strength of Carthage and settled for a peaceful alliance. Their disputes were, in fact, with a

Hellenized people: the Elymians of Segesta. Segesta, which lay to the north of Selinus, had been established as a settlement since the 12th c. BC, and the arrival of the new colony to the south created a continuing dispute over borders which flared into periodic warfare. The dispute was ultimately to have a destructive effect on Selinus. In 480 BC, when Gelon of Syracuse inflicted his crushing defeat on the Carthaginians at Himera, Selinus was lucky to escape reprisals. She had, after all, been on friendly terms with Carthage and hostile to the pro-Greek Elymians. But in 409 BC her luck ran out. By this time Selinus was a large prosperous city, allied to Syracuse and expanding with the trade she commanded from both the eastern and western Mediterranean. Segesta, feeling threatened, called on Carthage for support. The Carthaginians, who were opposed to the further expansion of Selinus and still embittered by their defeat by the Greeks at Himera 70 years before, responded with a massive invasion force which was landed at the port of Motya on the west coast and marched overland to Selinus. The Selinuntines, who had for so long enjoyed the security of their alliances, were totally unprepared for the attack. After only 9 days the siege-towers and battering rams of the Carthaginian army had broken the walls of the city and Selinus—denied help by her tardy allies in Syracuse and Akragas to the east—succumbed to the inevitable massacre and destruction.

For the remainder of its history, despite a brave attempt by Hermocrates of Syracuse ro resettle Greeks on the acropolis, the city remained in the hands of the Carthaginians. The end of Selinus came c. 250 BC when the Carthaginians, under pressure from the Romans during the First Punic War, abandoned the city for Lilybaeum (Marsala) on the west coast. In the process of evacuation the city was destroyed, and there is no evidence of further settlement.

Tour of the ruins A right turn from the road to Marinella leads to the area of the eastern temples, built by the Greeks in the palmy years before the Carthaginian takeover. In the midst of these enticing ruins the visitor will be somewhat disconcerted by the attentions of the determined sales squad from Marinella, proffering their own 'antiquities'. These scooter-borne predators, with their plastic bags full of bronze lamps, ancient terracottas, early Greek coins and Attic vases, are one of the hazards of a visit to Selinus, but not one that should be taken too seriously. If you are able to convince the earnest vendor that what he is offering as a genuine red-figure amphora of the 6th c. BC is in fact the product of a factory in Athens, skilled in the reproduction of antiquities, you can come away from Selinus with an attractive souvenir for a few hundred lire.

Temple, Segesta

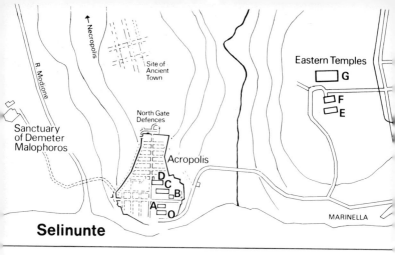

Selinunte

Although it is later than the other two temples on this site, most visitors will wish to commence their tour with **Temple E**. This building, whose columns were recently re-erected, provides an impressive reconstruction of a classical temple, whose basic plan, though a refinement of its archaic predecessors, helps in an understanding of the other ruins. Built in the early 5th c. BC the temple has a Doric peristyle (note the original stucco still visible on the columns of the north side) a *pronaos* at the east end of the *cella* and an *adyton* and *opisthodomos* to the west. The metopes from this temple, which are the best surviving examples of Greek sculpture in Sicily, are now in the Museo Nazionale Archeologico in Palermo. The earthquake which flattened Temple E

also devastated the temples to the north; but no attempt has yet been made to reconstruct them. **Temple F**, adjacent, has interesting differences to Temple E which signify its earlier date (*c.* 560 BC). At the east end, before the entrance to the *cella*, it had a second row of columns. More unusual was the walling up of the space between the outer columns, making a complete enclosure except at the east end, which had entrances between each column. A similar 'infilling' is found at the Temple of Zeus in Agrigento, built slightly later and perhaps in emulation of this temple.

More than twice the size of either of its neighbours is the massive **Temple G**, north of the road. Even with the knowledge that this is the second largest Greek temple in Sicily

(the largest was the Temple of Zeus, already mentioned), the heart of the keenest archaeologist may quail at the sight of this vast chaotic mound of stone, the aftermath of a violent earthquake. The dimensions of the temple are 113m long by 54m wide, the columns 16m high. The diameter of the columns at the base is over 3.3m, and the weight of a single drum has been measured at 100 tons.

At the time they started building the temple (mid 6th c. BC) the Greek Selinuntines were at the height of their power: unhappily the greatest symbol of their achievement was still unfinished when the Carthaginians conquered the city in 409 BC. The 150 years of its construction spanned the archaic and classical periods: evidence of this is in the different style of architecture of the east and west ends of the temple.

At the earlier eastern end the columns are cigar-shaped, with a sharp tapering like those of the Temple of Hera at Paestum in Italy (also mid 6th c. BC): the capitals are flat and pancake-shaped in the very early Doric style. The columns to the west, however, are more cylindrical, like those on Temple E and the Temple of Athena in Syracuse.

Apart from its size, Temple G differs from the other temples at Selinus in the plan of its *cella*. In order to support a roof, across a width of some 18m, the *cella* had to be divided by a double row of superimposed columns. An enclosure at the end of these, at the west end of the *cella*, was the cult room

Above: Temple E   Left & right: Temple G

in which the image of the deity and other sacred objects were kept. (An inscription, now in the Palermo Museum, shows that the temple was dedicated to the god Apollo.)

In the great shambles of broken walls and fallen columns these details may seem a little hard to discern: but the observant explorer will find plenty to instruct him in a scramble through the ruins. In the centre of each fallen drum he will see a recess: this held the pivot that was used to rotate one drum on top another, with abrasive sand between them. This ground the united surfaces to a perfect fit, and obviated the use of mortar. Many of the columns have not been fluted: the strongest evidence that the temple was never completed. Another interesting detail is the U-shaped cuts in the rectangular stones. Unlike the drums of the columns, which could be rolled, these blocks had to be hauled: the U-cuts were for the loop of the ropes which dragged them. Many of the blocks lying around the area of the temple, brought all the way from the quarry at Rocche di Cusa (12 km north-west of Selinus) were in fact never used.

Acropolis The acropolis of Selinus lies to the west of the three temples on the other side of the valley of an extinct river (now the Gorgo di Cottone). The road passes over the site of a harbour, now buried: one of the two harbours of ancient Selinus. Before entering the acropolis the visitor will pass the great **eastern wall**, about 10 m high, which is the largest part of the original defences. From the car park one reaches the central street which leads through the sacred area of the acropolis. To the west there are some ruins of small temples. First is **Temple O**, of which only the stylobate remains. To the north **Temple A** has some interesting features: a step between the *pronaos* and the *cella* and another between the *cella* and the *adyton*; and, just inside the entrance to the *cella*, the base of a round stairway which led to the roof of the temple. Both temples were built in the early 5th c. BC. The remains here are sparse, but one's understanding of them would be greater were it not for the indiscriminate 'tidying up' that has been done on the site. Instead of leaving the pieces in their

natural disorder, or carrying out reconstruction, those involved have re-arranged them in an arbitrary fashion, making walls out of odd bits of column and so on.

Running north of Temple A, and crossing the central street, is another street which traverses the width of the acropolis. At the east end of this is the tiny **Temple B**, built shortly before the evacuation of Selinus *c.* 250 BC. This consisted of a single chamber, like a small chapel, with a portico of four columns. Dominating the acropolis is the north colonnade, partly reconstructed, of **Temple C** (mid 6th c. BC). The lateral colonnades of this temple had 17 columns: those at front and rear, 6. Some of the columns lying around the site are monoliths: those re-erected are of the more classical fluted style which shows that—like Temple G—this temple was many years in construction. Part of the entablature and metopes of Temple C can be seen in the Palermo Museum.

To the north of Temple C, directly adjacent to the street, is the slightly later **Temple D** with 6×13 columns.

Since the founding of Selinus in the 7th c. BC the acropolis was a sacred site on which innumerable shrines and temples were built, including the early *megaron* type, a plain rectangular building without columns. Decorative work from these vanished temples, including the metopes from 'Temple Y', has been found in different parts of the site and can also be seen in the Palermo Museum.

At the north end of the acropolis are the **north gate defences**, with their bastions, ditches and concealed entrances—an intricate system which should appeal to the military minded. Beyond them is the site of the *ancient town*, and further north, the *necropolis*.

Situated to the west of the acropolis, on the west bank of the Modione (the ancient River Selinus) is the **Sanctuary of Demeter Malophoros**. This is one of the earliest sanctuaries to be built by the Greek colonists after their arrival at Selinus in the 7th c. BC. It was dedicated to Demeter in her role as the goddess of fertility (*Malophoros*: bearer of apples) by the local farmers. The propitiation of the goddess must have paid dividends in this luxuriant valley where the wild *selinon* which gave the ancient city its name still flourishes. A walk of 20 minutes, following a path and crossing the river by a footbridge, brings the visitor to the sanctuary. The site is mainly occupied by the *temenos* (sacred enclosure) demarcated by the outline of the ancient wall. Entrance to the *temenos* was by a *propylaeum*, of which traces of the steps, floor and colonnade remain. To the left of this is a secondary enclosure with an altar which was dedicated to another goddess, Hecate. She inhabited the underworld and was companion to Demeter's daughter Persephone, abducted there by Hades. Pilgrims to the main sanctuary were accommodated on a bench running along the wall to the right of the *propylaeum*. Inside the *temenos*, starting from the east, are the ruins of a long sacrificial altar, a curving stone aqueduct for channelling water from a nearby spring, and the small temple of the goddess, an early *megaron* of which part of the walls are still standing, enclosing a *pronaos, cella* and *adyton*. A short distance to the north of the *temenos* is another precinct, sacred to the minor deity Zeus Meilichios. Scattered to the west are a number of *stelae* or commemorative slabs, some of them carved with human heads. The strength of the cult of Demeter was dramatically revealed by the discovery in the *temenos* of thousands of terra-cotta figures of the goddess, offered at her shrine. A selection of these and other objects of the period is now in the Palermo Museum.

Rocche di Cusa The quarries of the ancient city are situated 3.5 km south-west of Campobello, a small town 10 km west of the SS115/115D junction north of Selinunte. It is interesting to see here the method by which the column drums were cut out of the rock.

Solunto (Soluntum, Solus) Ancient site, 17 km east of Palermo, reached by turning off the SS113 at S. Flávia to Porticello. In ½ km, turn left up side road to the site.

This city, wonderfully situated on the side of Monte Catalfano on the spur of land closing the Gulf of Palermo, was founded by the tyrant Timoleon in the middle of the 4th c. BC. It replaced an earlier settlement of the Phoenicians to the south-west, which has now disappeared. A hundred years later, after the Roman conquest of the island, the Greek city (named *Soloeis*) became the Roman *Soluntum*, or *Solus*. The ruins visible today are Roman but the city retains its original Greek plan.

Ancient city The site is approached by a path leading up from the small *antiquarium* overlooking the car park. The first remains, at the top of the path, are those of the *baths*: the path then joins the main street of the ancient city, identified currently as the *Via dell' Agora*. This is a fine example of the *decumanus* or principal thoroughfare of the Roman city, running straight through it on the long axis. It is finely paved with stone, in some places with terracotta in a chessboard pattern. An interesting detail in this road is the series of circular sockets running across its width at crossroads, used for fixing a movable bridge in position to connect side streets when the *decumanus* was awash in wet weather.

The greatest concentration of buildings is to the left of the *decumanus* on the slope of the hill. These are the *insulae*, the back-to-back dwellings of the ordinary people which were often used as shops. Some of these contain vestiges of frescoes and mosaic floors. One house, whose frescoes have been enclosed for protection, has a large cistern adjacent, part of the complex water system necessary to serve the population on this arid hill-side (note also the gutters running along the streets). A more prestigious dwelling is the one mistakenly known as the **Ginnasio**, with a partly re-erected peristyle consisting of six Doric columns with a section of the entablature in position.

Continuing northwards along the *decumanus*, the foundations of a gateway mark the entrance to the *agora*, a large open space with shops on one side. At the north end of the street is a public *cistern*, originally covered, and on the side of the hill opposite a tiny semicircular *odeon* or *bouleuterion* and a larger *theatre* of the Hellenistic-Roman period. Further on are more remains of *Roman houses* with floor mosaics and frescoes, and it is worth walking to the furthest point, not only to see one particularly fine example but also to admire the view. This is just one of the views from Solunto. On a clear day the most spectacular—from the summit of the ancient city—embraces Cefalù, the Aeolian Isles and Mt Etna. Excavations at this site are still in progress and it is estimated that three quarters of the city is as yet uncovered.

Stromboli Island see **Aeolian Is.**

Syracuse (Siracusa) (pop. 110,000) Provincial capital on south-east coast, situated partly on the mainland (**Achradina**) and partly on the connected small island of **Ortygia**.

The fame of this city springs from its place in antiquity, as the centre of Greek power in Sicily for more than 500 years. The virtues of the site will be quickly appreciated by the visitor. Ortygia lies as a salient protecting two harbours: to the north the *Porto Piccolo*, to the south the *Porto Grande*. The Porto Grande is Sicily's finest natural harbour, forming a 'C' with its two points—the tip of Ortygia and the headland of Plemmyrion to the south—only a mile apart. Behind Syracuse lies the long ridge of Epipolae, a natural rampart whose defence ensured the security of the city. To the south are the marshes around the Rivers Anapo and Ciane, which proved almost as effective as a natural barrier to invading armies.

History All these points commended the site to the Greeks from Corinth who founded a colony here *c.* 733 BC, driving out the Sicels who at that time were occupying the island of Ortygia. The development of Syracuse was *via* a number of outposts built to protect the inland routes to the settlement: one of these, Achradina, became eventually the mainland extension of Ortygia, connected to the island by a causeway. But the expansion of Syracuse went beyond this. Throughout the 7th c. BC she established splinter colonies in the south-east corner of Sicily, among them Akrai (Palazzolo Acréide) Netum (Noto Antica) Helorus (Eloro) and Kamarina (Camarina). By this means the colony became the city-state, with its own dependencies: but it was not until the 5th c. BC, when Syracuse started forming alliances with other Greek colonies in the island that her power became significant.

The agent of the first alliance was not however a Syracusan but **Gelon**, tyrant of the colony of Gela on the south coast. Gela, the settlement of Dorian Greeks from Crete and Rhodes, had for some time been at war with Syracuse: but Gelon brought the two cities together peacefully and established himself as the first tyrant of Syracuse (491–478 BC). He had earlier made an alliance with Akragas (Agrigento) to the west of Gela: this brought yet more territory to Syracuse (a cornerstone of which was the port of Himera on the north coast, a dependency of Akragas). Such expansion could not go unchallenged by the Carthaginians, whose position in the west of the island was threatened. The clash between the two powers—Greece and Carthage—proved, however, disastrous for the Carthaginians. At the Battle of Himera (480 BC) their army was routed by the combined forces of Gelon of Syracuse and Theron of Akragas, and with this victory Syracuse won its dominance of Sicily, which was to last until the Roman occupation.

Under Gelon the city greatly enlarged, and many temples were built, among them the Temple of Athena which survives today as part of the cathedral. Gelon's successor, **Hieron I**, increased the reputation of the city by inviting to his court the pick of Greece's poets and philosophers, including Aeschylus, whose works were performed in a theatre built by the tyrant (the predecessor of the existing theatre). Syracuse rapidly established itself as the most important city in Magna Graecia, and its influence inevitably provoked a contest with its arch-rival in the Greek world—Athens.

Athens, at this time in the middle of her campaigns against Sparta, decided to carry the war to Sicily. Her jealousy of Syracuse was aggravated by the fact that the Syracusans, with their Dorian ancestry, had tended to favour Sparta. In 415 BC the Athenians sent a war fleet to Syracuse and landed its army on the shores of the Great Harbour. A determined onslaught at this point might have won the city for the Athenians, but their leaders were cautious men and having gained a position on the ridge of Epipolae overlooking the city, they settled down to several months of extensive preparations, which included the construction of a system of walls, both to enclose the city and to defend their own position. The Syracusans responded by building their own walls across the line of the Athenians'. This caused further delays to their enemy, and in the meanwhile a relief force arrived from Sparta, which succeeded in trapping the Athenian fleet in the harbour. The Athenians were next to receive reinforcements, but these were mainly lost in an attempt on the Syracusan positions around Epipolae. The final battle, in the Great Harbour, resulted in the destruction of the Athenian fleet and the

rout of their soldiers, who were either killed in flight or rounded up and imprisoned in the notorious *latomie*, the great stone quarries of Syracuse.

If ever Syracuse needed a statesman, it was at this moment in her history. Although Syracuse had defeated Athens, the struggle had greatly weakened the city and the Carthaginians began to gain ground in the west, taking Selinus, Himera and Akragas. The threat to Syracuse was imminent, and the city was saved only by the political skill of its new leader **Dionysius I** (405–367 BC).

Dionysius, having concluded a peace treaty with the Carthaginians, made use of the breathing-space to rebuild the defences of Syracuse. The fortifications of Epipolae, including the magnificent Castle of Euryalus, date from this period, and it was these defences which saved the city from the eventual Carthaginian attack under Himilco (397 BC). Having ensured the security of Syracuse, Dionysius went on with a ruthless determination to make it the capital of the Greek world. In the 38 years of his tyranny he waged four wars against the Carthaginians, and although he was unable to expel them from Sicily he held them sufficiently in check to allow himself the freedom of other campaigns, notably in southern Italy. His greatest success here was the capture of the seaport of Rhegion (Reggio), which gave him control of the straits between Italy and Sicily. He went on to further conquests in eastern Italy, and established settlements as far away as Illyria, on the Dalmatian coast. Other settlements founded by Dionysius in Sicily itself include Halaesa and Tyndaris on the north coast.

During his tyranny Dionysius wrote many plays and poems for performance at the Olympic Games and similar festivals of ancient Greece; but they were rarely well received, not only because of their inferiority but because of the unpopularity of Dionysius' autocratic rule in the more democratic parts of the Greek world.

After Dionysius, Syracuse was ruled alternately by his son **Dionysius II** and his brother-in-law **Dion**. Despite the influence of Plato, (whom Dion had engaged to instruct the younger Dionysius) neither man was a successful tyrant and eventually, after a period of rebellion and political assassination the Syracusans had to appeal to the mother city of Corinth for help.

The man of the hour was **Timoleon**, a Corinthian general who with a small force of 1000 mercenaries landed at Tauromenion (Taormina) and marched on Syracuse (343 BC). Disposing of Dionysius II, Timoleon set about ensuring that no other tyrant would achieve a similar position of power by destroying the island fortress of Ortygia. This had been constructed by Dionysius I as a military headquarters, to protect himself and his followers, and Timoleon now restored it as part of the city, repopulating it with settlers from Corinth. He applied the same principle to other cities in Sicily, removing tyrants and settling Greeks from the mother country. He also defeated the Carthaginians in a great battle by the Krimisos River east of Segesta, a victory for the Greeks second only to Himera. The ensuing peace treaty settled the traditional boundary between the two powers: the Halykos River in western Sicily. It is extraordinary that in the seven or eight years of his rule (343–336 BC) Timoleon achieved so much: and regrettable that his example was so quickly forgotten. The next ruler of significance, **Agathocles** (317–289 BC) was a tyrant in the fullest sense of the word, consumed by a ruthless ambition that was nearly to prove the downfall of Syracuse. Renewing the conflict with the Carthaginians, he extended the campaign into North Africa itself. His bravado is best illustrated by the fact that he sailed for Africa while his own city, Syracuse, was being besieged by the Carthaginians (310 BC). It was a canny move, for a large part of the Carthaginian force surrounding Syracuse had to be withdrawn for the defence of their own city of Carthage, now threatened by Agathocles. This enabled the defenders of Syracuse to overcome their besiegers, and in the meantime Agathocles had conquered Tunis and was marching on Carthage. Although he never took the enemy capital, Agathocles conquered a large part of their territory, and in his moment of triumph declared himself a king. From this point he overreached himself. In his determination to dominate the other cities of Sicily he stirred up an enormous hatred in the island and an alliance led by Akragas opposed him. A later expedition to Africa was a failure and Agathocles spent the rest of his life warring on two fronts, against both Carthaginians and Sicilian rebels.

After Agathocles' death Akragas and Syracuse came together again in a common appeal to Greece for help against the Carthaginians. This time their champion was **Pyrrhus**, king of Epirus, a remarkable general who took time off from fighting the Romans in Italy to come and drive the Carthaginians out of Sicily (278–276 BC). This he all but succeeded in doing, taking every Carthaginian stronghold except Lilybaion (Marsala) on the west coast. This proved a calamitous omission. Lilybaion was the Syracuse of Carthage: a vital port, trading-post and military stronghold. When Pyrrhus withdrew from his siege of Lilybaion to return to Italy, the Carthaginians, their base intact, were able to quickly recover their lost territory.

The last tyrant of importance to rule Syracuse was **Hieron II**, one of Pyrrhus' generals who was elected King of Syracuse after Pyrrhus' departure from the island. During his long reign (265–215) the Romans, who had gained a strategic foothold at Messina, gradually won control of the island from the Carthaginians (First Punic War 264–241 BC). In this situation Hieron's problem was one of survival. As Greek ruler of Syracuse he had to perform a balancing act between the two warring powers to save his city. His support for Carthage could be taken to the point that the Romans were encamped outside his city: then, with supreme dexterity, he managed an alliance with the Romans.

This capacity for survival was Hieron's most remarkable quality. Unlike Dionysius or Agathocles he did not seek expansion of power but the exploitation of the *status quo*: in this case the position of Syracuse as a small and isolated city kingdom whose independent existence was at the disposal of her Roman masters. The relationship between the two

Syracuse
The Mainland

1 S. Nicolo
   (Tourist Information Office)
2 Roman Amphitheatre
3 Altar of Hieron II
4 Greek Theatre
5 Nymphaeum,
   Street of the Tombs
6 Sanctuary of Apollo,
   Linear Theatre
7 Latomia del Paradiso,
   Orecchio di Dionigi,
   Grotta dei Cordari
8 Latomia di S. Venera
9 S. Giovanni alle Catacombe
10 Latomia di Villa Landolina
   (site of new museum)
11 Catacomb of Vigna Cassia
12 Latomie dei Cappuccini
13 S. Lucia
14 Roman Gymnasium
15 Station
16 Tourist Information Office

Via Puglia

Via Bassa Acradina

Via Augusto von Platen

Via Torino

TYCHE

Riviera Dionisio il Grande

Viale Teocrito

Viale Luigi Cadorna

Via Monte Grappa

Corso Gelone

Via Agatocle

A C H R A D I N A

Viale A. Diaz

Viale R. Margherita

Porto Piccolo

PO

Corso Umberto I

Porto Grande

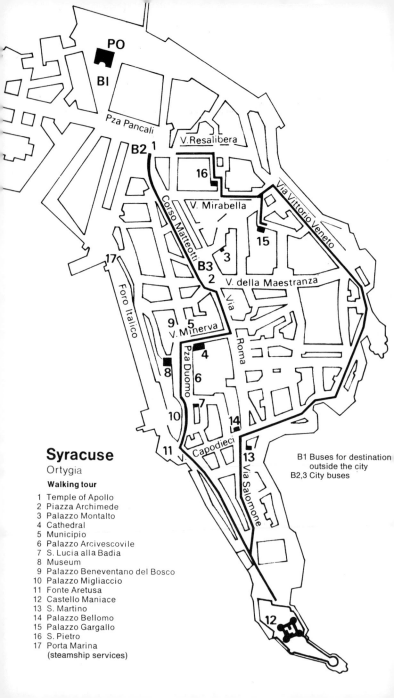

Syracuse

Ortygia

Walking tour

1 Temple of Apollo
2 Piazza Archimede
3 Palazzo Montalto
4 Cathedral
5 Municipio
6 Palazzo Arcivescovile
7 S. Lucia alla Badia
8 Museum
9 Palazzo Beneventano del Bosco
10 Palazzo Migliaccio
11 Fonte Aretusa
12 Castello Maniace
13 S. Martino
14 Palazzo Bellomo
15 Palazzo Gargallo
16 S. Pietro
17 Porta Marina
   (steamship services)

B1 Buses for destination
outside the city
B2,3 City buses

PO

B1

Pza Pancali

V. Resalibera

B2   1

16

V. Mirabella

Corso Matteotti

Via Vittorio Veneto

15

3

B3

2

V. della Maestranza

17

Via Roma

Foro Italico

9   5

V. Minerva

4

8

Pza Duomo

6

7

10

14

11   V.   Capodieci   13

Via Salomone

12

could best be developed by trade, with Syracuse the chief supplier of grain to the Roman forces in the island. The Romans, engaged elsewhere, were happy to allow Syracuse her autonomy, and for the next fifty years the city enjoyed the most prosperous period of her history, undisturbed by foreign adventures and unmolested from within. Much work was done on public buildings in this period, including the construction of the Altar of Zeus and the enlargement of the Greek theatre. Work was also carried out on the improvement of the city's defences, a task which Hieron assigned to the talents of the great mathematician Archimedes, who was a native of Syracuse.

After Hieron's death (215 BC) the splendid isolation of Syracuse came to a rapid and bitter end. This was the time of the Second Punic War (218–201 BC) and influenced by Hannibal's successes against the Romans in southern Italy, the Syracusans committed the fatal error of switching their alliance back to the Carthaginians. The result was a Roman attack on the city, commuted—after an effective defence by Archimedes' ingenious armoury of weapons—into a siege. The Syracusans, assisted by the Carthaginians, put up a strong resistance and the siege lasted two years (213–211 BC). In the end it was malaria (contracted in the marshes south of the city where they were encamped) that knocked out the Carthaginians: the Syracusans were defeated by treachery. When the Roman general Marcellus entered the gates of Ortygia (opened from within) he was amazed at the beauty and richness of the island city: so amazed that although he plundered its treasures he did not destroy the temples, palaces and other fine buildings that were the legacy of the tyrants and kings who had held this stronghold for five centuries.

Though it had now been conquered Syracuse retained its prominence as the capital of the Roman province of Sicilia. Under the Romans, however, the island's agriculture was badly mismanaged and her prosperity declined. The Romans made themselves owners of vast estates and employed Sicilian slaves—former prisoners of war—to work the land. These slaves, who were treated with extreme cruelty, twice revolted (135–132 and 104–101 BC), causing great destruction in the island.

Syracuse suffered particular despoliation at the hands of the Roman Verres. This man, appointed governor of Sicily, used the power of his office to plunder the city for his personal gain, ruthlessly executing any who opposed him. Though denounced by the orator Cicero, it was three years (73–71 BC) before he was deposed and exiled. But this was not the end of the city's impoverishment. In 43 BC Sicily became the stronghold of Sextus Pompey, the rival of Caesar's heir

apparent, Octavian. For seven years, during the ensuing civil war, he held the island, dividing his time between fighting Octavian and plundering the island's most important cities, including Syracuse. The most serious effect of the war, perhaps, was the suspension of trade between Sicily and Rome. Rome lost her granary, and Sicily her market. Syracuse, the port through which much of the corn had been shipped to Rome, lost her role as a merchant city and sank into oblivion.

After the defeat of Sextus (36 BC) it became the task of Octavian, the new Emperor Augustus, to revive the island. His first move was to recolonize Syracuse and restore its position as the chief city of the Roman province. The *Pax Romana* did the rest. 300 years of peace and an energetic programme of rebuilding put Syracuse back in the league of maritime cities: a key port-of-call for Mediterranean trade. In this period St Paul visited Syracuse, but his visit has only a token significance in the history of Christianity in the island. The apostle was not on a missionary journey but in the custody of the Romans, on the way to his trial in Rome. The great hero of early Christianity was St Marcian who became the first Bishop of Syracuse and was martyred here in the 3rd c. AD. A later martyr was St Lucy, the patron saint of Syracuse.

In the cathartic period of Rome's demise and the emergence of Byzantium, Sicily was beset by barbarian invasions: first the Franks, then the Goths and Vandals. It had to await the liberation of the Emperor Justinian's general Belisarius, who in 535 AD finally drove the barbarians from the island. Under the Byzantine Empire the Greek culture reasserted itself in Sicily and Syracuse became an archbishopric of the early Christian Church. For five brief and glorious years, when the Emperor Constans moved his court here from Constantinople, Syracuse became the capital of the Byzantine Empire: but after his assassination (668 AD) the capital reverted to Constantinople.

In this period the Arabs began their first raids on Sicily: 200 years later, in 878 AD, they were at the gates of Syracuse. There followed the most traumatic siege that the city had ever endured, in which the citizens had to resort to cannibalism for survival, only to be massacred when the Arabs eventually took the city. The accumulated treasures of more than 300 years of Byzantine rule were looted by the Arabs and the fortifications destroyed. This was the end of the Greek city, the only remission being a brief occupation by the Byzantine general Maniakes in 1038. Later on the Normans arrived in the island (1061) and began the process of driving out the Arabs.

Syracuse was not an Arab stronghold (their

capital was at Palermo) but when the Normans entered it they found an Arabized city. Although the Arabs had tolerated Christianity there had been no church building, or building of any importance in the city for 200 years. The city's recovery began under the Normans and continued under the rule of the Holy Roman Emperor Frederick II (Frederick I of Sicily) who fortified Ortygia with the Castello Maniace (1239).

In the 14th c. during the period of Spanish rule, Syracuse became the seat of the *Camera Reginale*, a royal domain given as a dowry to the Queen of Spain. As a result Syracuse returned to its former prosperity and many fine *palazzi* were built. Unfortunately many of these Renaissance buildings were destroyed in a disastrous earthquake in 1693, and much of the city's Baroque architecture—such as the rather overpowering façade of the Cathedral—dates from the subsequent rebuilding of Syracuse at the tail-end of the Spanish period.

The last damage that the city sustained, after 2,700 years of sieges, sackings, revolts and natural disasters, was in World War II, when the city was occupied by both German and Allied forces. Fortunately the air attacks were largely confined to the dock area.

The town Modern Syracuse includes the island of *Ortygia* and the adjacent borough of *Achradina*. This has kept its ancient Greek name, and the city also embraces three other ancient quarters, namely *Tyche, Neapolis* and *Epipolae*. Most of the business activity of the town is concentrated in Achradina, and most of the hotels and shops in the area of the Corso Gelone near the railway station. Local sightseeing is largely confined to the Island of Ortygia or Citta Vecchia (Old City) and Neapolis, with its vast Archaeological Zone. These two areas of antiquity, which even the casual sightseer will find fascinating, justify a visit of not less than two days: but if a longer visit is preferred, with time off for sea-bathing, there are resorts to the south of the city (*Lido Arenella, Ognina, Fontane Bianche*). These are Italian, rather than international resorts, although there is now an excellent new international hotel at Fontane Bianche. The most attractive part of the coastline is the lower curve of the 'C' of the Porto Grande (Great Harbour). This leads out to the Maddalena Peninsula and Plemmyrion Point, where there is a tourist village. The coast here is a mixture of rocks and sandy beaches. To the north of Syracuse the coast is unsuitable for bathing. The land rises steeply and the railway line girdles the cliffs.

Walking tour of Ortygia (see map p. 166) Starting point: **Piazza Pancali.** This square lies to the east of the Ponte Nuovo, the bridge connecting Ortygia with the mainland. In the south-east corner of the square are the remains of the **Temple of Apollo.** This temple,

which lies below the level of the square, was excavated in 1938. It is one of the oldest Doric temples in Sicily, corresponding in date to the Olympieion, outside the city, and the earliest of the temples at Selinunte (mid 6th c. BC).

Its plan is peripteral and hexastyle (6×17 columns) with a double colonnade at the front. All that remains now is the stereobate, partly rebuilt, two of the columns with part of the architrave, fragments of other columns and part of the south wall of the *cella.* Before excavation this temple was covered by buildings of the Spanish period, and before that it was used as a church by the Normans. The arched opening in the *cella* wall, some height above the original floor of the temple, is a survival of that Norman conversion.

From the Piazza Pancali follow the Corso G. Matteoti to the Piazza Archimede, the central square of the old city. The *fountain* in the middle is 20th c., but has the spirit of the Renaissance, depicting that legendary moment when the nymph Arethusa was changed into a spring. The buildings of the square, though commercial, have interesting details. The **Palazzo Lanza** on the south side (No 29) is 15th c., with a delicate *double window* of the period. The **Banca d'Italia** on the west side has a 15th c. *staircase* in its courtyard, in the Spanish Catalan style.

From the north-east corner of the square the Via Montalto leads to one of the saddest sights in old Syracuse: the rapidly crumbling **Palazzo Montalto.** This palace, built in 1397, is one of the few surviving examples of the Chiaramonte style of architecture in Sicily. It is little more than an echo of the grander palaces built by the Chiaramonte family and their followers elsewhere in Sicily earlier in the 14th c., but the two elegant *windows* on the north side, one double-arched, one triple-

Windows, Palazzo Montalto

along the north side of the cathedral. This is one of Sicily's most pleasant squares, not only for the architecture that surrounds it but for its unaccustomed and refreshing quietness: the special virtue of its location, tucked away in the corner of an island.

Dominating the square is the Baroque front of the **Cathedral** (Santa Maria delle Colonne). This is undoubtedly Sicily's most unusual building, for the simple reason that it combines in the one structure the most important temple of the ancient city with the most important church of the modern.

Visitors passing along the Via Minerva will already have noticed the Doric columns buried in the north wall of the cathedral. These belong to the Temple of Athena, built here by Gelon, the first tyrant of Syracuse, in the 5th c. BC. This temple (erected on the site of an earlier, archaic, temple) was built in celebration of the Greek victory over the Carthaginians at Himera, and was dedicated to Athena in her role of the Warrior Goddess. Her statue adorned the roof, and the temple was elsewhere lavishly decorated. Details of this decoration come to us from Cicero in the record of his attack upon the Roman praetor Verres, who pillaged and defaced the temple in the 1st c. BC. Before this plunder the temple was one of the most magnificent in the ancient world, with doors of ivory and gold and a series of wall paintings inside depicting the victories of Agathocles over the Carthaginians. There were also paintings of the tyrants and kings of Syracuse, which one can only wish had survived.

Of the temple itself, enough has survived to give an idea of its form, as will be seen on a tour of the cathedral. The temple was of the traditional Doric style with 6 × 14 columns. The colonnades of the peristyle have disappeared at the east and west ends but those on the north and south are largely intact, embedded in the walls of the cathedral. The architrave on the north colonnade (Via Minerva) is topped by a decorative Norman crenellation. The columns still rest on the three-stepped stylobate of the ancient temple.

Like the neighbouring Temple of Apollo, the Temple of Athena was converted into a church in the Byzantine period. In 640 AD Bishop Zosimus transferred the cathedral here from its original site in Achradina. The Normans made further alterations, and in the 18th c., after the destructive earthquake of 1693, the cathedral was rebuilt in the Baroque style. The front is impressive, with fine statues by Marabitti. Flanking the steps are *St Peter* and *St Paul*: on the façade, on either side of the *Madonna*, are *St Marcian*, first Bishop of Syracuse, and *St Lucy*, the city's patron saint.

arched, preserve the essence of the Sicilian Gothic. What remains of this palace is now propped up by temporary buttresses at the front and rear. The buildings to the east have disappeared and it is possible from this side to see the arcaded gallery at the first floor level which at one time must have overlooked a courtyard. While work is in progress on restoring other buildings of this period in Ortygia it is regrettable that this old palace has not received more immediate attention. From the Piazza Archimede the tour continues along the Via Roma. A right turn at the Via Minerva leads to the Piazza Duomo,

Entering the cathedral one can easily grasp the form of the ancient temple. The nave is in fact the original *cella*, the walls of which

Cathedral, Syracuse

have been pierced by eight arched openings to connect the nave with the aisles. At the west end, set into the wall on either side of the entrance, are two of the columns of the *opisthodomos* (rear vestibule) of the ancient temple. The columns of the peristyle can be seen in the aisles: on the north side, embedded in the walls of the cathedral; on the south side, separating the chapels from the south aisle. The effect of the various earthquakes which have struck Syracuse can be seen in these columns, some of which are shattered and out of alignment.

South aisle The first chapel (*baptistery*) contains a Norman *font* cut from an antique marble with a Greek inscription, resting on seven bronze lions. The mosaic vestiges on the wall behind it, in the Cosmatesque style, are also a relic of the Norman church. Next is the *Cappella di S. Lucia*, with bronze gates by Spagnuolo (1605). In this chapel is a silver statue of *St Lucy* (1599). The casket on which it stands (1610) and the altarpiece (1781) are also of silver (the statue, which is much venerated, is on show only a few days each year). The third and largest chapel, closed by 19th c. wrought-iron gates of special delicacy, is the *Cappella del SS. Sacramento*. This contains an altar with a marble relief of the *Last Supper* by Fil. Valle (1762) and above it a polychrome marble *tabernacle* (1752) by the Neapolitan architect Vanvitelli. At the end of the aisle is the *Cappella del Crocifisso* which contains, on the left wall, a painting of *St Zosimus* attributed to Antonello da Messina, Sicily's greatest native painter. Opposite, from Antonello's school, is a painting of *St Marcian*.

A door on the right leads to the *Sacristy of the Chapel*, from which a further door (left) leads on to the *Sacristy of the Church*. This contains fine carved *stalls* of the 15th c. There is at present no access to the Treasury.

The choir retains its Baroque decoration, stripped from the body of the church. The altar incorporates part of the entablature of the ancient temple.

North aisle The apse at the end of this aisle, to the left of the choir, is the only relic of the Byzantine church. In it stands a *Madonna della Neve* (of the Snow) by Antonello Gagini (1512). This sculptor is represented by another statue in the aisle itself, *St Lucy* (between the 4th and 5th columns). Other statues in this aisle are also by the Gagini.

The classical bareness of this cathedral (ignoring the vestiges of Baroque) makes it one of the most appealing religious buildings in Sicily.

Municipio Next to the cathedral, on the opposite side of Via Minerva, are the city's municipal offices, housed in the building of the old cathedral seminary. The building stands on the site of an *Ionic temple*—a rarity in Sicily. On either side of the entrance there is an exhibition of fragments from the

temple, with a reconstruction of capitals and columns. The foundation of the temple may be seen in the basement of the building, with relics of the earliest settlement (8th c. BC). The temple, which had 6 × 14 columns, was built *c.* 530 BC, 50 years before the Temple of Athena.

The other buildings in the Piazza Duomo (going clockwise around the square) are: next to the cathedral, **Palazzo Arcivescovile** (Archbishop's Palace). The lower two storeys date from 1618, the third storey from 1751. The building contains a library of classical and medieval manuscripts. Across the Via S. Lucia, in the south-east corner of the square, is the church of **S. Lucia alla Badia**, built after the 1693 earthquake in the Baroque style. Opposite the Archbishop's Palace is the museum building, and next to that the **Palazzo Beneventano del Bosco**, rebuilt in 1775. This fine building, which has a beautiful inner courtyard and pavilion, rounds off a charming square which must have looked much the same 200 years ago.

Museum (Museo Nazionale Archeologico) This museum, the National Museum of Syracuse, is shortly to be transferred to new premises at the Villa Landolina on the mainland. In view of this impending change, only a general description of the collection will be given (for opening times, see p. 25).

The museum is the headquarters of the *Soprintendente alle Antichita della Sicilia Orientale* (Superintendent of Antiquities, Eastern Sicily) and most of the collection comes from this region, covering all periods from the prehistoric to the Byzantine. From the *Palaeolithic* and *Mesolithic* periods are fossil bones and simple stone implements; then from the *Neolithic* period (c. 3000 BC) tools of flint and obsidian (the latter imported from Lipari) and the first pottery. Much of this pottery, which has impressed decoration (i.e. impressed on the clay before baking) was imported from the eastern Mediterranean and was found at Stentinello and other Neolithic sites in the vicinity of Syracuse ('Stentinello' culture). The *Bronze Age*, which began c. 1800 BC, is represented by finds from necropolises at Castelluccio, Thapsos and other sites. These include bronze weapons and jewellery. There are also models of the rock-cut tombs introduced in this period, which show how the underground chambers were constructed (note the use of channels to drain off rain-water). Of special interest are the carved *tomb doors* from Castelluccio, the only examples of prehistoric stone carving in Sicily.

The beginning of *Greek* influence in Sicily is best illustrated by the pottery of the 8th–7th c. BC, decorated in the Geometric style. From the various colonies in the south-east a great wealth of material has been recovered. This includes 'burial objects, figurines of deities, theatrical masks, pottery, armour and weapons. The richest hoard was from the Fusco necropolis (Syracuse), a cemetery in use from the foundation of the city by the Greeks (c. 733 BC) to the arrival of the Romans (211 BC). The pottery found in the tombs of this necropolis is particularly interesting, spanning 500 years of decorative development.

The best examples of sculpture and architecture belong to the archaic period of the Greek colony (6th–5th c. BC). The outstanding sculptures here are the **Kouroi**. These are three male figures (one a torso) from Megara Hyblaea, Lentini and Syracuse. From the same period are fragments of the *Temple of Athena*, discovered during excavations beneath the cathedral in 1912–17. These include a section of the terracotta frieze of the earlier Archaic temple, and a reconstruction of part of the cornice of the temple itself, with seven lion-headed waterspouts. Part of the frieze of the *Temple of Apollo* may also be seen, and vestiges of other buildings of the period. Perhaps the most remarkable piece of archaic sculpture is the seated figure of the **Goddess Suckling Twins** from Megara Hyblaea (6th c. BC).

From the *Roman* period comes the celebrated **Venus Anadyomene** or **Landolina Venus**. It is difficult to accept this beautiful statue (discovered in 1804 by the archaeologist Landolina) as merely a Roman copy of a Hellenistic original. The delicacy of the carving and the purity of the marble give the figure a superbly life-like quality. An original Hellenistic work is the statue of *Hercules* (300 BC). The museum is very rich in objects from the Hellenistic and Roman Syracuse, including mosaic pavements, caryatids from the Greek theatre, a head of *Zeus* from the Roman amphitheatre, and statues of *Muses* from the Nymphaeum.

The *Early Christian* (Byzantine) period is represented largely by finds from the catacombs: inscriptions, portions of frescoes,

Sarcophagus of Adelphia, Syracuse Museum

funerary lamps. The greatest treasure from the catacombs of San Giovanni is the marble **Sarcophagus of Adelphia** (4th c. AD). Adelphia was the wife of a magistrate, Count Valerius, and their portraits form part of the relief, enclosed by a sea-shell. The other reliefs depict scenes from the Old and New Testaments.

No-one visiting the Syracuse Museum should miss the unique **coin collection** (apply to the custodian), which includes the first coins struck in Syracuse (6th c. BC). A portrait gallery of the tyrants, from Gelon to Hieron II, exists in the heads on these coins—virtually the only record we have of their physical appearance. The most beautiful coins are those struck to commemorate special events, e.g. the large golden *decadrachms* marking the Syracusans' victory over the Athenians. One of these bears the head of the nymph Arethusa, surrounded by dolphins.

Palazzo Migliaccio This 15th c. building lies on the right of the Via Picherale, going south from the Piazza Duomo. It was incorporated in the old *Hotel des Étrangers*, but retains a fine balcony of marble decorated with chevrons of black lava. The Via Picherale leads down to the **Fonte Aretusa** (Fountain of Arethusa), one of the most romantic diversions of a tour of old Syracuse. The romance lies not so much in the fountain itself, which is now nothing more than a placid pool enclosed by stone walls, but in the legend attached to it. The ancients who first recorded this freshwater spring, issuing mysteriously from a grotto at the tip of Ortygia, found a home for it in legend. The most popular version was that a nymph, Arethusa, pursued by the river-god Alpheus in the Peloponnese, leapt into the sea and was changed into a spring by the goddess Artemis. To pursue her, Alpheus in turn changed into a river, and his waters crossed the sea to Ortygia to mingle with those of Arethusa. This legend was always very popular with the Greek colonists of Syracuse, for the associations it created with the mother country. The goddess they had transported with them to Syracuse reigned supreme as Artemis Arethusa.

The fountain had not only an emotional but a practical significance for the Syracusans. During the many prolonged sieges which the city endured, the fountain provided a vital supply of fresh water for the defenders. Visitors, too, sampled the water: most famously Admiral Nelson, who in 1798 brought his fleet into the Great Harbour and took on water here, saying: 'Surely, watering at the Fountain of Arethusa, we must have victory.' He went on to win the Battle of the Nile.

The pool, amply shaded and in a quiet corner of the island, is a pleasant spot to pause. Watching the mullet frisk beneath the fronds of the papyrus, one can idly wonder if this clear, fresh water has its origin, as the legend suggests, in the distant Peloponnese. Those preferring a short tour should return via the promenade of the Foro Italico to the Piazza Pancali. On the way is the *Porta Marina*, the only surviving gateway in the 15th c. Spanish fortifications.

A longer return route may be made via the east side of the island. Before embarking on this route a diversion may be made south to the **Castello Maniace**, at the very tip of the island. The castle is used by the military and may be visited on weekday mornings only (09.00–12.00). Permission to visit the castle must be obtained from the barracks (*Caserma Gaetano Abela*).

The castle was built by Frederick II in 1239 and has a square plan with round towers at each corner. The architecture is French and includes a fine marble *entrance* with a Gothic arch resting on Corinthian capitals. The niches on either side of the arch used to contain bronze rams of the Hellenistic period, one of which is now in the Palermo Museum. The vaulted *great hall* of the castle is now largely ruined, but retains its fine windows and fireplace. A staircase leads to a terraced roof, with generous views of the Great Harbour and eastern coastline.

From the Piazza Svevia, in front of the barracks which close off the approach to the castle, the Via Salomone and the Via San Martino lead north to the church of **S. Martino**, commemorating the 6th c. Bishop of Syracuse. This is one of the oldest churches in Syracuse, originally of the early Christian basilican style but rebuilt in the 14th c. with a Gothic doorway and rose window. Inside is a 15th c. triptych of the *Madonna and Child with Sts Marcian and Lucy.*

In the adjoining Via Capodieci is the **Palazzo Bellomo**, an interesting if rather severe building which combines the architecture of two periods. The lower and older part—considerably restored—belongs to the first half of the 13th c. (Frederick II) and the upper part, with its Catalan-Gothic windows, is 15th c. Inside, the *courtyard* is similarly mixed in style, preserving part of its 13th c. arcading and a later Catalan stairway. The portico and the first-floor loggia are of the same period as the stairway.

The Palazzo Bellomo houses the **Museum of Medieval and Modern Art**, a fine collection of Christian art which includes sculpture by the Gagini. Among the paintings in the gallery is an *Annunciation* by Antonello da Messina, sadly damaged. The museum has been enlarged by the extension into the adjoining *Palazzo Parisio*. The 14th c. courtyard of the latter building may be viewed by passing through the north portico of the courtyard of the Palazzo Bellomo.

From the Via Capodieci the visitor who has time (and energy) should continue eastwards along the road embracing the east side of the island. From here there are fine views of the crooked finger of Ortygia, its tip fortified by the Castello Maniace, and of the opposing Plemmyrion point. Some of Ortygia's finest *palazzi*, of the 17th and 18th c., may be seen on the Via Vittorio Veneto: then at the Via Mirabella leading off the Largo Bastione S. Croce a left turn should be taken. A further left turn (Via Tommaso Gargallo) leads to the courtyard of the **Palazzo Gargallo**. Now used as public offices, this palace was built in the 15th c. and has the graceful portico and complementary outer stairway in the Catalan style seen in other buildings of this period in Ortygia.

In the Via San Pietro, off the Via Mirabella to the north (entered by the Piazzetta del Carmine), stands the very early church of **S. Pietro**. This church is thought to have been built by Germanus, one of the first Bishops of Syracuse, in the late 4th c. The evidence is in its basilican form, revealed after careful study and excavation, and in the tradition which records that Germanus built four churches in Ortygia during this period, within the first century of official Christianity. Throughout its long history the church has undergone many alterations. First encountered is the elaborate *entrance* on the north side, added in the 14th c. Inside one can see the form of the original basilica with its three aisles separated by arches and, on the side walls, corresponding blind arches. The dividing arches have been greatly modified and the large central openings, which make a kind of crossing between the north door and the 14th c. *south chapel*, each replace a pair of smaller arches. The slight point in these larger arches show the Gothic influence. It will be noticed that the orientation of the church differs from the norm, with the apses at the west end. In the Byzantine period this orientation was reversed, with the altars moved to the east into a specially constructed apse which has now disappeared. The Via Resalibera, adjoining (turn left), leads back to the Piazza Pancali and the completion of the tour.

Walking tour of Neapolis Neapolis or 'new city' is the area to the north-west of Syracuse, the Archaeological Zone which contains extensive ruins of the great buildings that were the development of Greek Syracuse from its original site on Ortygia. There are also considerable ruins of the Hellenistic and Roman eras. (For opening times, see p. 25.)

The tour commences at the entrance to the **Archaeological Zone**, the Largo Anfiteatro (see map). To the north is the Norman church of **S. Nicolò**, now used as a Tourist Information Office, and the remains of a Roman *piscina*, a vaulted reservoir from which water was channelled to the amphitheatre to the south. On the other side of the road a short track leads through pine trees to the **Roman Amphitheatre** (Anfiteatro Romano). This dates from the late 2nd c. AD, and stands as a monument to the rituals of Imperial Rome, when a downward thumb could pass judgement on a man's life. This was the arena of the *munera gladiatoria*, when man fought man—and beast—to a gory finish.

The amphitheatre is approached from the north. It is elliptical and measures 140 × 119m. Like the Greek theatre nearby it was largely cut out of the rock which accounts for its good state of preservation. Building was concentrated on the south side, and most of the stones from here have disappeared, taken for use in other buildings. The main entrance was to the south, but there was also an entrance to the north, cut in the rock. The *arena* is enclosed by a wall, about 2m high, to separate the audience from the conflict. Resting on top of this wall are blocks engraved with the names of the leading citizens to whom the foremost seats were allocated. (Note the one on the east side engraved 'Locus Statilius' or 'Place of Statilius'). Behind the wall, and around the arena, runs a vaulted passage, with openings into the arena. This was used by the gladiators, and by the wild animals which were driven through it into the arena. In the centre of the arena is a rectangular pit, with connecting channels, thought to have been used for flooding the arena for aquatic battles. Outside the amphitheatre, to the south, is a large service area, where the horses and vehicles were kept. The size of this amphitheatre (only 12m shorter than the great Roman amphitheatre at Verona) gives some idea of the significance of Roman Syracuse.

Immediately to the west of the amphitheatre lies the vast **Altar of Hieron II**. This altar, built shortly before the Roman conquest of the city (212 BC) was used for animal sacrifices in honour of Zeus. The upper part of the building—once a piece of monumental architecture adorned with columns, statues and cornices—has now completely disappeared,

Roman Amphitheatre

173

much of it pillaged by the Spanish in the 16th c. for the construction of the fortifications on Ortygia. The base, hewn out of the rock, survives and its length (198m) conveys an idea of the scale of the complete building. The north and south entrances of the altar were approached by a ramp, and there were additional entrances with steps at either end on the west side. Diodorus records that at one feast 450 oxen were sacrificed at this altar.

The Romans were so impressed by the altar that they added a porticoed *court* to the west, planted with trees and embellished with an ornamental basin. On this side, in the earlier Greek period, there ran the ancient rock-cut street that connected the *agora* (near the harbour) with the theatre to the north-west.

Greek theatre The most spectacular monument of ancient Syracuse is reached by a path leading north from the Viale del Paradiso. The path brings the visitor to the top of the theatre, above the *cavea*: the best point from which to view this vast and beautiful ruin.

The first permanent theatre on this site was the inspiration of Hieron I, in the period of euphoria following the victory of the Greeks over the Carthaginians at Himera (early 5th c. BC). The great dramatist Aeschylus was active in Syracuse at this time, and it is certain that the first production of 'The Persians' was staged here. Excavated from the rock of the hillside, this theatre had an orchestra in the shape of a trapezoid, the outline of which can still be seen. The traditional semi-circular orchestra was cut at a later date by Timoleon, who also enlarged the theatre by cutting deeper into the hillside. The final enlargement of the theatre, to its present size, was the work of Hieron II c. 230 BC. In these further excavations—one of the most massive feats of architectural quarrying in antiquity—the *cavea* of the earlier theatre was erased and a new auditorium created, capable of seating 15,000 people.

Originally there were 59 rows of seats, but the top 17, which were not cut out of the hill but specially constructed, have been removed. The remaining 42 are divided into 9 wedges, with a stairway between each wedge. Halfway up, the *cavea* is divided by a gangway (*diazoma*), which helped people get to their seats more quickly. On the wall of this are Greek inscriptions, dedicating the

relating sections of the *cavea* to various members of Hieron's family and to the supreme deity, Zeus Olympios.

The most confusing part of the theatre is the area to the rear of the orchestra. This was the site of the proscenium and the scene building: an elaborate construction which served as a backdrop to the action of the play. There was a further small wooden stage in front of the proscenium: this had changing scenery that was moved up and down by scene shifters working in the long narrow trenches which run parallel to the diameter of the orchestra. The two front trenches belong to the Roman period: these had to be cut when the Romans altered the scene building and moved the stage forward.

The shoulders of natural rock at either end of the semi-circle of the *cavea* give some idea of what the stone cutters had to tackle when they were carving out the theatre. Separating these rock masses from the seating of the *cavea* are the passages which gave access to the theatre. These became obsolete as entrances during the Roman period, when they were blocked off by the more prominent stage. To replace them the

Romans cut two new tunnel entrances through the *cavea*, taking a section out of the first wedge of seats on either side.

Further Roman alterations to the theatre involved a rather ham-handed conversion to make it more suitable for their own special form of entertainment: gladiatorial combat. The main change was to the bottom 12 rows of seats, which were cut back to enlarge the orchestra for use as an arena. These seats, reserved for the leading citizens, were faced with marble. Other changes were the removal of the 17th row (to segregate the classes?) and the installation of a governor's box, which involved cutting out a section of the fourth, fifth and sixth rows. It is unfortunate that the Romans could not have built their amphitheatre sooner: this would have saved the defacement of a fine classical theatre.

Above the theatre, a terrace leads past a series of cavities cut in the rock-face. The largest of these, the **Nymphaeum**, is an artificial grotto, fed by an aqueduct. It was decorated inside by an architectural frieze, now barely visible, and contained statues (2nd c. BC, now in the museum) which show that it was sacred to the Muses. Other, smaller niches in the rock contained paintings and carvings of the Hellenistic period, representing Heroes—a form of ancestor worship. More direct tribute was paid to the dead of the Byzantine period, whose bodies were laid in the rock-cut tombs. More of these tombs, and votive niches of the Hellenistic period, can be seen in the **Street of the Tombs**, to the west of the terrace.

Two of the city's oldest ruins lie to the west of the theatre. One is the **Linear Theatre**, so named from the unusual arrangement of its seats, cut in 17 straight rows like a flight of steps. The other ruin, only recently excavated, is of the **Sanctuary of Apollo Temenites**. The few vestiges of this sanctuary—a rectangular enclosure, the remains of a number of altars—are a sparse record of one of the most venerated spots in classical antiquity. Temenites, meaning 'god of the sacred precinct', was an epithet of Apollo and the name given to the quarter of the city—and the hill—where lay his shrine.

To the east of the Greek Theatre lies the first of the **Latomie**, the notorious stone-quarries of Syracuse which have such a fascinating, if forbidding place in the history of the ancient city. These quarries, which run from here as far as the sea, were used for centuries as a source of building material for the city. Their notoriety stems from their other use as a prison for the Athenian soldiers captured after the unsuccessful siege of Syracuse (413 BC). The sufferings of the 7000 or so prisoners trapped by these mighty stone walls were recorded by the contemporary historian Thucydides, who

Greek Theatre 175

wrote of them 'crowded together in a narrow pit, where, since there was no roof over their head, they suffered from the heat of the sun and the closeness of the air; and then in contrast came on the cold autumnal nights, and the change in temperature brought disease among them . . .'

The quarries have now been turned into gardens, which provide a cool retreat from the hot work of exploring the Greek and Roman ruins. In the **Latomia del Paradiso** (entrance fee) is the celebrated **Orecchio di Dionigi** or 'Ear of Dionysius', an artificial cave 23 m high and 65 m long with a tall pointed opening and a winding interior which Caravaggio (who came to Syracuse during his exile from Rome) likened to an ear. The association with Dionysius belongs to a legend deriving from the acoustics of the cave (eagerly demonstrated by the guide) and the opening in its roof at the far end. This hole is supposed to have been the 'ear' of Dionysius I, which the tyrant used for eavesdropping on the whispered plots of the Athenian prisoners working in the cave below.

The north-west wall of the *latomia* opens into the interesting **Grotto dei Cordari** or 'Cave of the Rope-makers'. This cave was also created by quarrying, and one can see the seams cut by the picks in its geometrically-sculptured walls. For many centuries the rope-makers of Syracuse have used this cave as their 'factory', spinning the hemp-fibre on a hand-turned wheel, and using the floor of the cave as their rope-walk. A small twist of rope may be offered the visitor as a souvenir: a few lire should be offered in exchange.

The exploration of the *latomie* may be continued with the **Latomia di Santa Venera** to the north-east (note the niches carved in the walls, for the images of Heroes). Further north-east is the *Grotticelle cemetery*, a necropolis of the Roman and Byzantine period, which includes among its tombs one with a Doric pediment which is referred to (unfortunately without foundation) as the 'Tomb of Archimedes'.

Tyche and Achradina The names of two of the quarters of Greek Syracuse are retained in these boroughs of the modern city. Tyche has a special relevance to the early Christian era, for its abundance of catacombs. In the first centuries of Christian worship, the Romans prohibited burial within the city limits: but at that time the city was much smaller than it had been under the Greeks, and the catacombs, though in the old Greek quarter of Tyche, were well outside the Roman city. Like the *latomie*, the catacombs were cut out of the rock, and often followed the course of the subterranean aqueducts, then disused, which had been carved out by the Greeks.

The most famous catacombs are those of the

church of **S. Giovanni alle Catacombe**, north of the Viale Teocrito. After the cathedral this is the most important church in Syracuse. It was, in fact, the first cathedral of the city, built over the tomb of St Marcian (S. Marziano), the first Bishop of Syracuse. St Marcian was martyred in 254 AD, and the underground chapel, or crypt, built around his tomb was later incorporated in a basilica (5th–6th c. AD). In the 7th c. the Bishop Zosimus transferred the cathedral to Ortygia, a precaution which might seem to have anticipated the destruction of San Giovanni by the Arabs in 827. The church was subsequently rebuilt by the Normans and altered in the 14th c., only to suffer further destruction in the earthquake of 1693.

The elegant *arcade* on the south front was part of an attempt at a further rebuilding, utilising stones, capitals and other materials from the earlier church. The fine *rose window*, set proudly in its shattered wall, is a survival from the 14th c. structure. Although the church is a ruin, a monastery is attached and visitors will be conducted to the catacombs and Crypt of St Marcian by a monk, who may be summoned by a bell at the south entrance.

Of the interior of the *basilica* little remains except part of the 7th c. apse and fragments of columns. A flight of steps at the west end leads down to the **Crypt of St Marcian**, a Roman underground chamber converted into a chapel after the entombment of the saint. The plan is approximately a Greek

cross, the central pillars supporting low arches and decorated with Norman capitals. In addition to the three apses at the north, east and south arms of the cross there are various side-chapels and burial chambers. To the south-east, in an open recess, is the *tomb of the saint*, and near it an altar marks the spot at which it is suggested St Paul preached during his visit to the island. Other propositions are St Marcian's episcopal chair and the column against which he was flogged to death by the Romans (north-east chapel). Whatever the truth about these relics there can be no doubt that this chapel, whose walls retain vestiges of 4th and 5th c. frescoes, is one of the earliest places of Christian worship in Europe.

The Catacombs which adjoin the crypt, are entered from the east of S. Giovanni. Like the church they became an extension of the veneration of the martyr-saint, their proximity to his resting-place offering a surer hope of redemption to those entombed in them. The catacombs belong to the 4th–6th c. AD and consist of a large central passage, the *Decumanus Maximus* (an enlargement of a subterranean aqueduct) and innumerable side passages, some of them leading to circular chapels. (*rotonde*). The walls of the passages contain the niches in which the shroud-wrapped bodies of the deceased were laid. After the entombment, the niches were sealed with terracotta plaques: these were subsequently removed by tomb-robbers.

Further along the Viale Teocrito is the **Latomia di Villa Landolina**. This is much smaller and shallower than the other *latomie* of Syracuse, and contains a Protestant Cemetery. The site is now dominated by the new museum building (Museo Nazionale, see p. 171).

Across the Via August von Platen lie the **Catacombs of Vigna Cassia**. These are older than those of S. Giovanni (mid-3rd c. AD) and were the resting-place of some of the earliest Christian martyrs. The other catacombs of Syracuse, even more ancient, belong to the churches of S. Maria di Gesù, further along the Viale Teocrito, and S. Lucia, to the south-east (Piazza S. Lucia). Unfortunately, both these catacombs are now closed to the public.

Latomie dei Cappuccini The line of stone-quarries commencing at Neapolis ends here, in this deep chasm by the sea-shore in the north-east corner of Syracuse. In selecting a prison for their Athenian captives, this would certainly have been the Syracusans' first choice: one can only guess at the suffering of the men incarcerated here with scant food or shelter. In the words of Thucydides: 'They were crowded together in a narrow pit, where, since there was no roof over their heads, they suffered first from the heat of the sun . . . and then, in contrast, came on the cold autumnal nights.'

Happily the grimness of the towering limestone walls has been softened by foliage, and the quarry floor by a beautiful garden.

S. Lucia This church is historically the most important in Syracuse after the cathedral and S. Giovanni.

St Lucy (S. Lucia) is Syracuse's patron saint. She was martyred—traditionally at this very spot— in 305 AD, and the sunken **Cappella Sepolcro** (the Sepulchre Chapel to the south of the church) contains the tomb in which the saint's body lay until 1038, when it was removed to Constantinople. (This was during the temporary occupation of the city by the Byzantine general Maniakes: the saint's final resting place was Venice, where she was taken by the Crusaders who sacked Constantinople). This octagonal chapel belongs to the 17th c. and is the work of the great Syracusan architect Vermexio.

Much of the church was altered and restored at the same time and only the apse, portal and lower part of the tower survive from the original Norman building. The *rose window* is 14th c. The significance of the church lies not only in its association with the martyrdom and burial of Syracuse's patron saint but in the painting of the latter event by Caravaggio (1609). Unfortunately, the condition of the church is such that this painting, which originally hung in the apse, has been removed to Rome for safe-keeping.

To the south of the Piazza S. Lucia, the railway line must be crossed to reach the Porto Piccolo. In the Via dell' Arsenale to the south are two interesting relics of the ancient city. In an enclosure is the *Arsenale*, where one can see the long rectangular holes which were the foundations of the machinery used to hoist the ships into dry dock for repair. Adjacent, in the basement of the building erected over it, is a Byzantine *bath-house* (4th c. AD).

From the *Port Piccolo* boat trips may be made to Ortygia.

Roman Gymnasium (Ginnasio Romano) Isolated from the rest of the antiquities, in the south-west corner of the city, this interesting but largely unexplained ruin is easy to miss. It is situated to the north of the exit road to Noto (Via Elorina) and is hidden by trees, without the customary approach-road or car-park. The mystery of the town stems from its name. It was not in fact a gymnasium but a theatre surrounded by a portico: the haphazard description awaits the correction of detailed excavation.

The whole lay-out is extremely unusual: to the west a tiny theatre and fronting it a stage and the podium of a small temple, used as an architectural back-drop to the stage. Between the temple and the east portico was an altar, and surrounding it all the portico itself, of which only the base on the north and north-west sides remains. Excavation of the site has been hindered by the existence of a high water level in the area, and the orchestra of the theatre is invariably flooded. (The Romans would approve!)

Excursions from Syracuse

Euryalus Castle (Castello Eurialo) No visit to Syracuse can be complete without an exploration of this intricate and fascinating ruin, the most intact example of an ancient Greek fortification in existence. The castle is 8 km north-west of the city on the way to the village of Belvedere (so named for its striking views of Syracuse). There is a bus service to Belvedere (stopping at the castle) from the Piazza Pancali, Ortygia.

The castle stands at the western end of the plateau of Epipolae, north of Syracuse. After

the Athenians took these heights—and nearly took the city as well—in the siege of 413 BC, Dionysius I, who was elected tyrant of Syracuse in 405 BC, determined to make the ridge an impregnable part of the city's defences. He accordingly encircled it with a huge wall, 30 km long, and at its western extremity, on a height (172 m) commanding the road from the interior, built the castle. The work was completed in six years, in anticipation of a Carthaginian attack from the west. In the event, Euryalus was ignored by the Carthaginians, and during the Roman siege of Syracuse was passively surrendered. Recent study of the ruins has shown that much of the construction of the castle belongs to later periods, particularly the 3rd c. BC. This identifies the castle with Agathocles and Hieron II, and suggests that Archimedes, who carried out military works for Hieron II elsewhere in Syracuse, had some hand in the modifications.

The castle is approached from the west. It was protected by three ditches. The first (**A**) near the custodian's house and crossed by the approach road, was probably a moat. Dug as an obstacle to the siege engines of the enemy, it was also within range of the catapults fired from the high towers of the castle. There are two further ditches (**B, C**) with defence-works between them. Ditch C may be entered by a tunnel with steps (**D**) which was accessible to horses but could be sealed in an attack. In the west wall of this ditch are four tunnelled chambers, which served as stables and stores: in the east wall eleven entrances run into a linking passage from which further passages lead into the fortifications. The southernmost of the entrances is blocked by the first of three

stone piers (**E**) which supported a bridge. This bridge was a later addition and connected the main building to the forward defence-works.

Four passages lead into the fortifications. **1**, on the south, enters the outer ward via a deep ditch. **2** and **3** enter the outer fortifications to the west and north of the inner keep. **4**, a long winding tunnel of 180 m, leads from the north end of ditch C to a point on the inside of the north wall of Epipolae. (This tunnel gave the defenders of Euryalus an alternative supply or escape route to Epipolae if other routes were cut off.)

The main building consists of an *inner keep* (**F**) with a bastion to the west and a long wedge-shaped *outer ward* (**G**) to the east. The dominant feature of the keep is the *western wall* with its five massive towers on which the great *ballistas* (machines for catapulting missiles) were mounted. These towers were probably built in the time of Agathocles, when such siege weapons were coming into use, and suggest a similar date for the digging of the outer ditch (A) which came within their range of fire. The inner keep is connected on the east to the outer ward, and this in turn has in its north-east wall the main entrance from the town of Epipolae. The outer ward contains a number of cisterns, one of which was located in the tower (now ruined) at the easternmost point of the castle.

Epipolae fortifications The great wall encircling the Epipolae ridge, the work of Dionysius I, has now largely disappeared. The most interesting survival is the *gateway* to the north of the castle, (**H**), main entry to the city of Syracuse from the north-west. This gateway had three openings, the centre one

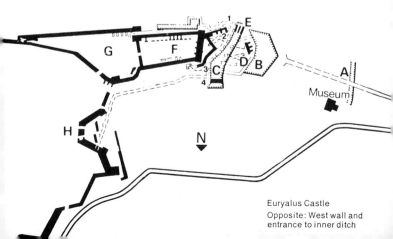

Euryalus Castle
Opposite: West wall and entrance to inner ditch

subsequently blocked, and was indented from the line of the wall so that anyone attacking it could be fired on from both sides. This 'pincer'-type gate is also found at Tyndaris, and in this connection it is interesting to remember that the two cities have a parallel history, Tyndaris being founded as a Syracusan outpost by Dionysius I and—like Syracuse—being later strengthened by Hieron II.

Visitors to Euryalus are recommended to pay a call at the small *museum* in the custodian's house after viewing the ruins. They will be shown various relics of the 1938–9 excavations, including lion's-head waterspouts from the towers of the west wall of the castle. The tops of these towers were used for catching rainwater which was channelled from them, via the spouts, to the cisterns.

Fonte Ciane (Source of the Ciane) This beauty spot 7 km to the south of Syracuse is best reached by road. (Take exit to Canicattini Bagni and bear left after 2 km to Fonte Ciane.)

The Fonte Ciane lays a rival claim to Lake Pergusa as being the place of Persephone's abduction by Hades. Cyane was a nymph of Persephone's who tried, unsuccessfully, to intervene. For her pains she was changed into the spring which bears her name.

The pool which marks the source of the Ciane River (formed, we are told, by the tears of Cyane) is fringed by the Egyptian papyrus which is also found along the river's banks. This is the only place in Europe where the papyrus—imported by the Arabs—grows in the wild.

Olympieion This 6th c. BC temple lies to the west of the SS115, 3 km south of Syracuse, near the outlet of the River Ciane, and may be reached by a track leading off the road to the south of the river bridge.

Only two columns (originally there were 6×17) and part of the stylobate remain, but a little bit of atmosphere is induced by the knowledge that the Carthaginians, Athenians and Romans all camped here during their sieges of Syracuse.

Taormina
Town and resort on east coast, 48 km south of Messina (SS114, A18).

History Originally a settlement of the Sicels (the early inhabitants of eastern Sicily) on the hill of Monte Tauro, the ancient town of *Tauromenion* was occupied c. 391 BC by the Greek tyrant of Syracuse, Dionysius I. Dionysius had earlier conquered the nearby Naxos (the first Greek colony in Sicily) and eventually Tauromenion became a fully Greek town with its own tyrant, Andromachus, brought in a new population of exiled Naxiots. It was this Andromachus who joined forces with the Corinthian general, Timoleon, when he sailed from Greece in a campaign against Dionysius' son, Dionysius

II, in 343 BC. Timoleon subsequently became the ruler of the whole of Greek Sicily, and history was repeated when Tauromenion became the landing-place, and ally, of another Greek leader, Pyrrhus, in 278 BC. Pyrrhus, the King of Epirus, carried Greek conquest to the western coast of the island, failing only to take the Carthaginian stronghold of Lilybaeum.

When the Romans conquered Sicily in 241 BC the town (renamed Tauromenium) was made a free city and ally of Rome, which gave it privileges above that of a purely subject city. During the Great Slave War of 135–132 BC Tauromenium became the hill-fortress of the rebel leader Eunus, but succumbed eventually to the retaliating forces of the Roman consul Publius Rupilius. A century later Tauromenium was again on the

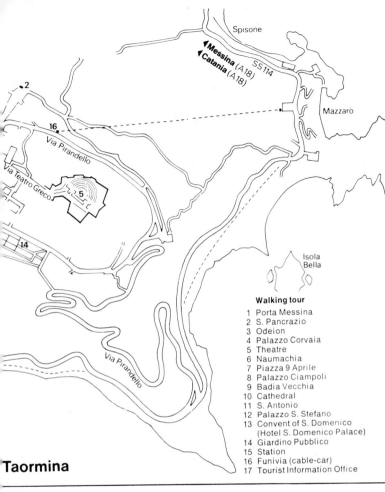

Spisone

◄ **Messina** (A18)
◄ **Catania** (A18)

SS 114

Mazzarò

16

Via Prandello

Via Teatro Greco

5

14

Isola
Bella

Via Prandello

Walking tour

1 Porta Messina
2 S. Pancrazio
3 Odeion
4 Palazzo Corvaia
5 Theatre
6 Naumachia
7 Piazza 9 Aprile
8 Palazzo Ciampoli
9 Badia Vecchia
10 Cathedral
11 S. Antonio
12 Palazzo S. Stefano
13 Convent of S. Domenico
   (Hotel S. Domenico Palace)
14 Giardino Pubblico
15 Station
16 Funivia (cable-car)
17 Tourist Information Office

Taormina

losing side when it accepted the domination of Sextus Pompey, the Roman general who became the great rival of Octavian during the struggle for power that followed the death of Julius Caesar. In 35 BC, after his triumph over Sextus Pompey, Octavian exacted a radical reprisal on Tauromenium: he deported the entire population. Later on, however, as the Emperor Augustus, master of the Roman world, he re-settled the city. But he made sure to reduce its status from that of a free city to a mere colony, a status that pushed it into the twilight until the occasions when its commanding site made Tauromenium an object of possession for invading armies.

This happened in 902 AD, when the Saracens captured and destroyed the city, and in 1078, when Count Roger and his Norman knights in their turn took it from the Saracens. Further destruction occurred during the civil strife following the death of Frederick II (1250) and almost nothing of the Norman town survives. The most significant single event in Taormina's history occurred in 1410 when the Sicilian Council met here to proclaim Ferdinand of Castile, husband of Isabella of Aragon, King of Sicily. This brought Sicily under the direct rule of Spain for the first time, and it is the architecture of the Spanish period which is to be found in the old quarters of the town.

The town In view of its unique site, terraced high above the sea in the presence of Mount Etna, it is unfortunate that the town itself no longer retains the beauty that up to the war made poets out of the travel writers who visited it. In World War II its use as a German

181

headquarters brought down the wrath of the Allied bombers: in recent years, with the advent of tourism and uncontrolled development, the destruction has been even more concerted—and certainly less selective.

If an example were to be sought of a town ruined by its popularity and the praise heaped on it by admirers, then Taormina would be the place. The attractions which have made it the most desirable—and exploitable—resort in Sicily are tailor-made for the brochures. The climate is perfect for most of the year. The views are a legend (Etna, Capo Schisò, Isola Bella, the Calabrian coast, Castelmola). The flowers are a fantasy, especially in spring.

Essentially there are the beaches, spread temptingly below the town. On successive bays, from the north, they are: Mazzeo, Spisone, Mazzarò, Isola Bella, and Giardini. Mazzarò and Spisone have a wide selection of hotels and pensions within a few minutes of their beaches, which saves the long haul up to Taormina: but for those who prefer to stay in the town (250 m above sea level) and make the journey to the beach, there is a *funivia* or cable car which leaves every ten minutes or so daily (between 08.15 and 21.45) from the top of Via Pirandello, Taormina, to Mazzarò.

Walking tour (see map, p. 180) Starting point: **Porta Messina**. This is the north-east gate of the town, at the summit of the steep climb from the coast. Cars may be parked in the square to the north, which fronts the church of **S. Pancrazio**. Like the cathedral in Syracuse and the little church of S. Biagio in Agrigento, this church has the unusual feature of incorporating in its walls and foundations the *cella* and stereobate of an ancient Greek temple.

Passing through the Porta Messina, the Piazza V. Emanuele Badia is entered. Behind the ruined church of *S. Caterina* lies an interesting relic of the Roman city: the tiny Roman theatre, or **Odeion**. This was in use at the same time as the main theatre (Teatro Greco) but unlike the larger theatre, adapted for gladiatorial combat, this theatre was used only for music and drama. The base of the scene building was originally the stereobate of a Greek temple of the 2nd c. BC.

Next to the church of S. Caterina and dominating the square is the lovely crenellated palace—Gothic at its most personable—of the **Palazzo Corvaia**. Built in 1372 around an old Saracen tower, the palace was the residence of a succession of noble Spanish families and was used in 1410 as a meeting-place for the Sicilian parliament, for the purpose of electing the new king, Ferdinand of Castile. Its walls are patterned with the black lava and white pumice found in the other palaces of Taormina and in the

churches of the region: the gifts of Etna. On the side of the palace opposite the church a gateway leads into a beautiful little *courtyard* with a stairway leading up to the first floor. The bas-reliefs decorating this stairway depict the *Birth of Eve*, the *Original Sin*, and the *Condemnation of Man to Work*. These figure-sculptures (a rarity in medieval Sicily) are strangely crude, in contrast with other more delicate features of the architecture (note the beautiful twin window and ogival door at the top of the stairs). This palace, restored in 1946, now houses the head office of the local tourist organization. Its *salons* are used for concerts and exhibitions. From the square, heading south, the visitor must run the gauntlet of souvenir shops in the Via Teatro Greco to reach the principal attraction of his tour, the Greco-Roman theatre.

Theatre Taormina owes much of its popularity to the irresistible post-card view of Mt Etna, taken through the collapsed *scena* of the ancient threatre situated on the spur of Monte Croce. The appeal 'of the theatre, in fact, rests wholly in its site. Although described as the 'Teatro Greco' the ruins are largely Roman and of massive construction, a conventional Greco-Roman adaptation. The original theatre is thought to have been built in the time of Hieron II, the last tyrant of Syracuse and ruler of Greek Sicily, just before the Roman occupation. Little of this Hellenistic theatre remains, and one must visit the theatre at Syracuse, built at the same time, to get an idea of its original form. The Roman modifications were made in the 1st c. AD, when the function of the theatre was changed from the presentation of music and drama to the Roman speciality of wild animal fights and gladiatorial combat.

Courtyard, Palazzo Corvaia

Entering from the west, the approach to the theatre is dominated by a large square building. This is one of the *parascenia* (**A**) erected by the Romans on either side of the *scena* (**B**). It was used to house the various scenic props that were employed by the Romans to give added effect to their 'productions'. To the left is the *scala regia* (**C**), the grand staircase which leads to the *cavea* (**D**). Before examining the building in detail it is best to ascend to the topmost tier of seats for a general view.

The seats were arranged in nine sections around the semi-circle of the *cavea*, each section divided by a flight of steps to the top. The only seats to survive from the original theatre are those that were cut from the actual rock of the hillside. Some bear dedicatory inscriptions in Greek (similar to those in the theatre at Syracuse). The masonry seats were inevitably pillaged and the ones that can be seen today are reconstructions. From the top of the *cavea* the Roman alterations can be clearly noted. The semi-circular orchestra (**E**) of the Greek theatre became the Romans' arena with the removal of the bottom six rows of seats and the construction, in their stead, of a semi-circular vaulted passage running along the foot of the *cavea*. This had openings through which the wild animals entered the arena.

On top of the passage, at the lowest audience level, was a podium. Here portable seats were installed for the benefit of the magistrates and other nobility. In the Roman theatre the seats were allocated according to rank, with the common people relegated to the seats at the top and furthest from the orchestra.

The rectangular pit (**F**) in the floor of the orchestra was covered in the Greek theatre by a wooden stage. This was to allow the actors access to the stage (note the connecting passage forming a 'T' at the entrance to the orchestra). Behind the orchestra rise the remains of the Roman *scena* or scene building. This consisted of a wall with a double colonnade and three openings. The latter did little to salvage the view of the coastline, effectively blocked by the structure; but happily time (and the Saracens) have taken their toll and the upper and central portions of the *scena* have collapsed, leaving a frame for the celebrated piece of genuine scenery which the Romans chose to ignore. The scalloped coastline, swinging out to Capo Schisò, leads the eye only momentarily away from the dominant mass of Mount Etna, sometimes stark and white-capped against a violently blue sky, sometimes only a shadowy presence in the haze.

Around the top of the *cavea* are the remains of a double gallery (**G**). The internal wall, behind the top row of seats, has openings corresponding to the eight flights of steps dividing the nine sections of the *cavea*: between each opening are niches for ornamental statues. The inner gallery served as a promenade: the outer gallery was in fact an entrance portico, covered by a vaulted roof supported by an arcade of 45 square columns. Some of this arcade (**H**) and roof has been reconstructed and the traditional Roman materials seen elsewhere in the theatre have been used: a central core of conglomerate, or stone and rubble mixed with cement, and a cladding of brick.

The tour continues eastwards past the remains of a Hellenistic temple (**I**) to the **museum** (**J**). (This is usually kept locked but

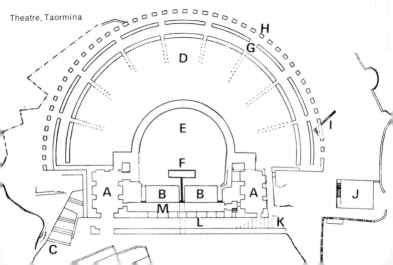

Theatre, Taormina

hillside town there is no way of siphoning off the traffic elsewhere. The streets on either side are merely flights of steps, and a brief diversion down one of these, the Via Naumachia, reveals another remnant of the Roman town, the so-called **Naumachia**. This is the outer wall of what could have been either a cistern or a bath-house. It is 122 m in length and contains a series of niches, presumably for statues.

Continuing west along the Corso we reach the small Piazza 9 Aprile, open on the south side to a magnificent view of the slopes below the town and of the coastline at Giardini. The important buildings in this square are the 15th c. church of **S. Agostino** (east side) with a Gothic doorway, which has now been made into the public library; the 17th c. Baroque church of **S. Giuseppe**, to the north; and the battlemented clock-tower, or **Torre dell' Orologio**. The smallness of the buildings is their most appealing feature, a reminder that Taormina was a gentle medieval hill town for a long time before its takeover by international tourism. Unfortunately the ar-

one of the attendants on the site may be summoned to open it.) The small collection includes a fine marble sarcophagus from the ancient necropolis of the city, oval in form and ornamented with a spirited procession of children; a marble column from the 3rd c. BC engraved with the names of the military leaders of Tauromenion; part of a theatrical mask made out of clay; and various architectural and sculptural fragments, mainly from the Roman period.

The round tour of the theatre is completed by descending steps (**K**) to the access portico (**L**). Parallel to this portico and immediately behind the *scena* is a corridor (**M**) connecting the *parascenia* for the use of the performers. At this point one can best appreciate the varied history and functions of this theatre. In the foundations of the *scena*, supporting the Roman masonry, are the great stone blocks of the Hellenistic period, all that is left of the scene building of the original theatre. The Roman adaptations to the orchestra and the *parascenia* already described can be seen more closely, as can the medieval adaptations that followed the Arab destruction (most apparent in the *parascenia*, which were converted into houses). One can also see the restoration that has been undertaken in the last 20 years to make this once more a living classical theatre.

Returning to the Piazza V. Emanuele the visitor commences the 'promenade' of Taormina, the Corso Umberto. This is the main street of the town, running from east to west, and as might be expected, is well served by the *arte locale*. Were it not for the insistent incursion of the motor-car the Corso would, in fact, rapidly become a street bazaar; and one can only regret that in this compact little

chitectural monstrosities spawned by this global phenomenon are giving us their own nudge in the ribs, elbowing into view behind the delicate mellowed façades and destroying the human scale of the old buildings.

Through the archway in the clocktower the visitor passes into the oldest part of the town, largely 15th c. On the right, after 100 m, the visitor will see the 15th c. **Palazzo Ciampoli**, now the *Hotel Palazzo Vecchio*. Behind this, at a higher level, is the **Badia Vecchia** (next to the *Continental Hotel*). This building, also of the 15th c., is the ornate tower of a defunct abbey, and shows the swallow-tail battlements, Gothic twin windows and variegated stone and lava walls seen elsewhere in Taormina's *palazzi*.

Returning to the Corso, the visitor reaches the Piazza Duomo, a pocket-sized square with a 17th c. fountain and small **Cathedral** (S. Nicola). Built in the 13th c., and subsequently much restored, it is a very plain little building, its squareness relieved only by the crenellation of its roof. The 17th c. *west door*, Renaissance in style, looks a little incongruous against the rest of the building.

Left: Scene-building of theatre
Above: Cathedral

The plain *interior* of the church is the result of the removal of the 17th c. decoration. The nave is very short, separated from the aisles by only three columns. The side aisles contain some small treasures. On the south, over the first altar, is part of a triptych of the *Visitation* by Antonio Giuffre (15th c.). The next altar has a *polyptych* by Antonello de Saliba (1504), and the first altar of the north aisle a *Madonna* by Alfonso Franco (17th c.). The chapel to the right of the high altar contains a venerated *Madonna and Child* in alabaster (15th c.).

The Corso ends at the *Porta Catania*, the west gate of the old town, through which we pass into the Piazza S. Antonio. A newly built post office has spoiled the character of this square but a little of the 16th c.—albeit bomb damaged—survives in the church of **S. Antonio**.

Lying to the south-east and pleasantly isolated from other buildings is the delightful 14th c. **Palazzo S. Stefano**, perhaps the best

example of the Taorminan Gothic style. This building also suffered in the Allied raids, and is still being restored. While this is in progress there is no access to the building, but it is worth knowing that the whole structure virtually depends on a single granite pillar inside, supporting the ribs of the vaulting which in turn supports the floors above. Note the original entrance at the front, now blocked. This would have been approached by a stairway, the steps at the side being an 18th c. addition. The most splendid features of the building are its windows and chequer-board cornice, considerably restored.

The main target of the Allied bombers in World War II was the vast Convent of **S. Domenico**, which can be reached by descending to the Piazzale San Domenico. This was Field-Marshal Kesselring's HQ during the Allied invasion of Sicily in 1943, and in the ensuing attack the church and convent were largely destroyed. Fortunately the late 16th c. cloister survived, and although the convent has now been reconstructed as a hotel, it is possible to get permission to view the cloister. From the Piazzale a pleasant walk may be made along the encircling Via Roma to the **Giardino Pubblico**, a beautiful botanical garden which is the endowment of an Englishwoman who loved Taormina, Florence Trevelyan. The personal touch of this lady can be seen in the follies, megaliths and other fantasies which adorn this garden. This walk offers splendid views from the vantage point of the town: for views of the town itself, and of the Greco-Roman theatre embraced by the wooden spur of Monte Croce, it is better to go up to the **Castello**. This is the ruined keep of a medieval castle overlooking the town, and can be reached by

Left: Palazzo S. Stefano
Above: Isola Bella

185

car (Rotabile Castelmola) or on foot (mule-track from the Via Circonvallazione). The castle stands on Monte Tauro (398m) site of the acropolis of the ancient city. There are two viewpoints: one from the castle and—if this is closed—from the belvedere of the *Sanctuary of the Madonna of the Rock*.

Castelmola (550m) If the Castello is Taormina's balcony, Castelmola is the 'Gods'. In ancient times this was the site of a fortress protecting Taormina from an inland attack. The fortifications are 16th c. and now very ruined: below is the village which must have become a little bored with being Taormina's belvedere. The panorama from here includes Mount Etna, the eastern coast and the tip of Calabria.

For routes to Mt Etna, see **Etna**

Términi Imerese (Thermae) Town on

northern coast 40 km east of Palermo, 34 km west of Cefalù (SS113, A20).

History This was part of the colony settled by the Greeks in the 7th c. BC and centred on Himera, 15 km to the east. Following the destruction of Himera by the Carthaginians in the late 5th c. BC the population shifted to Thermae, which became an important Carthaginian town. It was the Romans, however, who brought Thermae its greatest prosperity, and some remains of their public buildings can be seen in various parts of the town. The Roman name, *Thermae Himerenses* means 'Baths of Himera' and in ancient times, as now, it was a popular watering-place.

In the *Citta Bassa*, or lower part, stands the *Grande Albergo delle Terme*, which has been built over the remains of the Roman baths. The thermal waters which have for so long been a feature of the town can be sampled here. By the side of the baths a road leads up to the *Citta Alta* or upper part of the town. This was the site of the original settlement, and offers a more open and pleasing aspect than the congested lower part. For pedestrians, a flight of steps behind the baths offers a quicker ascent.

At the top is a broad piazza, dominated by the 17th c. **Cathedral**. Although in the Baroque style the façade is modern, incorporating early 16th c. statues in niches and part of a Roman cornice below the campanile. Inside one can view the work of the 18th c. sculptor Marabitti (4th chapel on right: *Madonna del Ponte*, chapel left of choir: *reliefs*) and, from the 15th c., a painted *crucifix* by Ruzzolone (3rd chapel on left).

On the opposite side of the square a street leads steeply down to the *Museo Civico*, where one can see amongst other antiquities of the area, the beautiful lion's-head water spouts from the Temple at Himera. Opposite the museum an alternative route, a series of graduated steps, leads down to the *Citta Bassa*, joining the Corso Umberto e Margherita.

Thapsos Ancient site on peninsula (Penisola Magnisi) on east coast, reached from Priolo. junction on SS114 14km north of Syracuse. This is the site of an interesting complex of rock-cut tombs, among the earliest discovered in Sicily and predating those at the great necropolis of Pantálica by more than a century.

History Thapsos was a Bronze Age settlement (c. 1400 BC) contemporaneous with other prehistoric settlements in eastern and north-eastern Sicily (notably that of the Milazzese culture in the Aeolian Is., which has produced similar pottery). It is not certain where these people came from, but much of the pottery discovered in the tombs was imported from Mycenae, and the influence of the eastern Mediterranean is also shown in the *tholos* or 'beehive' form of the tombs.

In 1270 BC the incursions of the Sicels and other tribes from the Italian mainland forced the inhabitants to retreat to the interior. The settlement of the great mountain fortress of Pantálica dates from this period. In the 8th c. BC Thapsos was temporarily settled by the Greeks who later moved on to found Megara Hyblaea to the north.

Tour The site is reached by a side road (leave SS114 at Priolo) which follows the coast across the neck of the peninsula. After 4.5 km, take the left hand track to the lighthouse. The area to the west of the lighthouse has the greatest concentration of **tombs**. The access to those inland was from vertical shafts: those on the shore are open to the sea and had small channels cut in the rock for draining off the rainwater. Excellent models of these tombs may be seen in the Syracuse Museum. Unfortunately the site has now been enclosed and access prohibited. Those interested in obtaining access should apply to the Soprintendenza delle Antichità di Sicilia Orientale.

Tíndari (Tyndaris) Ancient site on north

coast, north of road junction on SS113 67km west of Messina. (Hours: summer 09.00–13.00, 16.00–18.30; winter 09.00–13.00, 14.30–16.30) (SS113, A20).

History Founded by Dionysius I of Syracuse in 396 BC *Tyndaris* was one of the last settlements to be established by the Greeks in Sicily, as a defence against a possible Carthaginian attack on the north coast. The headland on which it was built gave it a dual advantage: impregnability and a commanding view of a large stretch of coastline. The only access was from the western side, along which a protecting wall was built.

A later tyrant of Syracuse, Hieron II, strengthened the defences when an army of mercenary troops in control of Messina, the Mamertines, threatened Tyndaris. The strategic link between Tyndaris and Syracuse prevailed until the First Punic War, when

Syracuse allied itself with the Carthaginians against the Romans. This alliance did not however have the support of the people of Tyndaris, who subsequently welcomed the Roman conquerors.

Two centuries of peace under the Roman Republic followed, but the focal position of Tyndaris, on the north coast of Sicily in proximity to the mainland and the chain of the Aeolian Islands, ensured its involvement in the civil war that followed the assassination of Caesar. Sextus Pompey, son of Caesar's great rival Pompey, seized Tyndaris, Messina and other key points on the north coast, all of which suffered destruction during the campaign by Octavian to recover the island for Rome. Later on, when Sicily had become part of the Augustinian Empire, Tyndaris was one of the six cities in Sicily designated a *colonia* by the Romans. This meant that its people were given the status of Roman citizens, and the commercial and cultural life of the city was greatly enhanced. Much of the building at Tyndaris that can be seen today dates from this period (end of 1st c. BC) and the subsequent centuries of Imperial Rule.

Tour of the ancient city The village of Tindari, dating back to the Byzantine period, now partly covers the site of the Roman city. To reach it, follow the turning off the SS113 for 1 km. On the way up to the acropolis, notice (to the left of the road) the **walls** built on the more vulnerable western flank of the promontory, with towers and openings at intervals and, in a curve in the road, the remains of a large main gate, with a double entrance, the first opening guarded by towers, the second a narrower gap between pincer-shaped walls. The road leads up to a large square, serving as a car park, which covers the sacred precinct of the original acropolis.

On one side is the *Hotel Tyndaris*: on the other the formidable modern church which encloses, in a small chapel, the much-revered *Icon of the Black Madonna*.

From the square a path leads along the rim of the promontory (view of the ancient walls below) to the entrance to the site. A further path takes the visitor down to the **museum**, where the exhibits include material from a Bronze Age occupation of the site (17th c. BC) and objects from the Greek and Roman periods. More interesting to the casual visitor, perhaps, are the water-colours of the 18th c. which show the most important building of the Roman period, the basilica, before the present unfortunate reconstruction. The museum also contains an interesting model of the scene building of the Greek theatre, which in the Roman modifications was demolished.

From the museum, follow the paved *decumanus* (main street) of the Roman city to the north-west, noting remains of *Roman houses* to the right. The **theatre**, on the left, belongs to the 4th c. BC, when Tyndaris was founded, but little remains of the Greek original. The *cavea* is divided into 9 sections, with 28 rows of seats. Originally there were 32 rows of seats, but when the Romans modified the theatre for gladiatorial combat, they removed the bottom four rows and built the existing low wall. Other alterations carried out by the Romans were the lowering of the orchestra to make an arena, the construction of access tunnels and openings, and the removal of the Greek scene building.

Returning to the museum, the visitor should pursue the *decumanus* and explore the main concentration of Roman houses and *tabernae* (shops) to the left. The finer houses had colonnaded courtyards and mosaic

floors, and one of the peristyles has been partly reconstructed. The best example of a mosaic floor is in one of the bathrooms of a house adjacent to the *decumanus*, under a protective roof. The hollow floor and closely stacked pipes for circulating hot air show that this was a *caldarium*.

Basilica At the end of the *decumanus* stands the monumental entrance to the *agora*, with four entrance arches. This building dates from the end of the 1st c. BC and consists of a passage, entered through the wide central arch, which gave access to the *agora*. On either side of the central passage were two flanking passages, also entered through arches. A fourth arch, to the west, is the survivor of two further outer entrances, leading to stairways. These stairways gave access to an upper floor, now partially reconstructed. The identification of this building as a basilica can be understood if one enters the central passage, which had a barrel-vaulting, and imagines the openings at either end closed off. This was, in fact, what happened when the space was used as an assembly hall. The entrances were closed and traffic diverted to the two flanking passages.

Beyond the basilica, the *agora* is largely covered by the village of Tíndari, and the only further visible remains are some walls of the Byzantine period. Tyndaris is a unique site, uniquely sited, and one can only express regret that its ruins are losing their appeal through over-restoration. In the case of the Roman houses the exercise should be

applauded, for here an intelligible plan has been created out of the rubble: in the case of the basilica it can only be deplored.

The basilica of Tyndaris is one of the most unusual and interesting Roman buildings in southern Italy. The ruin that survived the destructive forces of nature and man for so many years was not only extremely beautiful (as can be seen in the photographs and drawings in the museum) but also, by virtue of its relative intactness, easily comprehensible. Following the restoration of 1956, an unfortunate attempt has been made to reproduce the upper storey of the building using modern materials. (Most of the original stone from this level was lost, pillaged through the ages for house-building.) The result is an ungainly superstructure of reinforced concrete, which shows little more regard for the original than if it had been allowed by neglect to fall down.

Trápani (pop. 77,000) Provincial capital on west coast stretching inland from tip of sickle-shaped promontory to foot of M. Érice. A largely modern city, with a few architectural curiosities in the old part (*Citta Vecchia*), Trápani's significance lies in its port and local industries. These include salt —from the vast salt ponds to the south of the harbour—tunny-fishing and wine production.

History The modern name of the town comes from the Greek *drepanon* meaning 'sickle', a description of the shape of the spit of land which forms Trápani's harbour. Originally the port of the Elymian stronghold of Eryx

Trápani

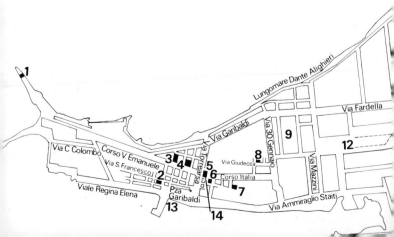

(Érice), the settlement here was enlarged by the Carthaginians and became a key fortress in their wars with Rome. In 241 BC, after the destruction of the Carthaginian fleet in a sea battle off the Égadi Is., the town was taken by the Romans. During the Roman period the town was overshadowed by the larger port of Lilybaeum to the south, and was later sacked by the Vandals. Trápani recovered its importance in the Middle Ages, as the link port for Spain, France and Africa. It was here that Peter of Aragon arrived as the first of the Aragonese princes to rule Sicily, following the departure of the detested Angevins (1282). In 1535 the Emperor Charles V, who used the port in his campaign against Tunis, conferred special favours on the town. In the last war the area around the harbour was totally destroyed by naval and aerial bombardment.

The town is entered by the Via Conte Agostino Pepoli and the wide Via Fardella. This is a popular race-track for the Trapanese, who —as one discovers after a short stay in the town—have their own way of doing things. Their independence may be the result of the isolation of their town on the west coast of Sicily, and a resistance to the domination of Palermo to the east. Despite its proximity to Érice and the Égadi Is., Trápani is one of the least visited towns in Sicily, and this must be considered as an oversight by those who enjoy prospecting for the vestiges of the disappearing past. Despite the obliteration of the last war and the sprawl of modern building on the east side of the town, Trápani has

some gems to offer the conscientious explorer.

The **port** lies to the west of the town. At the very tip of the 'sickle' is a Spanish fortification, the *Torre de Ligny*. To the south the *Isola Columbaia*, the island from which the Romans besieged the town in 241BC, has a fortification in part 14th c., now used as a prison.

The Viale Regina Elena—a pleasant tree-lined promenade—runs down to the Piazza Garibaldi, overlooking the quay. From here the Via Gen Giglio leads to the Via S. Francesco, two streets to the north. To the west this street is dominated by the 18th c. church of *S. Francesco* with its cupola of green majolica: at its east end is the 17th c. church of the **Purgatorio**.

This church is the home of the extraordinary tableaux known as the *Gruppi dei Misteri*. These realistic figures, representing scenes from the Passion, are paraded through the town on the night of Good Friday. (At present the Purgatorio is in restoration and the tableaux are being kept in the Church of *S. Domenico*, south of the Via Garibaldi.

Two streets to the north at the heart of the old city is the Corso Vittorio Emanuele with the 17th c. **Cathedral** (S. Lorenzo) and to the east the church of the **Collegio**, of the same period. In the sacristy of the latter church are finely carved *cupboards*, in walnut, by a local artist, Pietro Orlando (18th c.). Facing the end of the Corso is the old **Municipio**, an overwhelming 17th c. building laden with

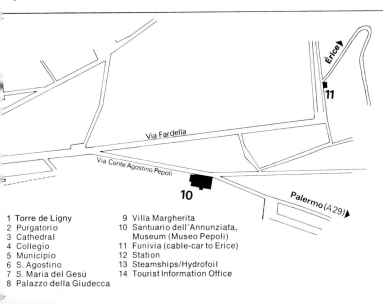

statues, cornices, columns and clocks. From the excesses of the Baroque it is pleasant to discover in the Piazzetta Saturno (turn down the left side of the Municipio) the more tranquil façade of the 14th c. church of **S. Agostino**. This beautiful little church, with its superb *rose window* and Gothic *portal*, was almost irreparably damaged by bombs in the last war. The church is now used as a concert hall.

East of S. Agostino lies the Corso Italia and, in a side street to the right, the church of **S. Maria del Gesù** (early 16th c.). The Gothic and Renaissance styles vie with one another in the west and south portals respectively, the latter having above it a fine relief of the *Annunciation*. Inside the church one discovers the same conflict of styles: the nave flanked by Romanesque round arches but the central apse with a Gothic arch and vaulting. In the chapel at the end of the right aisle is one of the gems of Trápani: the glazed terracotta *Madonna of the Angels*, a beautiful and typical work of the Florentine Andrea della Robbia. The rarity in Sicily of terracotta of the della Robbia school makes the discovery of this masterpiece a special joy. The marble *baldacchino* surmounting the work is appropriately by Sicily's master sculptor Antonello Gagini (1521).

The Corso Italia leads east to the Via 30 Gennaio. To the north, in the Via Giudecca, is the **Palazzo della Giudecca**, which is an example—unusual in Sicily—of the Spanish plateresque style of the early 16th c. The style is best illustrated by the elaborate mouldings of the windows, and the tower with its embossed *punta di diamante* stonework is reminiscent of another palace of the same period—the Steripinto, in Sciacca. Unfortunately this palace, like so many others in Sicily, has been used as a dwelling-place by families and allowed to disintegrate.

Other places of interest in Trápani

Villa Margherita This large garden at the west end of the Via Fardella is used for the music festival which takes place here in July.

Santuario dell' Annunziata (Bus No 1 from the Corso V. Emanuele) Trápani's principal religious monument, originally outside the town, now stands in a square to the south of the Via Conte Agostino Pepoli. The building was founded in 1315, but all that remains of the original is the *façade* with its Gothic portal and rose window, and the *north doorway*. The sculptures over the small doors on either side of the west entrance are 16th c. The campanile was added in 1650, and the main body of the church rebuilt in 1760. The accretions of different periods completely marred the *interior*, which is now undergoing a new restoration. Three chapels should be noted: one of which has particular importance as the shrine of the 'Madonna of Trápani'.

Cappella dei Pescatori (Fishermen's Chapel) This chapel, on the right side of the church, has a fine 14th c. blind arch in the Chiaramonte style and an octagonal cupola. Through a door to the left of the presbytery is the 16th c. **Cappella dei Marinai** (Seamen's Chapel) with the half-dome of its apse in the form of a sea-shell. Access to this chapel may also be made from the north side of the church in the Via Pepoli. Similarly, one may enter from here the **Cappella della Madonna**, which is situated behind the high altar of the church. At the east end of the chapel is a marble arch, decorated with reliefs of the *Eternal Father* and *Prophets*, by Antonio and Giacomo Gagini. This frames the entrance to the inner sanctuary (note fine 16th c. bronze *gate*). Beneath a rich *baldacchino* is the celebrated marble statue of the *Madonna col Bambino*, thought to be the work of the 14th c. Pisan sculptor, Nino Pisano. This statue, greatly venerated by the Trapanese, is at the centre of a cult of worship which may be considered a legacy of the ancient cult of the Venus (like the Madonna, a protectress of seamen) whose shrine stood on the mountain of Eryx.

Museum (Museo Nazionale Pepoli) To the south of the Santuario dell'Annunziata is its former convent which houses a collection of antiquities, sculptures, paintings and minor arts, the gifts of Count Pepoli and other benefactors (for opening times, see p. 25).

The museum is entered through a late-Renaissance cloister. On the *ground floor* are architectural fragments (*Room 1*) and Renaissance sculptures by the Gagini and others in *Room 2* (note particularly the fine figure of *St James the Great* by Antonello Gagini).

On the *first floor* is the entrance to the *art gallery*, containing for the most part works given to Trápani by Gen. G. Fardella. In *Room 3* are some fine Byzantine and Renais-

Santuario dell'Annunziata, Trápani

sance works, including 12th c. frescoes. Among the paintings is an early 15th c. polyptych, of the *Virgin and Child Crowning St Catherine, with Saints,* and a fine *Pietà* by the Neapolitan master Oderisio (*c.* 1380). *Rooms 4 & 5* have other works of the 15th and 16th c., and *Room 6* paintings of the 17th c. Outside *Room 6* in the corridor is a painting by Titian, *Stigmata of St Francis* (1530). *Rooms 7–11* carry the 17th into the 18th c., with an impressive bronze *model of the equestrian statue of Charles II* by G. Serpotta in Room 10. The actual statue was destroyed during a rebellion against the Neapolitans in Messina (1848).

Rooms 12–21 (Decorative Arts) contain the works of Trapanese craftsmen, between the 17th and 19th c. These include Nativity scenes and other *miniature tableaux* of the most intricate detail, made out of a variety of materials including coral, sea-shells, alabaster and wood. There is also a superb *crucifix* made out of a single piece of coral and a *lamp* in copper and coral, the work of Fra Matteo Bavera (1630 and 1633). Other treasures include altar cloths, vestments and chalices. *Room 11* has some fine ceramics, including three 18th c. majolica pavements showing fishing scenes (note the *matanza*). *Room 22* contains engravings and drawings, *Room 23* antiquities, *Room 24* coins and *Room 25* 18th and 19th c. relics including the flag of the steamship in which Garibaldi sailed to Sicily, the *Lombardo*.

Excursions from Trápani
Érice see **Érice**, cable-car service.

Égadi Is., Pantelleria and **Palermo** For boat services, see p. 17.

Troina (1120 m) Highest town in Sicily, to the west of Mt. Etna.

Traces of Greek walls may be found in this old town which was one of Count Roger's first conquests in his march through Sicily (1062). To commemorate his victory he made Troina the first Norman bishopric, a status it has since lost. He also built a castle at the highest point of the hill. This has now disappeared, but the fabric of a Norman church, built near the castle, survives in the *Chiesa Matrice*.

Tyndaris see Tíndari

Ústica (pop. 1300 area 8.6 sq km) Island 57 km north-west of Palermo. For boat services, see p. 17.

This volcanic island lacks the craters and thermal phenomena of its neighbours to the east, the Aeolian Is. Its mountainous area, in fact, is confined to a low ridge across the centre of the island whose highest point, *M. Guardia di Mezzo*, is only 244 m. On either side of this ridge the island is flat and fertile and cultivated over most of its area. There is also plentiful fish and this, coupled with the

clear water and variety of the coast, make Ústica a popular underwater fishing centre.
History Ústica has a sparse history. There is no natural water here and it is recorded that the name of the island is from a Greek word meaning 'ossary' which relates to the discovery here of skeletons of 6000 Carthaginian mutineers who were abandoned on the island in ancient times without food or water.

Evidence has been found of Punic and Roman occupation, and there was a Saracenic settlement which succumbed like the rest of Sicily to the Normans. The history of Ústica diverged from the rest of Sicily when later on the Barbary pirates raided the island and destroyed the Norman town which stood on the site of the present town of Ústica. After these destructive raids the island became deserted and was not repopulated until the 18th c. when the Bourbons established a garrison here and introduced some new inhabitants from the Aeolian Is. The population has suffered further depletion from emigration, but it is hoped that the process will be arrested by the development of tourism.

The town of **Ústica** has four hotels and a number of pensions. From its port, the *Cala S. Maria,* one can make excursions either by rowing boat, motor boat or hydrofoil. The attractions include the volcanic coast and grottoes on the east and south side of the island, the fishing on the west side (*Cala Sidoti*) or—for those with little time—the round trip by hydrofoil, which takes only ¾ hour. Distances in Ústica are short enough to make walking a great pleasure. The less energetic are however recommended the assistance of a donkey for trips to the *Guardia di Mezzo* and *Semaforo,* with their overall view of the island. Nearer the town is the *Boschetto,* a wooded beauty spot, and the view points of the *Fortezza,* the *Punta di Omo Morto* and the *Capo Falconiera.*

Vittória Town 25 km west of Ragusa, south of the SS115.

In 1607 Vittoria Colonna, wife of the Count of Módica, founded this town, which belonged for the next two centuries to the county of Módica. The town has the fine Baroque architecture which typifies the other 'Spanish' towns of this region. Unlike Ragusa and Módica, however, which are built on hills, Vittoria stands on a plain to the west of the Monti Iblei, a site which allowed its streets to be laid out in a rectangular plan. Driving through the grid of narrow streets it is a relief to come into the central Piazza del Popolo with its fine neo-classical *Teatro Communale* and pretty, curved façade of the church of the *Madonna della Grazie.*

Vulcano Island see Aeolian Is.

Guide to archaeological terms

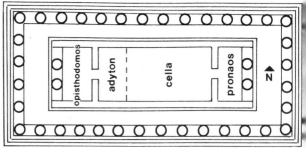

DORIC TEMPLE/PLAN

ELEVATION

cornice
triglyph
frieze
metope
architrave
abacus
capital
echinus

entablature

pediment

shaft

stylobate
stereobate

adyton inner shrine of temple
agora market-place
amphora classical two-handled vase
archaic period 7th-early 5th c. BC
atrium entrance court
cavea theatre auditorium
cella (or *naos*) sanctuary of temple
decumanus (Roman) main street

THEATRE

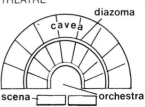

diazoma corridor in centre of *cavea*
forum open-air meeting-place
Hellenistic period late 4th c. BC to 1st c. BC
hexastyle (temple) with 6 columns at either end
hypogeum underground vault
in antis (temple) with side walls extended to form porch
kouros archaic male figure
necropolis ancient Greek cemetery
nymphaeum shrine of the nymphs
odeion small concert theatre
opisthodomos western vestibule of temple
peripteral surrounded by columns
peristyle enclosure of columns
portico colonnade supporting roof
pronaos eastern vestibule of temple
propylaeum entrance gateway to sacred area
scena scene building of theatre
stelae stone slabs with inscription
stoa similar to portico
temenos sacred area around temple